AN AMERICAN IN HITLER'S BERLIN

AN AMERICAN IN HITLER'S BERLIN

Abraham Plotkin's Diary, 1932–33

Edited and with an Introduction
by Catherine Collomp
and Bruno Groppo

UNIVERSITY OF ILLINOIS PRESS
Urbana and Chicago

Frontispiece: Abraham Plotkin, 1955.
Source: AP Coll., 6036/016, B2, F21,
Kheel Center, Cornell University.

∞ This book is printed on acid-free paper.

Library of Congress Cataloging-in-Publication Data
Plotkin, Abraham, 1892–1988.
An American in Hitler's Berlin : Abraham Plotkin's diary,
1932–33 / edited and with an introduction by Catherine
Collomp and Bruno Groppo.
p. cm.
Includes bibliographical references.
ISBN 978-0-252-03361-2 (cloth : alk. paper)
ISBN 978-0-252-07559-9 (pbk. : alk. paper)
1. Plotkin, Abraham, 1892–1988—Diaries.
2. Plotkin, Abraham, 1892–1988—Travel—Germany—Berlin.
3. Americans—Germany—Berlin.
4. Berlin (Germany)—History—1918–1945.
5. Labor movement—Germany—History—20th century.
I. Collomp, Catherine. II. Groppo, B. (Bruno) III. Title.
DD857.P53A3 2009
943'.155086092—dc22 [B] 2008021747

CONTENTS

ACKNOWLEDGMENTS

Working in archives is always a pleasure for historians building the world they are trying to re-create with fragments of evidence. But it is not so frequent when one discovers a manuscript of such literary and historical quality that deserves publication. Patrizia Sione, archivist at the Kheel Center for Labor-Management Documentation and Archives at Cornell University, first drew my attention to the papers of Abraham Plotkin. As soon as I opened the boxes and folders containing Plotkin's Berlin diary and papers, I was seized with the emotion of discovering a treasure, one that demanded I temporarily suspend my more general, but not unconnected, research on the Jewish Labor Committee—the New York–based anti-Nazi organization born from the ranks of the American Jewish labor movement—to immediately consider an edition of Abraham Plotkin's diary. From that moment on, many of my close historian friends in the United States have energetically contributed to the project, if only by sharing my enthusiasm.

But this first-person introduction will give way to the shared experience of having developed the project in collaboration with Bruno Groppo. A specialist of European twentieth-century political history, Bruno provided the necessary background on the fall of the Weimar Republic and the beginning of the Nazi regime. His knowledge of the German language was another indispensable asset for the bibliographic research on Plotkin's interlocutors in Berlin and the events reported. I, on the other hand, specializing in U.S. labor history, focused on the American aspects of the manuscript and Plotkin's own story before and after his Berlin trip. We both worked on the significance of Plotkin's journey and narrative in the context of transatlantic labor history during the Nazi years.

At every stage of the editing process in the United States, France, and Germany we have relied on the precious help and support of friends, archivists, librarians, and colleagues. The whole team of the Kheel Center has contributed to this project. We thank them all collectively and personally. Its former director Richard Strassberg and its reference archivist Patrizia Sione helped us trace the identity of Abraham Plotkin, whose name is hardly recorded in the history of American labor in spite of his constant activism through most of the twentieth century. Melissa Holland made the collecting and duplicating of documents easy and pleasant, while Barbara Morley brought her professional expertise for the choice and reproduction of relevant illustrations for the book.

Several historians read the text at various stages of the project and gave the advice and encouragement that eventually led to this University of Illinois Press edition. We thank them all—Nick Salvatore, Ann Sullivan, Vicky Caron, Donna Gabaccia, Fraser Ottanelli, and Dorothee Schneider—for their attentive reading and efficient support through written reports or conversation. For Mark Meigs, my colleague at the Université Paris VII, who closely followed the project from its early stages, Plotkin has become a new and familiar icon of the 1930s. Both he and Dirk Hoerder (then at the University of Bremen, Germany) read the Introduction and most of Plotkin's diary to help check facts, style, and spelling.

We have been especially grateful to Stephen Shatz in Massachusetts and to the late F. James Dallett in Connecticut, who offered legal and genealogical expertise concerning the property rights of the text. Gail Malmgreen, at the Robert Wagner Labor Archive Center (New York University), supported this project in many ways connected to the history of the Jewish Labor Committee whose archives she organizes and has edited. We wish to thank the staff at the Southern California Library for Social Studies and Research (Los Angeles) who provided copies of documents from the Abe Plotkin Papers collection. Finally, our thanks go to Robert Reynolds, archivist at the George Meany Memorial Center, for the authorization to reproduce Abraham Plotkin's *American Federationist* article.

In France, the staff at the Bibliothèque de Documentation Internationale Contemporaine provided material and intellectual support. Jean Luc Evard and Jean Claude Mouton helped locate and reproduce relevant photographic illustrations concerning Berlin in the early 1930s. And the Université Paris VII–Denis Diderot Research Center on American Studies participated in the financing of some journeys to the United States.

In Germany, the contribution of several libraries and archive centers was crucial. We want to thank the library of the Friedrich-Ebert-Stiftung in Bonn (especially for its online biographical databanks), the Archive of the German Social Democracy (Archiv der Sozialen Demokratie) in Bonn, the Bildarchiv of the German Historical Museum (Deutsches Historisches Museum) in Berlin, the Bildarchiv Preussischer Kulturbesitz in Berlin, the Staatsbibliothek in Berlin, and the library of the Institut für Soziale Bewegungen in Bochum. We received useful indications from Professor Michael Schneider (Friedrich-Ebert-Stiftung) and Dr. Jürgen Mittag (Institut für Soziale Bewegungen), both historians. Dr. Edith Pichler (Humboldt Universität, Berlin) helped in finding a map of Berlin at the beginning of the thirties.

Finally, we want to thank all those who partook in the joys and preoccupations related to the editorial process: our respective families in Nanterre for their patience and supportive interest and those who hosted us during our research trips. Among the latter our gratitude goes to Christoph Links in Berlin, to Ann Sullivan and Nick Salvatore in Ithaca, New York, and to Christine Luneau in New York City. Their generous hospitality made these research trips exceptional moments of warmth and friendship. Our last thanks will go to the editorial team at the University of Illinois Press, whose rigorous and intelligent editing and presentation of the text have improved its final publication. For all who helped us, we hope Abraham Plotkin's restored voice in this volume will make his presence more real.

ABBREVIATIONS

Political and Labor Organizations

ACWA	Amalgamated Clothing Workers of America
ADGB	Allgemeiner Deutscher Gewerkschaftsbund (General Federation of German Trade Unions)
AFL	American Federation of Labor
DAF	Deutsche Arbeitsfront (German Labor Front)
DDP	Deutsche Demokratische Partei (German Democratic Party)
DNVP	Deutschnationale Volkspartei (German National People's Party)
DVP	Deutsche Volkspartei (German People's Party)
IFTU	International Federation of Trade Unions
ILGWU	International Ladies' Garment Workers' Union
JLC	Jewish Labor Committee
KPD	Kommunistische Partei Deutschlands (German Communist Party)
LSI	Labour and Socialist International
NSDAP	Nationalsozialistische Deutsche Arbeiterpartei (National Socialist German Workers' Party)
SA	Sturmabteilungen (Stormtroops)
SPA	Socialist Party of America
SPD	Sozialdemokratische Partei Deutschlands (German Social Democratic Party)
SS	Schustzstaffel (protection squads)

Archival Collections

AP	Abraham Plotkin
AP Coll.	Abraham Plotkin Collection, Kheel Center for Labor-Management Documentation and Archives, Cornell University, Ithaca
AP Diary	As edited in this volume
AP OH	Abraham Plotkin, ILGWU Oral History Interviews, Kheel Center
AP Papers	Abe Plotkin Papers, Southern California Library for Social Research, Los Angeles

INTRODUCTION

Catherine Collomp and Bruno Groppo

Origin of the Diary

This volume presents the first edition of the diary written by an American labor activist, Abraham Plotkin, who was in Berlin from November 1932 to May 1933 and witnessed the downfall of the Weimar Republic and the beginning of the Third Reich. Perhaps Plotkin did not quite know why he was going to Germany when he left New York in the fall of 1932. And he surely did not know that he would stay as long as he finally did. His intentions were both adventurous and motivated by the more political desire to be fully acquainted with the functioning of the German labor movement. Once in Berlin, however, in the fateful winter of 1932–33, he was caught in the vortex of events that led to Hitler's seizure of power. Finding himself invested with an unforeseen higher testifying mission on the beginning of this reign of terror, he stayed until May 1933.[1]

In the fall of 1932, at the nadir of the Great Depression, like millions of workers in the United States, Plotkin was unemployed. With the little money he had saved he decided to break away from American life, and embarked on a journey of intellectual discovery. An American citizen of Russian Jewish origin, he had been active since the early 1920s as an official of one of the main trade unions in the clothing industry in the United States, the International Ladies' Garment Workers' Union (ILGWU). Serving as the Pacific Coast organizer, he had successfully created and maintained several local unions in Los Angeles and San Francisco. By the end of 1931, however, because of the depressed state of the garment industry, the ILGWU restricted its payrolls and relieved him of his functions.[2] Plotkin's choice to leave for Germany, rather than try his luck at other ventures in the United States, was linked to his political curiosity for what was happening in Europe, a continent his parents had left in 1901 when he was eight or nine years old.

Alarmed by the depth of the economic crisis on both sides of the Atlantic and concerned by the problem of massive unemployment in America, Plotkin wanted to see how German labor responded to the crisis. His longtime involvement in both the trade union movement and the Socialist Party of America naturally guided him to study the advanced model of labor relations that the German Social Democratic Party (Sozialdemokratische Partei Deutschlands [SPD]) and labor movement had jointly shaped. With a letter of introduction from ILGWU president David Dubinsky in his pocket,[3] Plotkin intended to receive from the main labor leaders and Social Democratic Party officials in Berlin an introduction to a more advanced stage of labor relations than existed in the United States in these pre–New Deal years. Feeling that "real developments" might take place in Germany that winter, he was moved by the sudden impulse to be there: "I was tired of reading about things that happened elsewhere," he said to one of his interlocutors. Little could he imagine, of course, what would happen in the following months.

Leaving New York on October 25, 1932, Plotkin crossed the Atlantic aboard a freight ship bound for Le Havre. He spent a week in Paris and reached Berlin on November 22. Staying there until May 8, 1933, he witnessed the last months of the Weimar Republic, Hitler's seizure of power in January, and the confirmation of the Nazi regime in its first four months. Observing the effects of the Third Reich's immediate destruction of democratic life, he witnessed the Nazi attacks against German labor until the first week of May, when the whole movement was destroyed. Having been personally acquainted during the preceding months with the labor leaders who were now incarcerated, not only did he become a persona non grata to the new regime, but he also was one of the first eyewitnesses through whom information on German events could be channeled to other European countries and the United States. Stopping in Amsterdam and Paris on the way home, he transmitted information to international labor leaders on the fate of their German comrades.[4] Whether he was forced to leave Germany by the authorities or his lack of funds, Plotkin came back to the United States with little luggage, as he later recalled, other than "the clothes on his back, his cane and his typewriter," not mentioning his manuscripts in this terse description.[5]

During the first four months of his stay Plotkin wrote a diary. And certainly his trip to Europe was a literary experience. The value of the diary, however, cannot be separated from its political and social contents. The historical qualities of his testimony are linked to the time span covered and the particular angle of vision from which it is written. His pages offer the rare point of view of an American observer sympathetic to the particular situation of German labor, and reporting on its main leaders' own interpretations of the crisis. The moment of this observation, in addition, is crucial. Plotkin arrived in Berlin at a time when the Nazi takeover was not inevitable. His report thus captured the initial fluidity of the moment and the pervasive sense of uncertainty. In January, from day to day, he reported on the escalation of violence and the political maneuverings that finally led to Hitler's appointment as chancellor on January 30. In the following weeks, the Social Democrats remained dubious as to the longevity of the new coalition. Plotkin recorded the reactions of the most important leaders of the main labor organization, the powerful General Federation of German Trade Unions (Allgemeiner Deutscher Gewerkschaftsbund [ADGB]), and several Social Democratic Party experts. From the beginning of his stay he had interviewed them on the present situation as well as more general policies concerning unemployment, social insurance, housing, public health, labor relations, and the state of the German economy. He also met some leaders of the International Federation of Trade Unions (IFTU), whose headquarters were then in Berlin. Through the first months of his stay Plotkin thus recorded these leaders' political preoccupations. From day to day, these contacts were the fabric of Plotkin's life in Berlin recorded in his diary. At the same time, his direct observation of ordinary men and women, on the streets or in their homes, offers penetrating glimpses of everyday life during the crisis. As the pace of political events quickened, the nature of his writing took a new turn. Caught up in the surrounding political fever, Plotkin continued writing every day. He attended Nazi, Communist, and Socialist mass meetings. He read newspapers and met friends he had made from the world of German labor with whom he discussed the situation. The style becomes more brisk. Plotkin, of course, moved away from the solitary journey of investigation he had embarked upon. The larger issues of the destruction of all democratic life subsumed his initial interest in the German labor movement. What he encountered and reported now constituted much more than the personal narrative of a trip to Europe, much more too than the introduction to the world of German social democracy he had initially sought. He saw the end of the Weimar Republic, the downfall of social democracy, and the rise of a reign of terror.

By mid-February, Plotkin stopped making entries in his diary.[6] The first direct attacks on the Social Democratic Party and on the labor movement as a whole by the suppression of their press, as well as the incarceration of Communist leaders in February 1933, created a stasis in Plotkin's narrative. Not only were the leaders now unavailable to answer Plotkin's questions on the nature of their movement, but Hitler's repression of German labor and Socialist and Communist movements had interrupted Plotkin's voluntary mission of discovery. Until the end of his stay, rather than day-to-day entries, Plotkin now wrote essays in hopes of synthesizing his impressions and analysis of the situation. They covered such subjects as the last Social Democratic meeting in Berlin, the March 5 elections that confirmed the new coalition in power, and Hitler's characteristic first measures.[7] This change of format in Plotkin's writing was also suggested by his friend Richard Rohman in New York to whom Plotkin had entrusted parts of his diary, hoping for publication in some American magazine. Rohman's advice, by mid-February, was that a diary "[could] not be sold," but that "separate, complete articles" might be easier to place for publication.[8]

Upon his return to the United States, in July 1933, Plotkin had no time to edit his papers.[9] He was immediately sent by David Dubinsky to organize the garment workers in Kansas City. These were the days of labor revival in the United States under the auspices of the New Deal and the National Industrial Recovery Act. For the first time in U.S. history, the federal government legalized and encouraged labor unionism. Action was also necessary for the sake of the imprisoned German labor leaders whom Plotkin had met. And Plotkin, as we shall see, was instrumental in initiating an American network of relief and support for some of them. Only one article written in 1933 was published upon his return, "The Destruction of the Labor Movement in Germany." It appeared in the August 1933 issue of the American Federation of Labor's monthly organ, the *American Federationist,* and is reprinted at the end of this book.[10]

It is not known when Plotkin attempted to edit his diary. He may have started on the way back to the United States during the two-week transatlantic crossing and the several weeks he spent in Amsterdam and in Paris before he finally reached New York on July 1, 1933.[11] Or perhaps he undertook this work after he finally retired from the ILGWU in 1959. Editing remarks appear in the margins of the manuscript but are not dated. He may have taken up the manuscript again between 1977 and 1978. In these years, Plotkin was extensively interviewed for an ILGWU oral history project by Enoch Mendelsund and Ethel Goldwasser.[12] The typescripts of these oral interviews, focusing extensively on Plotkin's organizing activities for the ILGWU, give us precious insight into his life before and after the trip to Germany. The German episode is, however, only briefly mentioned in these talks. Such silence on a dramatic moment of his life may indicate that Plotkin at that late stage had abandoned the project of publishing these papers, or, on the contrary, that he intended his German story and manuscript to be kept for separate scrutiny, and separate publication. Yet no publication appeared. Abraham Plotkin died at age ninety-five on May 28, 1988, in Los Angeles, where he had retired.[13]

Not commissioned by anyone, Plotkin could maintain an entirely free and independent voice on the events he witnessed in Germany. Unlike foreign correspondents for American newspapers, for instance, he was not subjected to any kind of censorship or pressure, stylistic or political.[14] Financially independent, though pressed for funds,[15] he was not constrained by any imposed request from American labor officials to investigate the German labor movement for specific purposes. Certainly, his observations were informed by his own experience as a labor activist and as one who had had to contend with specific political and economic situations. The extremely high level of unemployment in the United States (twelve million unemployed in 1932, at least one-fourth of the labor force) and the lack of adequate unemployment insurance motivated him to make this journey. But beyond his obvious sympathy for the social democratic movement, Plotkin's attention was drawn to many other aspects of life in Germany. His notes therefore convey the sense of an unusually creative and open-minded person. He attended all kinds of political meetings, Nazi, Communist, and Socialist. He went to museums, concerts, and cafés, and enjoyed the company of friends on strolls through the city. At the same time that his perception of the political situation built, he maintained his own point of view within the comparative structure that his American experience and his German interlocutors provided.

The Roots of Plotkin's Social Consciousness

Abraham Plotkin was born on August 22, 1892, at Tackmack, near the Ukrainian city of Ekaterinoslav, in the southeastern part of the Zone of Settlement in the Russian Empire.[16] His father, like his grandfather before, was a butcher in the small Jewish community. Plotkin recorded that "the one who had the greatest influence on the family was an uncle who had emigrated to the United States some time around 1895" and who, in a classic pattern of family chain migration, had enticed his brother, Abraham's father, to join him in America. In this country, he claimed, "there was absolutely no anti-Semitism."[17]

In the United States, where they arrived in 1901, Plotkin's family led a life similar to that of countless Jewish immigrants. In Philadelphia, Abraham's father tried his luck in a dry goods store. Three years later, in New York, he was peddling his wares in a pushcart, while young Abraham supplemented the family income by selling newspapers in the streets after school or by entering prizefighting contests at Miner's Burlesque Theatre in the Bowery. Finally, like so many Jewish children, Abraham entered the garment trade. But he hated the small, overcrowded, and unsanitary knitting sweatshop where he worked. In 1907, after many odd jobs in New York and Albany, he landed in Chicago, working in the post office pneumatic department.[18]

Plotkin first heard about socialism from fellow workers in Chicago. He attended meetings and heard the names of Bill Haywood, Vincent St. John, Morris Hillquit, and Victor Berger. He read Edward Bellamy's *Looking Backward* and Upton Sinclair's *The Jungle,* which made him pine for "the dream of a road toward a new society."[19] He learned about the splits among socialists between the De Leonites, the Industrial Workers of the World, and Eugene Debs's Socialist Party of America. He soon spoke on street corners for the Cook County Central Committee of the Socialist Party. But his older comrades encouraged him to get an education and complete his studies. This he did "with a vengeance," thus opening a new phase in his life dominated by the constant desire to expand his education—it was the same intellectual curiosity that later led him to Germany in 1932—while supporting himself doing any job available. Thus, in the following years, Plotkin's life was marked by this fundamental complementary commitment to higher learning and the practical application of his socialist dedication. He read widely from Marx, Engels, and utopian socialists to more general literature (Balzac, Hugo, Zola, Ibsen, Shaw, or Hauptmann), and attended night courses in New York City, where he spent part of the following decade.[20] Between 1914 and 1922, he even intermittently attended law school in Denver, where he worked at several jobs, including one stint as a repairman in a railroad yard. In that city he lived with Zelda Wright, a court officer for a judge doing work on behalf of women and children. Together they attended law school, and he at times "was permitted to try justice of the peace cases." But he never completed his degree, recognizing that "he would not be happy doing anything else than what he was doing and that was union organizing."[21]

Indeed, from an early age Plotkin was involved in the labor conflicts of the industries where he happened to be working and in Socialist Party campaigns. He volunteered to give speeches in the 1909 dressmakers' strike in New York that was to launch the ILGWU toward a more advanced stage of organization. Sensitive to the fact that these workers were mostly women, he later recalled that their coming out in full force broke the prejudices of both the trade union movement at large and the Socialist Party, whose spokesmen kept repeating that women could never be organized.[22] In 1910, he supported the cloak makers' strike that eventually led to the 1914 foundation of the union in the men's clothing industry, the Amalgamated Clothing Workers of America (ACWA). In 1910–12, Plotkin was sent by the Socialist Party on speaking tours through the main industrial cities of New York State and the Midwest.[23] Being part of the Jewish labor movement in the garment trades, he was close to Morris Hillquit, who supported their umbrella organization, the United Hebrew Trades, affiliated with the American Federation of Labor (AFL). In this context, Plotkin was on the side of the reformist leaders of the Socialist Party who favored AFL trade unionism as opposed to the Industrial Workers of the World's syndicalist, direct-action methods. More important in view of Plotkin's later interests, it is in these socialist circles that he first heard about the German model of compulsory social insurance. Meyer London, for instance, whose campaign for a second term as Socialist Party representative for New York in the U.S. Congress Plotkin supported in 1916, had launched the first congressional hearing in the United States on a national program of unemployment, sickness, and old-age insurance based on the German model.[24]

When the United States was about to declare war against Germany, in the winter and early spring of 1917, Plotkin adhered to the party's majority position against the entry of the United States in the war. At its emergency convention held in St. Louis on April 7, 1917, the Socialist Party of America reaffirmed its opposition to the war in the name of international working-class solidarity. Registered but never drafted for military service, Plotkin organized meetings in New York and St. Louis to build a peace movement, and, like many other Jewish socialists, he enthusiastically discussed the Russian Revolution with his comrades.[25]

Through the rest of his working life, with two brief exceptions—among which the German trip was one—Abraham Plotkin dedicated himself to labor organizing. In the 1920s he was active on the West Coast, working first (1922–23) as a manager for the Amalgamated Clothing Workers of America and, from November 1923, as manager and organizer for the International Ladies' Garment Workers' Union.[26] The situation he found in Los Angeles, the fourth-largest garment center in the United States, was appalling. Workers there, he later recorded, experienced a terrible fear of death, and funerals were frequent events among fellow workers. Many of them had come to California "as graduates for the sanatoria," hoping to find a cure for tuberculosis in the sunny climate. More workers were stranded there than anywhere in the country. The average yearly employment in the garment industry was not more than eighteen weeks. In this city, "the fortress of capitalism," where bankers foreclosed their loans to managers as soon as they heard of unionizing drives, Plotkin imagined solutions that preceded what later became the basis of New Deal labor policies. He envisioned that industrial development was not independent from the workers' welfare. Battles for union recognition were fought to improve the workers' conditions but also to create jobs by shortening the working day and raising the workers' standard of living to that of consumers. He conferred with employers. suggesting that, instead of depending on New York producers, they create designing departments and force the big department stores to buy at least 10 percent of their goods from the local market. He went to Portland, Oregon, to devise a plan for Los Angeles manufacturers to buy 75 percent of their wool from the local sheep growers, and encouraged a West Coast line of garments. In a few months of working with employers and workers to establish more stable industrial conditions, Plotkin was able to create ILGWU local unions in Los Angeles and San Francisco.[27]

Along with the struggles against the local manufacturers' associations, Plotkin also had to face the fierce internecine war in the garment trades' unions. This was the period when the Communist Party of the United States adopted the Comintern-dictated strategy of "boring from within" to capture the leadership of the existing unions. The garment trades were designated targets in this tactic. And on the West Coast the "civil war in the unions" became more intense in 1926–27 as a consequence of the major strike the Communists were waging, and finally lost, in New York City. Plotkin enforced rules to try to keep control of the California locals. But, for a year, in 1927–28, a Communist-guided coalition forced him to resign his position as manager of Los Angeles Local 52.[28] Yet he was soon back in the battle among garment workers in 1928 when the ILGWU Executive Board revoked Local 52's charter and appointed him organizer for the West Coast and in charge of Local 65. As he remembered many years later, the four years that followed, spent reorganizing the depleted union ranks in the midst of violently opposed factions, were "among the stormiest of [his] life."[29]

The onslaught of the Great Depression in 1929 did not make things easier.

By 1932, ILGWU membership had declined to 40,000, down from 170,000 in the early 1920s. Already in debt when the Depression started, to retrench in harder times, the union rescinded its payrolls and reduced the number of officers. The American Federation of Labor, with which it was affiliated, was not faring any better. Its traditional policy of organizing workers by crafts, as opposed to by industry, and its reluctance to consider state-sponsored policy regarding social welfare and the unemployed proved even less adaptable to a period of economic crisis than in more prosperous times. In the summer of 1932, however, the AFL for the first time reversed its stand on workers' voluntarism and started advocating federal unemployment compensation. But its political weakness, as well as its precipitous decline in numbers since the end of World War I, prevented it from making a breakthrough for social reform. Only the Communists acted on behalf of the unemployed, but in their "third period" policy (1929–33) they stigmatized any cooperation with "reformist" organizations: the Socialist Party or the mainstream labor unions. One of Plotkin's concerns in the 1920s had precisely been to tie the unemployed to the labor market by keeping their names on union rolls and to offer them jobs when there were openings. But by 1932, with unions indebted, wage cuts in all factories, plant closings, massive unemployment, widespread poverty, bread lines in all cities, and a chasm between America's revolutionary and progressive movements, no solution was in sight.[30]

Germany had long been the model of social modernism for many American progressive reformers. Since the adoption of workers' social insurance plans in the 1880s by the Bismarck government, which thus preempted socialist programs, Germany had become the birthplace of social reform concerning sickness, old-age, and unemployment insurance. And, as Daniel T. Rogers has shown, most attempts in the United States to enact workers' protective legislation were inspired by the German model, which by World War I offered the most elaborate system of social insurance in Europe. Many American reformers in the 1920s and early 1930s made trips to the Weimar Republic to learn about recent developments in social policy. Dozens of housing experts, for instance, visited Berlin and Vienna or Paris.[31] Plotkin, as we have seen, had early been in contact with the ideas of social insurance in the Socialist circles to which he belonged. Outside of labor or Socialist groups, he also had the opportunity to engage in more general projects for workers' protection and the improvement of public life. In 1927–28, when ousted by the Communists from his position as union manager, never short of ideas, Plotkin became the editor of the *Community Builder,* a Los Angeles journal dedicated to urban and community planning whose first issue came out in

December 1927. His friend Carol Aronovici, the founder of the journal, was a specialist of town planning with a particular interest in German housing reform. Plotkin, although entirely new to the field, enjoyed imagining that "slums could be eliminated, and a whole new way of life created through the building of public housing, control of traffic, and the elimination of a host of other evils plaguing our cities."[32] Although incomplete, this experiment, like his previous attempt at law school, helped him articulate larger concepts of social justice, labor policies, and community life, which are apparent in his discussions with German ordinary citizens, labor leaders, and SPD public policy planners.

However, it is in the Jewish labor movement in the United States that Plotkin participated in the most consistent and concrete implementation of workers' mutual insurance programs. Founded by Jewish immigrants, with a large Jewish and an ethnically mixed membership, the clothing workers' unions were pioneers in the field of worker education and welfare. The ACWA in particular had opened the way in the early 1920s with its housing programs and labor banks. Both the ILGWU and the ACWA had implemented a range of benefits and educational programs. Both unions were built on the industrial model. Thus, Plotkin came from what in all respects was the vanguard of the American labor movement. ACWA president Sidney Hillman and ILGWU president David Dubinsky, like many of these unions' less prominent officials and rank-and-file members, were first-generation immigrants whose early lives had been shaped by political struggles in the czarist empire. In the United States they had adapted their revolutionary activism to the more pragmatic goals of labor organizing and American progressive values. Of all American unions, theirs were the closest to the European social democratic model. Yet by 1932, these unions' mutual-help benefits and programs were all shattered by the Depression.[33]

In the Weimar Republic, Plotkin hoped to learn how social welfare policies survived in a country that, with six million unemployed, one-third of the labor force, was proportionally more affected by the economic crisis than the United States.

Plotkin's Perception of German Events

The tragic irony of Plotkin's presence in Berlin is that he observed German social democracy at the very moment when the movement was about to be destroyed. The nature of his conversations with labor and SPD leaders is therefore paradoxical. He captured both the dramatic sequence of events and these leaders' illusory belief that their long history of resistance had given them the strength to survive what they saw as just another crisis. Plotkin thus discovered the historical and organizational strength of the German social democratic movement at the same time that he witnessed its fragility and complete defeat.

Reaching Berlin in late November 1932, he arrived at a particular juncture of time whose significance gradually unraveled before him. The moment was barely two months before Hitler's seizure of power, a development that still seemed vastly unlikely to most observers. The advantage of hindsight, of course, gives us the full measure of the changes to come, but to contemporary observers a Nazi takeover was only one of the possible outcomes of the crisis.[34] At first not anticipating the importance of the Nazi Party (Nationalsozialistische Deutsche Arbeiterpartei [NSDAP]), Plotkin did not immediately evaluate its strength. The party's impact had risen dramatically from a 2.6 percent electoral return in 1928 to 37.3 percent of the electorate (13.7 million votes) in July 1932. Yet Plotkin's arrival in Berlin coincided with a less ominous turn than in the preceding months. A few weeks earlier, in the November 6 parliamentary elections to the Reichstag, the Nazi Party had received a slightly smaller proportion of the votes (33.1 percent). The return indicated a relative decline of Hitler's party since the July elections. The loss of 2 million votes was interpreted as a disaster by the Nazis themselves but as a positive sign by the rare optimists who still saw a future for the republic. Preceded by a vote of no confidence against Chancellor Franz von Papen, these elections announced the formation of a new cabinet. Amid this political instability, the heads of the General Federation of German Trade Unions (ADGB), whom Plotkin first encountered, were cautiously and critically awaiting what new developments would now prevail.

The Social Democratic Party, obtaining only 20.4 percent of the votes, had suffered new setbacks in the November elections, and was poised between bad and evil forces.[35] Its leaders opposed any labor or SPD collaboration with Kurt von Schleicher, von Papen's successor, who was trying to make overtures to ADGB leaders for their support.[36] Confronted on the Right since 1930 with a succession of reactionary governments and the alarming rise of the Nazi Party, they also had to contend on the Left with the increasing appeal of the Communist Party (Kommunistische Partei Deutschlands [KPD]), whose growing share in the electorate (16.9 percent in November 1932) included many former SPD supporters. With constant clashes between Nazis and Communists, or Nazis and Socialists, the summer months of 1932 had been a kind of civil war.

Table 1. Results of legislative elections obtained by the three leading parties, the SPD, KPD, and NSDAP, from 1928 to 1932

Party	1928	1930	July 1932	November 1932
SPD	28.8	24.5	21.6	20.4
KPD	10.6	13.1	14.6	16.9
NSDAP	2.6	18.3	37.3	33.1

Source: Möller, *Die Weimarer Republik* (Munich, 2004).

Note: Figures are percentages. The Catholic Centrum remained stable, polling successively 11.8, 12.4, and 11.9 percent of the electorate. All other parties' results were below 10 percent. In the March 5, 1933, elections, the NSDAP obtained 43.9 percent of the votes and established a majority by adding the 8 percent returns from the nationalist DNVP (Deutschnationale Volkspartei).

Through the years of the Weimar Republic, the German labor movement[37] had certainly been the most impressive in Europe. Relying on massive memberships in labor unions and political parties, it had a wide representation in parliament and benefited from a solid structure of experts, bureaucrats, and associative networks of solidarity. On the international scene, the SPD,[38] with nearly one million members, was one of the strongest pillars of the Labour and Socialist International (LSI). And the General Federation of German Trade Unions, its labor corollary, had an equivalent position in the International Federation of Trade Unions, whose seat had just been transferred in 1931 from Amsterdam to Berlin in recognition of the growing strength of German labor unionism in the international federation. The German Communist Party, on the other hand, was the Comintern's largest national organization outside of the USSR; its electoral impact had increased since 1930. Although the SPD's losses accrued to the KPD, as well as to the Nazi Party,[39] to outside observers German labor as a whole seemed to present a bulwark against the rise of Nazism.

Numerical and political strength, however, did not prevent internal and fatal weaknesses. The main source of fracture resulted from the deep-seated hostility between Communists and Socialists. Dating back to the severe repression of the Spartacist upheaval in 1919 by the Social Democratic government—which had led to the assassination of the two main founders of the Communist Party, Karl Liebknecht and Rosa Luxemburg—this rivalry was now fueled by the discontent of the urban proletariat beset by massive unemployment. The two parties did not have a symmetrical impact in the working class or its institutions. The SPD, with a stronger electoral basis and membership, also controlled vast sections of the labor movement. The Communists, on the other hand, had not been able to capture any sizable portion of organized labor.[40] By 1932 the KPD's increasing, but volatile, membership was mostly composed of unemployed workers, more vocal in the streets and in the polls than at the workplace. Strictly adhering to the Comintern's third-period diktats, the KPD denounced Socialists as "Social fascists," a discourse that, beyond words, not only precluded any possibility for a united labor front against the rise of Nazism but at times allowed Communists to prefer joint action with the NSDAP rather than to combat it. They had taken such positions in the referendum against the Social Democratic government in Prussia in April 1932 and when they colluded with the Nazis in the Berlin transportation workers' strike of early November 1932.

Social democracy, by far the most numerous and powerful component of the German labor movement, had sunk deeper roots in working-class institutions and politics. Surviving the antisocialist laws of the Bismarck period and decades of hostile imperial governments, the SPD had headed the first democratic government in the country at the end of World War I. Adopting a resolutely reformist policy, it was the only party that fully supported the Weimar Republic, the others either being hostile to parliamentary democracy, like the Communists, the Nationalists, or the Nazis, or giving it only lip service. In this context, the SPD had been the central political force of the republic. At the regional level, in Prussia, the largest of the German *Länder,* the party had governed for twelve years, with Otto Braun as prime minister of a center-left coalition.[41] Nationally, the party had led the government in four administrations.[42] In the years 1928–30, under Hermann Müller's chancellorship, the SPD, at the height of its electoral strength (9 million votes, or 28.8 percent of the electoral returns), implemented a program of mandatory unemployment insurance, voted in 1927, whose financing caused the collapse of the coalition in March 1930 once the depression set in. Since then the SPD had adopted a policy of "toleration" of the conservative Brüning cabinets, which, in spite of their constant antilabor policies, it saw as a "lesser evil" than the threat of an NSDAP government. The dilemma that confronted SPD leaders was whether to accept "presidential governments" ruling without parliamentary majorities and whose policy of economic austerity directly hurt their electorate of working and unemployed people or to overthrow these governments but thus risk paving the way to the subversion of radical Communist or Nazi forces.

The troubled history of German social democracy had created a mythical past and a set of principles that, not without some condescension, party officials and many labor leaders were proud to impart to their American visitor. The existence of long-established cooperation between the SPD and the unions gave a high degree of maturity to the German labor movement.

The ability to survive setbacks, to accept political compromises rather than shun political responsibility, had shielded it against its more radical critics and certainly given its leaders a sense of superiority over representatives of American labor, a movement known for its acceptance of capitalism, hostility to state intervention, and antisocialist choices.

Many of the labor leaders Plotkin encountered had taken a special interest in the United States. They shared the general fascination among German industrialists for the managerial and technical progress of American industry. Business leaders had often made the trip to the United States in the mid-1920s. They admired in particular the scientific rationalization of the work process in the automobile industry. In their eyes Henry Ford was the symbol of modern capitalism, including in the aspects of welfare capitalism and wage policy.[43] This explains why German labor unions were also interested in the American example. In 1925 the ADGB and several affiliated unions had sent delegates to report a labor view of that modernity.[44] Among them were ADGB president Theodor Leipart, secretary Wilhelm Eggert, executive board member and president of the Wood Workers' Union Fritz Tarnow, and the federation's chief statistician, Franz Joseph Furtwängler. Among other union representatives was the president of the Clothing Workers' Union, Martin Plettl.[45] In Germany Plotkin interviewed and met most of these leaders several times. Their openness to the *Amerikaner*'s questions partly derived from their own interest in the United States, which had become an inescapable reference in economic debates.[46] At the same time, they had observed American labor relations. Their notions about American wealth and industrial rationalization were thus tempered by the observations they had made of a labor movement still mostly organized according to obsolete trade or craft union structures. Hence, they showed a pedagogical willingness to explain the superiority of the German model of labor relations. Conversations with Plotkin thus compared two visions of progress and modernity. Yet both German notions of material progress in the United States and Plotkin's own quest for social progress in Germany were challenged in the two countries by a present inability to fight the Great Depression.

The first difference between the two labor movements was one of scale and structure.[47] The ADGB, the largest German confederation, had counted nearly 8 million members in the early 1920s. By the end of the decade its membership had dwindled to 4.5 million. By 1932, eroded again, its membership had declined by another million members. Yet the adoption of the principle of industrial unionism had allowed the organization of much larger sections of the working class than in the United States.[48] From the fifty-two independent labor unions that existed at the time of its foundation in 1919, the ADGB had formed twenty-eight large industrial unions. Together, six big unions made up more than 50 percent of its membership. In the metal, textile, transportation, and construction industries, workers were organized in single industrial unions, regardless of their specific skills or trades. Plotkin's admiration of these unions, their imposing buildings, multiple services, expert officers, and abundant press, underlined by contrast the fragmented and limited achievements of most contemporary American unions. The office building of the 870,000 strong Metal Workers' Union (Metallarbeiterverband) and that of the Municipal Workers seemed to Plotkin the "modern Temples of a modern movement."[49]

The fact that the labor movement was not limited to the blue-collar and industrial sectors also drew his admiration. The Federation of Employees (AfA-Bund, Allgemeiner freier Angestelltenbund), organizing white-collar workers, and the Federation of Civil Servants (Allgemeiner Deutscher Beamtenbund) were entirely new developments to him. That professional associations such as draftsmen, architects, engineers, teachers, civil servants, and also—but separately—unions of agricultural workers could be part of the labor movement was unimaginable for American trade unionists. These federations cooperated with the ADGB in political, economic, and social decision making. The combined membership of the three organizations still represented a 5 million–member labor movement in 1932 when unemployment affected at least one-third of the labor force.[50] Together, they worked for the defense of the republic.[51]

Beyond numbers, it was the scope of the governmental social services and labor institutions that Plotkin especially admired. He reported extensively on the municipal and statewide labor exchanges (*Arbeitsamt*) established in practically every city. He sat through hearings in one of the labor courts with special jurisdiction to solve grievances in the workplace. He was told about the unions' cooperative programs for public housing projects. Plotkin investigated the various systems of unemployment insurance. Looking at the unions' own programs, national unemployment benefits, and municipal assistance (*Wohlfahrt*), he surveyed the extent and limits of compensation or assistance for the jobless.

Unemployment insurance, as he discovered, was a subject of bitter conflict in German politics. A majority in the Reichstag had enacted the national Law on Employment Service and Unemployment Insurance in July 1927. Financing it, however, brought about the downfall of the Müller government in 1930 when no compromise could be reached between the ADGB-

SPD demand that the benefits be raised to maintain the standard of living for the unemployed and the employer-backed conservative parties that did not wish to pay for it. Initially planned to cover a maximum of 1.1 million unemployed workers for twenty-six weeks (or thirty-nine weeks in case of emergency), the program quickly became inadequate. In 1929, 81 percent of the unemployed were covered by this system of compensation. But by 1932 that proportion had fallen to only 31.2 percent of the unemployed, while 26.4 percent had to claim emergency benefits and 42.4 percent fell on public assistance (*Wohlfahrt*) or received no compensation at all. Each responsible authority was now imposing restrictive definitions of unemployment in order to reduce the number of claimants.[52]

The Berlin streets, however, more than formal explanations, completed Plotkin's education in German social problems and politics. The social geography of the city mapped itself out as he strolled through its various neighborhoods. By visiting working-class areas, entering tenements, and investigating the living conditions of families, he fathomed the depth of the depression, discovering the reality of hunger, disease, and demoralization. His notes therefore convey a firsthand account of the social and economic effects of the depression at its darkest moment. Struck by the widespread poverty, he reported on families' meager diets and appalling housing conditions. Unemployed men milling in the streets to keep themselves away from heatless rooms, emaciated girls selling boxes of candy on street corners, prostitutes, gaunt children, and women producing insufficient meals while still having to choose between the cost of food and paying the rent, these were the figures he met while wandering about Alexanderplatz or in his visits to working-class Wedding.

The streets were also the theater of German politics. This was particularly true in Berlin, the capital of the nation as well as of the state of Prussia.[53] By attending many political meetings, Plotkin personally witnessed the violence of the Nazi confrontations with Communist or Socialist forces. In successive demonstrations and counterdemonstrations, the paramilitary forces of one organization defied another. From the Nationalist Steel Helmet to the Socialist Eiserne Front (Iron Front) or the Communist Rotfront (Red Front) demonstrators in their Soviet-style uniforms, political formations swept across the city, asserting their control over the streets, against one another, or against the police, making the political landscape visible and dangerous. Violent clashes, murders, and rumors were reported in the press and in the next moment commented upon in cafés and on street corners.[54]

After following the evolution of German politics for six months, and observing the Hitler government's "First Steps," Plotkin was the witness of the final Nazi attack against the ADGB and affiliated labor organizations in the week of May 2. In the article published in the *American Federationist* in August 1933, he reported the arrest of the leaders, the raiding of the unions' headquarters, the confiscation of their property, and their complete destruction at the hands of the Nazi storm troopers. In this article—the only American testimony on these events by a labor activist—Plotkin, as he rarely did, threw himself into the task of analyzing as well as describing what had happened. Wondering whether another course of action on the part of the SPD and ADGB could have been possible, he tried to explain the paradox that such a powerful and well-organized labor movement could have been defeated practically without resistance on its part.

Plotkin was not alone in looking for answers. Debates about the causes of the disaster took place among social democratic circles in Germany, in Western countries, as well as in the international labor movement (especially within the Labour and Socialist International and the IFTU). A debate on the "German Catastrophe" was at the heart of the LSI conference held in Paris in August 1933. So wide were the divergences among Socialists that no other international congress of the LSI was gathered after 1933.[55] Since then, historians have never stopped interpreting the causes of the collapse of the Weimar Republic. Plotkin's own evaluation of the crisis is important because it bears the mark of his main interlocutors, the front-rank German leaders of the labor and social democratic movement.

He naturally defended their point of view. Anticipating questions or criticisms, he argued that trade unionists and Social Democrats had "opened the road to socialism in Germany through democratic means, but in the process had greatly weakened themselves," especially in the economic context compounded by the situation created by the Versailles Treaty reparation debts and massive unemployment. At the time of the Nazi takeover, the SPD and trade unionists were not able to resist the devastating attacks inflicted upon them. Graphically describing Nazi methods of terrorist violence, Plotkin made clear on what side the responsibilities lay. His article in part tried to contradict those critics, "the nit wits and those who are blind," who "condemn the German trade union leaders for being without a program" and for "too much conservatism." Rather, he maintained that German labor leaders should be honored for having avoided a bloodbath by useless resistance.

> They met both their fate and the issues that confronted them with genuine courage. It took courage to avoid pitfalls that might have led to the slaughter of tens of thousands of workers and victimization of thousands more. It was doubly courageous to remain at their posts, as practically all of the national leaders did, until the guns of the Nazis ordered them into

> the lorry on their way to the military barracks. These leaders knew what was awaiting them. And they faced their arrests unflinchingly.[56]

In this evaluation, as well as in his general account of the political maturity of German labor, perhaps Plotkin overestimated the SPD-ADGB cohesion. Or, rather, he did not perceive or muted the unions' criticism of the SPD's lack of action in the face of adversity, a paralysis often held responsible for the defeat of May 1933. Several grievances had been expressed among union leaders in the preceding months. The SPD's refusal to endorse the program of job creation that the ADGB had advocated in 1932 (*Arbeitsbeschaffungsprogramm*) was one of them.[57] The SPD's lack of political response to the von Papen coup of July 1932 against the Prussian government led by Otto Braun was another instance of its policy of "toleration" of the "lesser evil" for fear that more radical positions would lead to immediate conflict or civil war. Nationalist proclivities expressed in labor ranks, and the temptation for some ADGB leaders to accept a compromise with von Schleicher in December 1932, which the SPD adamantly refused, were yet other sources of dissension or disagreement. Furthermore, the SPD's tradition of respecting the legal paths of action and its fatalistic interpretation of the economic crisis as a natural phenomenon inherent to capitalist economies also added to the impression of apathy. The SPD's fear of a return of the hyperinflation of the early 1920s constrained its decisions in economic matters.

It is not clear who were the "left-wingers" to whom Plotkin attributed such criticism of SPD inaction. That judgment may be a replica of American discourse typically charging the "radicals" with divisive tactics in the failure of labor struggles. In reality, left-wing currents were only a minority among the cadres of German labor, strongly controlled by the reformists. If the notion was a displacement of the Communist proposal for a general strike, Plotkin was correct in underlining the many reasons a general strike was impossible and would have been suicidal. Historians have concurred in recognizing that massive unemployment and the Nazis' readiness to exploit the discontent doomed a general strike to failure. Likewise, the hypothesis that had Communists and Socialists been able to form a united front—an unlikely possibility, given the former's resolute hope for a revolutionary Germany on the Soviet model—they could have saved the republic is still a matter of conjecture.

Plotkin did not isolate the labor movement from other forces that led to Hitler's seizure of power. He was well aware that the German industrialists' offensive against the unions in the previous years, as well as the particular interests of the large landowners in East Prussia (the Junkers), played a decisive role in Hitler's accession to power. The old ruling classes and the military held the key that opened the door to Hitler, hoping they could sway his forces to their advantage. The dubious role played by Alfred Hugenberg, president of the nationalist Deutschnationale Volkspartei (DNVP), who traded off his personal hostility to Hitler for silence on the Junkers' scandalous appropriation of farm-relief funds, implicated the aristocratic elite. And Plotkin recognized von Papen's conspiracy to recover his lost powers by negotiating with President Paul von Hindenburg for Hitler's appointment as chancellor as another conservative force bringing about the worst possible denouement to the crisis.[58]

Plotkin's Jewish Identity

Anti-Semitic violence in Berlin made Abraham Plotkin rediscover problems that now revived his Jewish identity.[59] In the United States, Plotkin's thinking had been more influenced by the universal quality of socialism than by things strictly Jewish. The degree of his American integration can be measured in the fact that his first wife, Jean Bangs, with whom he was still married when he went to Germany, belonged to an old Protestant family of "descendants of the Mayflower," as he reported.[60] Yet, working in the Jewish world of the garment trades in New York and on the West Coast, Plotkin lived in the midst of the *Yiddishkeit.* He could speak Yiddish with his fellow workers. But no specific concern about Jewish culture in his pre-German years appears in his later autobiographical records.[61] Once in Germany, however, his interest in the peculiar situation of Jews in that country became vivid.

No doubt when speaking German, Plotkin's accent betrayed the influence of the Yiddish language upon his pronunciation. Although generally recognized as an American when he spoke German, he could also be marked out as a Jew. "I do not speak to Jews" was the terse response of a woman whom Plotkin and his companion addressed at a Nazi meeting in January 1933.[62] Plotkin, however, did not need such extreme reminders of his own identity to take note of the plight of Jews in the brutally anti-Semitic climate of Nazi Germany. Just as he had done with other social problems, he investigated the situation through several encounters with Jewish people. With young man Herschel and his family, he shared the warmth of a Jewish moment in their grocery store. With them he understood the bitterness of Jews who could neither assimilate nor defend themselves. And from representatives of Jewish organizations he understood the social structure of the German

Jewish population as well as the plight of the more recent nonnaturalized Jews who were shut out from any form of public help.[63]

Investigating the Jewish situation, however, had not been Plotkin's primary goal. Entries explicitly addressing Jewish problems are less numerous in his diary than those devoted to labor and general social questions. Two factors may explain his perspective. On the one hand, the SPD and labor leaders whom Plotkin met did not directly address that issue. In their view, anti-Semitism would be solved within the larger context of universal labor and democratic progress. Of all German political, religious, or social institutions in the Weimar Republic, left-wing labor unions and the accompanying political parties were the only ones not to contain any anti-Semitic clause, platform, or practice.[64] On the other hand, if attacks against Jews were part and parcel of Nazi strategy long before the fall of the Weimar Republic, Plotkin, whose main concern was labor and unemployment, may not have immediately recognized the specific harassment of the Jewish community. In the initial weeks of the Third Reich, in addition, the Nazis' first and most systematic attacks were directed not against Jews but against Communists and all forces on the Left. Did Plotkin perceive that in Nazi ideology Jews and "Bolsheviks" were often interchangeable and equally condemnable identities or social groups? It would be hard to point out precisely what he perceived since the diary stopped before the savagery against Jews was unleashed in April 1933 when Hitler launched the boycott of Jewish trades and restrictions on Jewish professionals.

But he captured the ultimate meaning of that policy in an essay devoted to the "Jews in Germany." In this essay, probably written in June 1933,[65] Plotkin outlined the reasons that had made political anti-Semitism possible. In a classic analysis of Jewish life in Germany, he ascribed to the financial elite a central role in the transition from feudalism to the modern industrial state. The structural causes of what Hannah Arendt later called "modern anti-Semitism" appeared, Plotkin noted, when Jews, who had been the "catalytic agents" of the development of commercial and capitalist Germany in the nineteenth century, were no longer so useful.[66] Their real economic power, he suggested, had declined after World War I, or had been merged into larger business concerns. "From that moment [the Jew] was marked as a victim," Plotkin noted clear-sightedly, "or perhaps the fore-runner of the victims to come." Exposing the demagogic, anticapitalist aspects of Nazi anti-Semitism, Plotkin did not, however, fully perceive—and it would be anachronistic to imagine that he could—that the Third Reich's anti-Semitism was not simply an incremental step from the anti-Semitism of previous decades or a repetition of the czarist persecutions that Plotkin's family had known in the Russian Empire. But he clearly underlined the threatening irrationality of their arguments. Illogical in terms of economic interest, the boycott against Jewish trades and professionals, he understood, served symbolic rather than real political functions or economic needs in German society. The essay ended with a somber and prescient warning: "After spending six months in Germany, the writer hasn't a moment's hesitation in answering that Hitler, Goering and Goebbels will have no hesitation, if it serves their purpose, [. . .] in deferring the day of judgment by turning the blame for their failures on the Jews. Already the signs are not wanting that this is being prepared."[67]

Consequences of Plotkin's Trip: American Labor's Rescue of German Labor and Socialist Leaders

For Plotkin himself, the German experience was eventually a source of political disenchantment. The German model of labor relations he so admired was now shattered. Its leaders were violently attacked, interned in concentration camps, or forced into exile. Even Plotkin's belief in the Marxist canon that social progress is positively linked to the degree of class consciousness and labor organization of a nation was also shattered. What he had seen in Germany, on the contrary, was a country whose highly organized working class had not prevented the course of history from going backward. "I considered myself a Marxian until I saw the tragedy in Germany," he later said. "I realized that other factors determine men's thinking [than] class interests."[68] The simple fact that he entirely devoted himself body and soul to labor organizing for the rest of his life in the United States and did not engage in political activism as he had done in the heyday of the Socialist Party of America is another sign of his definitive acceptance of the pragmatic form of American labor politics.[69]

This, however, did not prevent him from organizing the support of German comrades once Nazi repression fell upon them. Plotkin was one first link in the chain of international solidarity building up for the support of the German movement. He offered moral, material, and political help in Germany, in Europe, and finally in the United States. After Hitler's seizure of power, Plotkin used his American Express Company address as a front for German leaders whose mail was now raided. He served as an underground courier between them and international labor organizations. He claimed that he helped IFTU assistant secretary Georg Stolz protect the archives of the International Federation by personally carrying part of them to Prague and Paris.[70]

On the way back to the United States, he stopped in Amsterdam and Paris to report on the situation of the German comrades. He was especially active on behalf of the president of the German Clothing Workers' Union, Martin Plettl, whom he had befriended in Berlin. After being arrested, brutally beaten, and jailed by the Nazis, Plettl had been able to escape to Amsterdam, where he stayed in the home of Tonnis Van der Heeg, the secretary of the International Federation of Clothing Workers. In Paris Plotkin alerted the French Federation of Clothing Workers on Plettl's behalf and more generally asked for their cooperation in helping the refugees.[71] In the following months, having returned to the United States, Plotkin corresponded with refugees from the world of German and international labor he had known in Germany. He was in contact with IFTU secretary Walter Schevenels and his assistant, Georg Stolz, as well as with Valtin Hartig, leader of the German union of transportation and municipal workers. All of them had precipitately reached Paris and were seeking means of supporting themselves and helping their comrades. Hartig, who attended the Labour and Socialist International conference that took place in Paris in August 1933, as well as the IFTU Congress in Brussels in July of the same year,[72] complained about the weakness and inefficiency of these international bodies. "We wept," Hartig said speaking of Plettl and himself, when we "thought of our people at home hoping the International would do something for them, our people always the most severely attacked because they were internationalists. And the only practical help for them was a [collection] for which each delegate gave 30—today maybe 40—American cents. [. . .] We wept."[73]

In the United States, Plotkin immediately alerted the cadres of the American labor movement to the plight of the German trade unionists. Published in the August issue of the *American Federationist,* his article titled "The Destruction of the Labor Movement in Germany" described the extent of the Nazi attack on German labor in May 1933. Plotkin reported in a letter to Stolz that his article "apparently had its effect because our President used it as a basis for the boycott that the Federation passed at its convention last month."[74] AFL president William Green did in fact deliver a long speech that in parts echoed Plotkin's own words, describing "the absolute annihilation of one of the finest organized trade union movements ever established under the sun." Underlining the complete destruction of the German unions and the leaders' imprisonment, he also affirmed his absolute condemnation of anti-Semitism, and successfully moved the federation to enact a boycott of German-made goods and services.[75]

Plotkin was also able to arrange support for Martin Plettl by inviting him for a series of lectures on the German situation for American labor audiences. This decision not only helped Plettl and his secretary, Dorothea Heinrich, survive but also initiated a series of other similar invitations of German refugees, a policy that soon expanded into the foundation of the Jewish Labor Committee (JLC). For Plettl's invitation, Plotkin had gathered the support of a committee composed of the leaders of the main Jewish labor organizations: ILGWU president David Dubinsky, ACWA secretary-treasurer Joseph Schlossberg, manager of the *Jewish Daily Forward* Baruch Charney Vladeck, and Joseph Baskin, who headed the Workmen's Circle (the Jewish socialist mutual-help organization). From November 1933 to February 1934, Plettl toured a number of American cities, speaking to labor audiences. Dubinsky wrote to all Joint Board ILGWU correspondents in Chicago, Boston, Philadelphia, Baltimore, Cleveland, and St. Louis to organize local lectures. "Brother Plettl is the first prominent labor refugee to come to America [. . .]. Money from these lectures or dinners will go in part for covering the expenses for his tour and partly for the Fund for Labor and Socialist German Refugees in Europe."[76]

The Jewish Labor Committee, founded in New York in February 1934, quickly institutionalized and developed on a larger scale what had spontaneously been organized for Martin Plettl. Headed by B. C. Vladeck and supported by the ILGWU and the ACWA and by the Workmen's Circle, the JLC now made it its task to "give aid to Jewish and non-Jewish labor institutions overseas; to assist the democratic labor movement in Europe; provide succor to victims of oppression and persecution and to combat anti-Semitism and racial and religious intolerance abroad and in the United States."[77] Gathering the main organizations of the noncommunist Jewish Left, its founders believed that a united front of labor and secular Jewish organizations was necessary to combat the Nazi antilabor and anti-Semitic persecutions. Linked to the American Federation of Labor and later to the Congress of Industrial Organizations, through its constituent unions, the JLC became the vanguard of American labor's struggle against Nazism and fascism. It launched a wider fund-raising drive, which the AFL joined, run by David Dubinsky, who was its treasurer. It organized the support of many European socialist and labor leaders through the 1930s. During 1940–41, when the German armies had invaded Western Europe and Poland, the JLC was able to rescue hundreds of the German, Austrian, Italian, Polish, and Russian labor and socialist leaders who had found refuge in France through the 1930s, or in Lithuania after September 1939, when Poland had been invaded. Once these countries had fallen to Nazi or Soviet rule, these refugee labor leaders found themselves in a death trap.[78]

Plotkin himself did not participate in the JLC work and rescue operations. In the mid-1930s he had become ILGWU general organizer for the Midwest, and was involved in battles to win union recognition for garment workers in Kansas City, Milwaukee, Chicago, and Alpena, Michigan. Among the refugees for whom the JLC secured passage to the United States in 1940–41 were several of the prominent men whom Plotkin had met in Berlin. The exiled Menshevik leader Rafael Abramowitch, for instance, was Plotkin's first interlocutor in Berlin. Friedrich Stampfer, the former editor of the German *Vorwärts,* and IFTU assistant secretary Georg Stolz were some of the leaders he had met, talked to, or corresponded with whom the JLC liberated from "the clutches of Hitler's assassins."[79]

Plotkin as a Writer

Plotkin's trip to Germany was also a literary adventure. The first evidence of this is the diary itself, not simply because Plotkin kept it from the moment he left New York but because of the compelling urge to write that it reveals. By writing, Plotkin was experiencing another form of life. And through the pages we also see him experimenting with different forms of style. These range from romantic descriptions of sunsets or the sea when crossing the Atlantic to notes on social mores in Paris and Berlin and vivid recollections of street life, cafés, and encounters with different social types. Self-taught Plotkin was not without a literary introduction for his German explorations. Widely read in modern literature, he was certainly influenced by Alfred Döblin's recent novel *Alexanderplatz.*[80] To a certain extent Plotkin's initial wanderings through Berlin echoed those of Döblin's protagonist, Franz Biberkopf. His first long explorations of the city were precisely devoted to the centers of Berlin's working-class life: Alexanderplatz and Wedding. What he saw and felt there was not unrelated to Döblin's expressionist fiction: tramps, pawnbrokers, prostitutes, hucksters, and ill-nourished families on the dole, living in the cramped rooms of damp tenements.[81] Discovering that, although fantastic or grotesque, Döblin's world was not unrealistic, Plotkin continued in this vein when describing the extent of poverty or the inadequacy of the *Wohlfahrt* in his reports. To a great extent, these descriptions offer a counterpoint to the more idealized and rational world of reforms and planning that Plotkin's social democratic friends exposed to him.

As a narrator and autobiographical writer, Plotkin himself, unwittingly, became a literary figure. A *flâneur,* like the contemporary German writer Walter Benjamin for whom the Paris streets and passageways were the essence of the nineteenth century,[82] Plotkin strolled through Berlin, drawing a mental topography of the city now epitomizing all the social ills caused by the depression. In this respect Plotkin's diary must be added to the series of works whose subject is life in Berlin in the Weimar or early Third Reich years.[83] Together, these works constitute a Berlin genre in which the fascination for the extremes of decadence or modernity is combined with nostalgia for a world destroyed by Nazi violence. Ironically, Plotkin's steps as a wandering Jew prefigured in reversed manner those of the German exiles (Jews or Gentiles) who, like Benjamin but also like Plotkin's friends from the German labor movement, were soon to seek refuge in Paris or other cities, and whose aimless meanderings became the leitmotif of their new condition.

The fluidity with which dialogues are reported in the diary is another mark of his literary merit. Voices answer one another without the usual punctuation marks, reproducing the manner of speech of the persons Plotkin talked to as well as his own. One nearly hears these voices as the conversations proceed through questions and answers, just as one hears the oratorical style of the speakers in political meetings. From encounter to encounter, a multivoiced evocation of life in Berlin emerges, finally silenced by the blasting violence of Nazi takeover.

That the diary ends at this juncture is significant. Although Plotkin stayed in Berlin another three months, the initial optimistic desire to faithfully chronicle what he discovered belonged to a genre that no longer applied to the new reality. Words and descriptions had become useless and therefore meaningless. This may partly explain why Plotkin did not publish his diary. Had he had the time to do so upon his return, it is not certain that he would have published it as it was. The initial intentions that had led to its writing no longer corresponded to what needed to be said about Germany. Both in Germany and in New Deal America, the situation had changed to unforeseen and directly opposed circumstances. The fact that Plotkin had turned to writing essays rather than daily descriptions from the moment Hitler seized power also underlines this observation. In Germany, the fluidity of democratic life, time, and language had been interrupted and perverted.[84]

Editing Plotkin's Diary

Methodology

This first edition of Abraham Plotkin's diary is a selection. The length of the manuscript, the multiple versions of some of its pages, and the incomplete character of these revisions required making choices.

From the moment he left New York on October 25, 1932, to February 15, 1933, Plotkin wrote nearly every day. He wrote quickly, reporting major events, impressions, and conversations of the day. But the typescripts and the style of some passages indicate that some parts were rewritten for publication, while others remained in rougher drafts. No final version of the diary was ever completed. The quality of the writing and the attention to details of spelling and sentence construction are therefore uneven, and Plotkin was well aware of this. When he hurriedly sent parts of the manuscript from Berlin to his friend Dick Rohman, probably in late May 1933, he accompanied the document with this note: "I see all of its weakness, names, deletions, etc., but part of it is because I was compelled to leave material behind. It is so damned badly written that you may have to rewrite it."[85] Although this note leaves us with the knowledge that Plotkin would have corrected the manuscript and further revised it had he had the desire and opportunity to do so, we have kept the present edition as close to the original as possible while making the necessary corrections for the sake of legibility.

Considerations of space, thematic consistency, and progression guided our choices. For instance, we have not reproduced the batch of forty-one typed pages contained in folder 1 where Plotkin described the transatlantic crossing as well as his first week abroad in Paris. Although the pages in this section introduce his style, manner of speech, and intellectual curiosity, we did not reproduce them here, thinking that they would distract the reader from the real focus of Plotkin's final main themes: his discovery of the world of German social democracy and his testimony on Hitler's rise to power. For the same reason, we kept the intellectual and political aspects of descriptions devoted to the scope and structure of labor organization as well as to unemployment insurance or public assistance, but we cut some of the more technical passages related to these subjects. In all instances, we indicate cuts with square brackets: [. . .]. At times, to avoid long and technical descriptions, we have summarized the information contained in these entries. These summaries appear in italics.

When several versions of the same day, event, or conversation existed, our decision was guided by comparing their stylistic and informative quality while reconstructing the chronological order of day-to-day entries. The obviously rewritten passages are only partial. For instance, Plotkin had revised most of the December 1932 entries (folders 4 and 5). For January and February 1933, however—the most politically eventful weeks covered in the diary—two sets of entries are organized in the archives as two batches within folder 6 (which we called F6.1 and F6.2). F6.1 is quicker and less technical than F6.2, but the chronological order of events is split within these two batches, indicating that Plotkin at some time was in the process of reorganizing these pages. We chose entries from the two sets and tried to eliminate repetitions by signaling cuts with [. . .] while reintroducing the chronological sequence of political events and Plotkin's activity. For every diary entry we indicated its archival classification at the Kheel Center (box, folder, and batch number within folder 6).

Only two of the seven essays in the collection are included in this volume. Plotkin's article published in the *American Federationist,* "The Destruction of the Labor Movement in Germany," is reprinted at the end of the book.[86] Its importance for the awakening of the American labor movement to the antilabor reality of the Nazi regime has been noted above. Plotkin's trip of optimistic discovery thus ends on his account of the brutal attack against the persons and institutions he had encountered and admired in the previous months. Here again, names were corrected for the sake of consistency and historical accuracy. In the same line, we also reproduced Plotkin's account of the last Social Democratic meeting in Berlin held on February 27, 1933. Two versions of this event exist in folder 2. We chose the most complete one, "Berlin bleibt rot" ("Berlin Remains Red") and borrowed its subtitle, "The Last Social Democratic Meeting in Berlin," from the shorter essay that duplicates only a part of the former one. Although these pages were classified along with the other essays, and were probably intended for separate publication, they bear the same firsthand quality of personal observation as the diary entries. For this reason, we published this essay as the final entry of Plotkin's diary in February.

Spelling and Punctuation

An immigrant of Jewish origin, Plotkin had had little formal education. His style is compelling, but being neither a journalist nor a confirmed writer, he made spelling or typing mistakes in English. For instance, he wrote "lig" instead of "league," "marter" for "martyr," "musik" for "music," and so on. We silently corrected these mistakes, not seeing much interest in reproducing them. Together, they would have made the text difficult to read. Sprinkling some of the most frequent mistakes about did not make much sense, either. We have used square brackets when we introduced an obviously missing word in a sentence structure. Similarly, in most cases, German names and words had to be corrected. For instance, the word *Reichstag* is never spelled correctly. Plotkin's spelling in German was often phonetic, inaccurate, and irregular. Rarely were the names of the persons he met consistently and correctly written. We corrected these names (German labor leaders, politicians, SPD experts). In most cases, we were able to ascertain who they were and provided a footnote to identify them.[87] Very few of the persons Plotkin met or talked about remain unidentified. In itself, this is an indication of the public character of his interlocutors. Correction was necessary for the sake of historical usefulness and to avoid confusion between two names (for instance, President Paul von Hindenburg and President of the German National People's Party Alfred Hugenberg, the latter's name being regularly misspelled as "Hugenburg"). Plotkin often used German words in his text without italicizing them. We introduced italics and capitals when necessary, according to German usage—for example, *Polizei* or *Bahnhof*. But we have not italicized the names of German institutions, such as Reichstag or ADGB Gewerkschaftshaus.

The structure of Plotkin's original punctuation has been kept. We kept his way of reproducing dialogues without introducing the interlocutor's voice by a dash, but we introduced modern-usage punctuation marks when sentence structure or sequencing was not clear. We silently introduced a question mark when it was missing.

Plotkin's use of capitals for institutions or political names has been kept—for example, the *C* in *Catholics* when speaking of members of the Catholic Centrum. But frequent occurrences of the words *communists* or *socialists* are without capitals.

Notes

1. Abraham Plotkin's diary, essays, and correspondence are in the Abraham Plotkin Collection, 6036/016, boxes 1–4, Kheel Center for Labor-Management Documentation and Archives, Martin P. Catherwood Library, Cornell University, Ithaca (hereafter cited as AP Coll.).

2. ILGWU president Schlesinger to Abraham Plotkin (hereafter AP), December 10, 1931; ILGWU general secretary-treasurer Dubinsky to AP, December 11, 1931; AP to Dubinsky, December 1, 1931, AP Coll., B1, F25; Dubinsky to AP, October 1, 1931, AP Coll., B1, F10.

3. President Dubinsky, "To whom it may concern," October 17, 1932. "This will introduce Bro. Abraham Plotkin, our representative on the Pacific Coast for a number of years. Bro. Plotkin is making a tour of several countries of Europe and is particularly interested in visiting Socialist and labor institutions abroad" (AP Coll., B1, F10).

4. See Lefkovits to AP, May 23 1933, letter addressed in care of International Federation of Clothing Workers, Amsterdam, Holland, B1, F14; Plettl to AP, June 13, 1933, sent to his Paris address, 3 rue Bonaparte, Paris 6eme, France, in care of the Fédération des Travailleurs de l'Habillement, AP Coll., B2, F9.

5. Abraham Plotkin Oral History Interviews, ILGWU Records, 5780/110, B15, F5, p. 426.

6. The last diary entry is that of February 15, 1933.

7. "Berlin bleibt rot"; "The Last Social Democratic Meeting in Berlin," the latter essay a part of the former one; "The German Elections"; "First Steps"; "The Boys Must Play"; "The Terror in Germany"; "Jews in Germany"; "The Destruction of the German Labor Movement in Germany." These essays are to be found in AP Coll., B4, F2, and B4, F3. For reasons explained in the methodology section of the Introduction, we have reproduced only two of these essays in this volume.

8. Richard Rohman to AP, February 16, 1933, in Abe Plotkin Papers, MSS 060, B1, F32, Southern California Library for Social Studies and Research, Los Angeles (hereafter AP Papers). Richard Rohman was a labor journalist, then employed at the WEVD radio station in New York.

9. Plotkin was back in New York on July 1, 1933 (AP Coll., B2, F15).

10. *American Federationist* (August 1933): 811–26. We have not found any other article published by Plotkin on the German events after his return to the United States.

11. This is suggested in AP's Oral History Interviews, typescript, ILGWU Records, 5780/110, B16, F15, p. 426.

12. Abraham Plotkin's Oral History Interviews done in Los Angeles and New York, from August 1977 to January 1979, typescript, ILGWU Records, 5780/110, boxes 15 and 16 (hereafter cited as AP OH).

13. Plotkin lived in Los Angeles after retiring, and had worked there in the 1920s. This is why part of his papers are held at the Southern California Library for Social Studies and Research.

14. On the Third Reich's attempts to influence foreign correspondents, see Deborah Lipstadt, *Beyond Belief: The American Press and the Coming of the Holocaust, 1933–1945* (New York: Free Press, 1986), 6–7.

15. Through these months, Plotkin lived on a budget of nine hundred dollars from his own savings, three hundred dollars that the ILGWU owed him from his previous employment, and money that he borrowed from manager of ILGWU Local 35, Joseph Breslaw, who also intervened on his behalf with Dubinsky to obtain payment of his debt (Dubinsky to AP, October 7, 1931, AP Coll., B1, F10; Breslaw to AP, December 13, 1932, February 15, 1933, AP Coll., B1, F15; AP OH, B16, F3, p. 855). In his biography of Dubinsky, Robert D. Parmet mentions these debts to Plotkin and budget difficulties (*The Master of Seventh Avenue: David Dubinsky and the American Labor Movement* [New York: New York University Press, 2005], 68).

16. Plotkin mentions 1892 as the year of his birth in the oral interview records (AP OH, B15, F1, p. 1). This date also appears in the only known biographical note about him in *Who's Who in Labor,* edited by M. Dickerman and R. Taylor (New York: Dryden Press, 1946), 282. Yet his death certificate (Plotkin died in Los Angeles, California, on May 28, 1988) bears August 22, 1893, as the date of his birth. The one-year gap may be due to differences between the Jewish calendar

and the official one in czarist Russia. It may also simply be an error in the U.S. records, as often happened with many immigrants.

17. AP OH, B15, F1, pp. 1–5.

18. Ibid., pp. 19–24.

19. Ibid., pp. 24–43.

20. Ibid., pp. 34–48.

21. AP OH, B15, F2, p. 143; F3, pp. 190, 211–12.

22. AP OH, B15, F1, p. 55. Through his career as an ILGWU organizer, especially after the mid-1930s, given the predominantly female composition of the labor force, Plotkin organized mostly women workers.

23. AP OH, B15, F1, pp. 48–55.

24. The Socialist Party of America had included a social insurance plank in its platforms since its foundation in 1901. U.S. Congress, House Committee on Labor, *Commission to Study Social Insurance and Unemployment,* 64th Cong., 1st sess., 1916, House Report 914; Morris Hillquit, "Socialism and Social Insurance," *National Conference on Social Work Proceedings* (1917): 525–28, quoted in Daniel T. Rodgers, *Transatlantic Crossings* (Cambridge: Harvard University Press, 1998), 242. See also Norma Faun Pratt, *Morris Hillquit: A Political History of an American Jewish Socialist* (Westport, Conn.: Greenwood Press, 1979), 99–114.

25. AP OH, B15, F3, pp. 260–63; F4, pp. 246–53. See Morris Hillquit, *Loose Leaves from a Busy Life* (New York: Rand School Press, 1934), which Plotkin mentions in relation to the splits occasioned in the SPA in the war context (145–277).

26. Abraham Plotkin's personal record in AP Papers.

27. AP OH, B15, F3, pp. 216–25; John Laslett and Mary Tyler, *The ILGWU in Los Angeles, 1907–1988* (Inglewood, Calif.: Ten Star Press, 1989), 15–22; Mike Davis, "Sunshine and the Open Shop: Ford and Darwin in 1920s Los Angeles," *Antipode* 29 (1997): 356–82.

28. AP OH, B15, F4, pp. 312–20, 394–418; B15, F5, 415–21, 444–54. The "civil war in the unions" refers to these internecine battles between Communists and Socialists (or apolitical trade unionists) to capture the leadership of the garment unions. On this subject, see Melech Epstein, *Jewish Labor in America* (New York: Trade Union Sponsoring Committee, 1953), 124–56; Irving Bernstein, *The Lean Years: A History of the American Worker, 1920–1933* (Boston: Houghton Mifflin, 1960), 136–41; and Stanley Nadel, "Reds versus Pinks: A Civil War in the Unions," *New York History* 66, no. 1 (1985): 48–72.

29. AP OH, B4, F5, p. 418; Laslett and Tyler, *ILGWU in Los Angeles,* 24.

30. Bernstein, *Lean Years,* 336–37, 345–55; Craig Phelan, *William Green: Biography of a Labor Leader* (New York: State University of New York Press, 1989), 49–60; Fraser Ottanelli, *The Communist Party of the United States: From Depression to World War II* (New Brunswick: Rutgers University Press, 1991), 17–48; Harvey Klehr, *The Heyday of American Communism: The Depression Decade* (New York: Basic Books, 1984), 49–69.

31. Daniel T. Rodgers, *Atlantic Crossings: Social Politics in a Progressive Age* (Cambridge: Harvard University Press, 1998), 209–76, 386–92. See also Kathryn Kish Sklar, Anja Schüler, and Susan Strasser, eds., *Social Justice Feminists in the United States and Germany: A Dialogue in Documents, 1885–1933* (Ithaca: Cornell University Press, 1998).

32. AP OH, B15, F5, pp. 394, 401–2. Carol Aronovici (1881–1957), Ph.D., *German Housing Reform* (1914), was the author of *Housing and Town Planning* (Philadelphia: Academy of Political and Social Science, 1914), and with Elizabeth McCalmont he later wrote *Catching Up with Housing* (Newark: Beneficial Management Corporation, 1936) and *Housing the Masses* (New York: J. Wiley and Sons, 1939). His interest in German housing and architecture brought him to Berlin again in 1932 when Plotkin was there.

33. On the ILGWU and ACWA, see, for instance, Parmet, *Master of Seventh Avenue;* Steve Fraser, *Labor Will Rule: Sidney Hillman and the Rise of American Labor* (New York: Macmillan Free Press, 1991); Irving Howe, *World of Our Fathers* (New York: Simon and Schuster, 1976); Joseph Brandes, "From Sweatshop to Stability: Jewish Labor between Two World Wars," *Yivo Annual of Jewish Social Science* 16 (1976): 1–150; Isaiah Trunk, "The Cultural Dimension of the American Jewish Labor Movement," *Yivo Annual of Jewish Social Science* 16 (1976): 342–93; and Melech Epstein, *Jewish Labor in the USA, 1914–1952* (New York: Trade Union Sponsoring Committee, 1953).

34. On the succession of decisions, meetings, and compromises that led to the appointment of Hitler to the chancellorship and the initial unlikeliness of that outcome, see Henry A. Turner, *Hitler's Thirty Days to Power, January 1933* (Reading, Mass.: Addison-Wesley, 1996). More generally, among the many books on the Weimar Republic, see Karl Dietrich Bracher, *Die Auflösung der Weimarer Republik* (Düsseldorf: Droste, 1978); Heinrich August Winkler, *Weimar, 1918–1933: Die Geschichte der ersten deutschen Demokratie* (Munich: Beck, 1993); Hans Mommsen, *The Rise and Fall of Weimar Democracy,* translated by E. Foster and L. E. Jones (Chapel Hill: University of North Carolina Press, 1996); Horst Möller, *Die Weimarer Republik: Eine unvollendete Demokratie* (Munich: Deutscher Taschenbuch Verlag, 2004); Detlev Peukert, *Die Weimarer Republik: Krisenjahre der klassischen Moderne* (Frankfurt am Main: Suhrkamp, 1987); Eric Weitz, *Weimar Germany: Promise and Tragedy* (Princeton: Princeton University Press, 2007); and Eberhard Kolb, *The Weimar Republic* (New York: Routledge, 2004).

35. Results of legislative elections obtained by the three leading parties, the SPD, KPD, and NSDAP, from 1928 to 1932. See table 1.

36. Gerard Braunthal, *Socialist Labor and Politics in Weimar Germany: The General Federation of German Trade Unions* (Hamden, Conn.: Archon Books, 1978), 72–74.

37. By "labor movement" here we include labor organizations as well as parties and associations emanating from the working class. Among a voluminous

bibliography on German labor, most useful have been Arno Klönne, *Die deutsche Arbeiterbewegung: Geschichte, Ziele, Wirkungen* (Cologne: Diederichs, 1980); Richard J. Evans, ed., *The German Working Class, 1888–1933: The Politics of Everyday Life* (London: Croom Helms, 1982); Helga Grebing, *History of the German Labour Movement: A Survey* (Oxford: Oxford University Press, 1985); Heinrich August Winkler, *Der Weg in die Katastrophe: Arbeiter und Arbeiterbewegung in der Weimarer Republik, 1930 bis 1933* (Berlin: Dietz, 1987); Richard J. Evans and Dick Geary, eds., *The German Unemployed* (London and Sydney: Croom Helm, 1987); Klaus Schönhoven, *Reformismus und Radikalismus: Gespaltene Arbeiterbewegung im Weimarer Sozialstaat* (Munich: Deutscher Taschenbuch Verlag, 1989); Conan Fischer, ed., *The Rise of National Socialism and the Working Classes in Weimar Germany* (Providence: Berghahn Books, 1996); Peter Stachura, ed., *Unemployment and the Great Depression in Weimar Germany* (London: Macmillan, 1986); Wilhelm L. Guttsmann, *Workers' Culture in Weimar Germany* (New York: Berg, 1990); Michael Ruck, *Bollwerk gegen Hitler? Arbeiterschaft, Arbeiterbewegung und die Anfänge des Nazionalsozialismus* (Cologne: Bund, 1988); and Stefan Berger, *Social Democracy and the Working Class in Nineteenth and Twentieth Century Germany* (London: Longman, 2000).

38. See Richard N. Hunt, *German Social Democracy, 1919–1933* (New Haven: Yale University Press, 1964); Richard Breitman, *German Socialism and Weimar Democracy* (Chapel Hill: University of North Carolina Press, 1981); Susanne Miller and Heinrich Potthof, *A History of German Social Democracy from 1848 to the Present* (Oxford: Oxford University Press, 1986); Eberhard Heupel, *Reformismus und Krise* (Frankfurt am Main: Campus, 1981); and Donna Harsch, *German Social Democracy and the Rise of Nazism* (Chapel Hill: University of North Carolina Press, 1993).

39. Estimates indicate that blue-collar workers provided 39 or 40 percent of the NSDAP vote in every Reichstag election from May 1928 to March 1933 (Detlef Mühlberger, "A Workers' Party or a Party without Workers?" in *Rise of National Socialism,* edited by Fischer, 47–79).

40. In 1931, the KPD controlled less than 2 percent of the ADGB local councils, and, like in the United States, the dual unions it had launched (Rote Gewerkschaftsopposition [RGO]) with one hundred thousand members did not make a significant breakthrough. See G. Braunthal, *Socialist Labor and Politics,* 10; and Werner Müller, *Lohnkampf, Massenstreik, Sowjetmacht: Ziele und Grenzen der "Revolutionären Gewerkschafts-Opposition" (RGO) in Deutschland 1928 bis 1933* (Cologne: Bund-Verlag, 1988). On the German Communist Party during the Weimar Republic, see Hermann Weber, *Die Wandlung des deutschen Kommunismus* (Frankfurt am Main: Europäische Verlagsanstalt, 1971); Siegfried Bahne, *Die KPD und das Ende von Weimar: Das Scheitern einer Politik, 1932–1935* (Frankfurt am Main: Campus, 1976); Ossip Kurt Flechtheim, *Die KPD in der Weimarer Republik* (Hamburg: Junius, 1986); Conan Fischer, *The German Communists and the Rise of Nazism* (Houndsmill, Basingstoke: Macmillan, 1991); Klaus-Michael Mallmann, *Kommunisten in*

der Weimarer Republik: Sozialgeschichte einer revolutionären Bewegung (Darmstadt: Wissenschaftliche Buchgesellschaft, 1996); Lore Heer-Kleinert, *Die gewerkschaftliche Politik der KPD in der Weimarer Republik* (Frankfurt am Main: Campus, 1983); and Eric D. Weitz, *Creating German Communism* (Princeton: Princeton University Press, 1997).

41. Chancellor von Papen deposed the Prussian government (which had lost its SPD majority in April 1932) in a coup on July 20, 1932, and replaced Prime Minister Otto Braun by instituting himself as commissar of the Reich.

42. The 1919 cabinet, Philipp Scheidemann; the 1919–20 cabinet, Gustav Bauer; the 1920 cabinet, Hermann Müller; and the 1928–30 cabinet, also Hermann Müller. The SPD had also participated in the coalition governments led by Chancellor Joseph Wirth in 1921–22 and by Chancellor Gustav Stresemann in 1923.

43. Henry Ford's autobiography and other writings had been translated into German: *Mein Leben und Werk* (Leipzig: List, 1923); *Das grosse Heute—das grösserer Morgen* (Leipzig: List, 1926); and *Und trotzdem vörwärts* (Leipzig: List, 1930). Other studies had appeared on the Fordist model, such as Friedrich Gottl-Ottlilenfeld, *Fordismus: Über Industrie und technische Vernunft* (Jena, 1926); and Jakob Walcher, *Ford oder Marx: Die Praktische Lösung der sozialen Frage* (Berlin, 1925). On this subject, see Mary Nolan, *Visions of Modernity: American Business and the Modernization of Germany* (New York: Oxford University Press, 1994).

44. ADGB, *Amerikareise deutscher Gewerkschaftsführer* (Berlin: ADGB, 1926). The German delegation was received by the AFL at its 1925 convention in Atlantic City (*Proceedings of the American Federation of Labor 1925 Convention* [Washington, D.C.: Law Reporter Printing, 1925], 108–9).

45. ADGB, *Amerikareise*, 6.

46. The ADGB delegates had concluded that the real "miracle" of the American economy resided in its capacity to match the rate of growth of productivity and that of the workers' purchasing power. In the 1930s ADGB leaders were therefore slow to recognize that the 1929 crash and the ensuing depression were caused by the actual imbalance between the growth of productivity and lagging wages.

47. Plotkin's comparison of American and German labor is more fully developed in Catherine Collomp, "Abraham Plotkin, un syndicaliste américain observateur à Berlin, 1932–33, du mouvement syndical allemand et de sa chute," *Transatlantica* (2006): 1 (available at http://transatlantica.revues.org/).

48. Since 1922, the largest unions had advocated the principle of industrial organization. The line was adopted at the ADGB 1925 convention. A number of original trade unions, however, resisted this movement to protect their specific trades (G. Braunthal, *Socialist Labor and Politics*, 98–100).

49. AP Diary, December 8, 1932.

50. Owing to the high number of those who were only partially employed, the rate of unemployment was difficult to ascertain. It was higher among the

unionized or formerly unionized sectors (43.7 percent in 1932); these workers' discontent accrued to the Nazi or the Communist Party (Klönne, *Die deutsche Arbeiterbewegung,* 231–32).

51. Other labor federations existed besides the major social democratic ones, but Plotkin did not investigate them. The 700,000 membership of the Christian Deutscher Gewerkschaftsbund (DGB) mostly resided in the southern and western regions. Allied to the Catholic-dominated Center Party (Zentrum), the DGB sometimes cooperated with the ADGB on issues of wages and working conditions. The Hirsch-Duncker unions, on the other hand, maintained their separate national-liberal position that was clearly opposed to any link with the SPD or socialist labor organizations. The communist RGO never outgrew its 100,000 membership. As to the Nazis, hardly present in the workplace, they claimed about 400,000 members before 1933 through their NSBO federation (NS Betriebszellen Organisation [NS Shop Floor Organization]). Gunther Mai suggests a 250,000 NSBO membership ("National Socialist Factory Cell Organization," in *Rise of National Socialism,* edited by Fischer, 121).

52. G. Braunthal, *Socialist Labor and Politics,* 158–60; Klönne, *Die deutsche Arbeiterbewegung,* 231; Richard J. Evans, "The Experience of Unemployment in Weimar," in *The German Unemployed,* edited by Evans and Geary, 8.

53. By his 1932 coup, von Papen had taken over control of the Prussian police.

54. On the problem of political violence in the streets in Weimar Germany and especially in Berlin, see Dirk Schumann, *Politische Gewalt in der Weimarer Republik, 1918–1933: Kampf um die Strasse und Furcht vor dem Bürgerkrieg* (Essen: Klartext, 2001); Marie-Luise Ehls, *Protest und Propaganda: Demonstrationen in Berlin zur Zeit der Weimarer Republik* (Berlin and New York: de Gruyter, 1997); Eva Rosenhaft, *Beating the Fascists? The German Communists and Political Violence, 1929–1933* (Cambridge: Cambridge University Press, 1983); and James M. Diehl, *Paramilitary Politics in Weimar Germany* (Bloomington: Indiana University Press, 1977).

55. On the LSI conference and IFTU congress, see Julius Braunthal, *History of the International* (London: Nelson, 1967), 2:399–402.

56. AP, "Destruction of Labor Movement," 824–25.

57. The ADGB had proposed a vast public works program that could have created one million jobs. The SPD, clinging to its legislative privilege, did not support this plan in the name of its anticapitalist orthodoxy. The plan would have been a precursor to Keynesian deficit spending that was to be the hallmark of the New Deal. See Michael Schneider, *Das Arbeitsbeschaffungsprogramm des ADGB: Zur gewerkschaftlichen Politik in der Endphase der Weimarer Republik* (Bonn–Bad Godesberg: Verlag Neue Gesellschaft, 1975).

58. AP Diary, February 15, 1933.

59. Plotkin's father's and grandfather's trade as butchers in the Jewish small community where they lived in the Pale had placed them at the heart of Ortho-

dox ritual practice, but once in the United States the family did not remain very religious.

60. AP OH, B15, F1, p. 307; B15, F3, pp. 211–12. After living with Zelda Wright, Plotkin married Jean Bangs in the early 1920s. They were divorced in 1935. In 1949, Plotkin married Sarah Rotblatt, and the ceremony was performed by Rev. H. Rotblatt, rabbi of the Pinsker Shul Congregation at Montreal (AP Papers, MSS 060, B1, F5).

61. Plotkin mentioned that, understanding Yiddish from an early age, he really learned to speak the language when he organized the cloak makers in Los Angeles (AP OH, B16, F3, p. 804).

62. AP Diary, January 7, 1933.

63. Ibid., December 5, 21, 1932; January 7, 20, February 6, 1933.

64. George Mosse, *The Crisis of German Ideology* (New York: H. Fertig, 1964); Enzo Traverso, *The Marxists and the Jewish Question* (Atlantic Highlands, N.J.: Humanities Press, 1984), 190.

65. "Jews in Germany" (AP Coll., B4, F2) is not reproduced in this volume.

66. Hannah Arendt, *The Origins of Totalitarianism* (New York: Harcourt, Brace, 1951), pt. 1, "On Antisemitism." Leon Poliakoff also insists on late-nineteenth-century construction of modern anti-Semitism, in *History of Anti-Semitism* (New York: Vanguard Press, 1965–85). For more recent evaluations of the interpretations of Nazi anti-Semitism, see Saul Friedländer, *Nazi Germany and the Jews* (New York: Harper Collins, 1997). On the situation of the Jews in Germany during the Weimar Republic, see Wolfgang Benz, Arnold Paucker, and Peter Pulzer, eds., *Jüdisches Leben in der Weimarer Republik* (Tübingen: Mohr, 1998); Walter Grab, ed., *Juden in der Weimarer Republik* (Stuttgart and Bonn: Burg, 1986); Donald L. Niewyk, *The Jews in Weimar Germany* (New Brunswick, N.J., and London: Transaction Publishers, 2001); Cornelia Hecht, *Deutsche Juden und Antisemitismus in der Weimarer Republik* (Bonn: Dietz, 2003); Michael Brenner, *The Renaissance of Jewish Culture in Weimar Germany* (New Haven: Yale University Press, 1996); George Mosse, *Masses and Man: Nationalist and Fascist Perceptions of Reality* (New York: H. Fertig, 1980), in particular "German Socialists and the Jewish Question in the Weimar Republic"; and Reinhard Rürup, ed., *Jüdische Geschichte in Berlin: Essays und Studien* (Berlin: Hentrich, 1995).

67. "Jews in Germany," AP Coll., B4, F2.

68. AP OH, B16, F3, p. 799.

69. After his German trip, Plotkin uninterruptedly devoted his life to organizing for the ILGWU. He was general organizer for the Midwest and Chicago area from 1933 to 1953, then was appointed in the same capacity to the Miami area, which in part led him to work in Puerto Rico, and ended his career as general organizer in Hawaii (1958–59). Plotkin's ability as an organizer was remembered by contemporary ILGWU organizer and labor activist Rose Pesotta in *Bread upon the Waters* (1944; reprint, Ithaca: Cornell University Press, 1987), 186. Historian

Melech Epstein appreciated Plotkin as "one of the most intelligent and conscientious organizers in the ILGWU" (Epstein to AP, April 2, 1954, AP Coll., B1, F11). See also Epstein, *Jewish Labor in America,* 418, 440. When he retired, Plotkin participated in the ILGWU Leadership Training Institute with Gus Tyler.

70. AP OH, B16, F3, p. 840.

71. Schevenels to AP, June 3, 1933, 3 rue Bonaparte, Paris, AP Coll., B2, F15; S. Bonnet, general secretary of the French Federation of Clothing Workers, Federation des Travailleurs de l'Habillement, "Au Camarade Plotkin," June 2, 12, 1933, AP Coll., B1, F5.

72. On these meetings, see J. Braunthal, *History of the International,* 2:399–402; and Geert Van Goethem, "Conflicting Interests: The International Federation of Trade Unions, 1919–1945," in *The International Confederation of Free Trade Unions,* edited by Anthony Carew et al. (Berne: Peter Lang, 2000), 121–26.

73. Plotkin's correspondence in AP Coll., B1, F5; B2, F9; B1, F23; B2, F18; Hartig to AP, September 4, 1933, AP Coll., B1, F17.

74. AP to Stolz, November 14, 1933, AP Coll., B2, F15.

75. American Federation of Labor, *Proceedings of the Fifty-third Convention* (October 1933): 465–73. On the boycott of German-made goods and services, see Moshe R. Gottlieb, *American Anti-Nazi Resistance, 1933–1941* (New York: Ktav Publishing House, 1982).

76. AP to Martin Plettl, July 14, November 1, 1933, AP Coll., B2, F9; Dubinsky Correspondence, ILGWU Records, 5780/02, B134, F4, November 9, 1933; Joseph Schlossberg's Correspondence, ACWA Records, Kheel Center, 5619, B143; ILGWU 1934 Convention, *Proceedings,* 166; ILGWU organ, *Justice* (December 1933): 7; (March 1934): 17; Dorothea Heinrich, "Women in Hitler Germany," *Justice* (August 1934). Plettl and Heinrich definitively stayed in the United States, receiving a monthly stipend from both the ILGWU and the ACWA.

77. "Jewish Labor Committee Constitution," Holocaust-Era Records of the Jewish Labor Committee, Robert Wagner Labor Archives, Bobst Library, New York University, B1, F1.

78. On the Jewish Labor Committee, see Gail Malmgreen, "Labor and the Holocaust: The Jewish Labor Committee and the Anti-Nazi Struggle," *Labor's Heritage* 3 (October 1991): 20–35; Malmgreen, "Comrades and Kinsmen: The Jewish Labor Committee and Anti-Nazi Activity," in *Jews, Labour, and the Left, 1918–1948,* edited by Christine Collette and Stephen Bird (Aldershot: Ashgate, 2000), 4–20; Jack Jacobs, "A Friend in Need: The Jewish Labor Committee and Refugees from the German Speaking Lands, 1933–1945," *Yivo Annual* 23 (1996): 391–417; Catherine Collomp and Bruno Groppo, "Le Jewish Labor Committee et les réfugiés en France," in *1940: La France du repli, l'Europe de la défaite,* edited by Max Lagarrigue (Toulouse: Privat, 2001), 211–47; and Collomp, "The Jewish Labor Committee: American Labor and the Rescue of European Socialists, 1934–1941," *International Labor and Working Class History* (Fall 2005): 112–33.

79. In his later interviews, Plotkin mentioned the JLC's rescue activity, but attributed its achievements mostly to Dubinsky (AP OH, B16, F2, p. 747).

80. Alfred Döblin, *Berlin, Alexanderplatz: Die Geschichte von Franz Biberkopf* (Berlin: S. Fischer, 1929), translated into English by Eugene Jolas as *Alexanderplatz, Berlin: The Story of Franz Biberkopf* (New York: Viking Press, 1931).

81. AP Diary, November 24, December 10, 1932.

82. Walter Benjamin, "Paris, capitale du XIXeme siècle" (1935), in *Das Passagenwerk* (Frankfurt am Main: Suhrkamp, 1983), translated as *The Arcades Project* (Cambridge, Mass.: Belknap Press, 1999).

83. To Döblin's *Alexanderplatz,* one must add Christopher Isherwood, *Good-bye to Berlin* (New York: Random House, 1939); Siegfried Kracauer, *Strassen in Berlin und anderswo* (Frankfurt am Main: Suhrkamp, 1964); Franz Hessel, *Spazieren in Berlin* (Munich: Rogner und Bernhard, 1968); Harry Graf Kessler, *Tagebücher, 1918–1937* (1961), translated as *Berlin in Lights: The Diaries of Count Harry Kessler, 1918–1937* (New York: Grove Press, 2000); Otto Friedrich, *Before the Deluge: A Portrait of Berlin in the 1920s* (New York: Harper, 1972); Joseph Roth, *Joseph Roth in Berlin: Ein Lesebuch für Spaziergänger* (Cologne: Kiepenheuer und Witsch, 1997), translated as *What I Saw: Reports from Berlin, 1920–1933* (New York: W. W. Norton, 2003); and Jean Michel Palmier, *Retour à Berlin* (Paris: Payot, 1997).

84. On the Nazi perversion of the German language, see Viktor Klemperer, *LTI: Notizbuch Eines Philologen* (Berlin: Aufbau Verlag, 1947), translated as *Language of the Third Reich: LTI, Lingua Tertii Imperii, a Philologist's Notebook* (London: Athlone Press, 2000).

85. AP Coll., B4, F2.

86. A copy of the article is contained in AP Coll. in B4, F3. Authorization has been granted for reproduction by AFL-CIO archivist Bob Reynolds at the George Meany Memorial Archives, Silver Spring, Maryland, July 2005.

87. Most useful to identify labor, political, or intellectual personalities on the Left were Jacques Droz, ed., *Dictionnaire biographique du mouvement ouvrier allemand* (Paris: Éditions Ouvrières, 1990); Biosop Online: Biographien sozialdemokratischer Parlamentarier in den deutschen Reichs- und Landtagen, 1867–1933, Datenbank, Universität Köln/Friedrich Ebert Stifttung, http://biosop.zhsf.uni-koeln.de/index.html; Deutsches Historisches Museum, LeMo: Lebendiges Virtuelles Museum Online, Datenbank Online, http://www.dhm.de/lemo/home.html); and Hermann Weber, *Andreas Herbst, Deutsche Kommunisten: Biographisches Handbuch, 1918 bis 1945* (Berlin: Dietz, 2004).

ABRAHAM PLOTKIN'S DIARY

OCTOBER–NOVEMBER 1932

[Tuesday], October 25, 1932

B4, F1

Off at last. Don't know what I am heading for. I probably would have changed my mind about going if some occult wisdom had given me foresight. Here is to prayer that my hindsight will prove to be as exciting as my lack of foresight.

This is my second sea voyage . . . The first one was thirty years ago. The year McKinley was shot.[1] I came to the shores of the land that became my native land with wonder and dreams and the vague hopes of a child. Or was it the sense of escape from the dark shadows of terror that hovered over Czaristic Russia. The ghetto in old Russia then was neither picturesque nor pleasant. Those qualities of the ghetto, I suspect were discovered in America. Now I am going back. What for? I hardly know. Perhaps I am going so as to escape the humdrum of everyday city life in my own country. Perhaps my eyes have gotten tired of seeing the forms and people and things. I don't really know. I mean that if I have any motive in going it's stuck deep down in me, so far down that as yet I haven't seen either sight or sound of it. Perhaps later when and if I become aware of it I'll feel as silly as I look. One never can really tell how foolish one is.

So far it's been quite exciting. When the impulse hit me I decided that I was going, and going in my own way. No passenger ship with all that a passenger ship implies for me. I had no intention of being nursed and coddled by a lot of stewards. Neither did I want a swarm of tourists to help pass the

---

1. President William McKinley, assassinated in September 1901.

time. I wanted something else. I wanted to go, but not in the usual way. So here I am. One of five passengers on a freighter bound for [Le] Havre, five hours out of New York, not a bit seasick, and hoping for the best. I'm on my way.

From October 26 to November 16, 1932, in his diary Plotkin recorded impressions noted during the transatlantic crossing and then during his one-week stay in Paris. There, he enjoyed strolling through the Latin Quarter and discovered the churches, Saint Etienne du Mont, Saint Séverin, La Sainte Chapelle, and Notre Dame. He visited the Louvre, went to a concert, watched the Armistice Day parades, including the antimilitarist Communist and Socialist demonstrations, and generally observed French class distinctions in the public places. He also noted the palpable memory of the world war and the insecurity linked to unemployment and the fear that another war might take place. His last day in France was devoted to a visit to Chartres, where he admired the architecture, sculptures, and the "unsurpassed beauty" of the stained glass windows of the cathedral. He then took a train for Berlin.

◇ *Tuesday, November 22, 1932*

B4, F2

Arrived seven in the morning. Rain. Came into Potsdam station. Checked my bags and looked for a coffee shop. Found everything closed. Asked for American Express and was advised that its office is on Charlottenstrasse and that it probably doesn't open until 9 o'clock. Nothing else to do but walk. Along Friedrich-Ebertstrasse to the Brandenburg Gate and then turned up Unter den Linden. Wide paved streets reflecting both the hush of dawn and rose streetlights. Rain not unpleasant. Brought with it mist that silhouetted trees and buildings and giving everything a sense of unreality. Only a few going to work on their bicycles, scattered policemen who eyed me suspiciously and an occasional beggar. Gradually it became brighter. The street lamps were extinguished, concierges began to open the doors of their houses and to look out upon the gray morning. Daylight had arrived.

I walked Unter den Linden. I realized that the stores would stay closed until 9 o'clock regardless. Began to feel the weight of my small portable, when I noticed the sign of the Adlon.[2] Plucking up my courage I walked in and

2. Luxurious hotel, situated near the Brandenburg Gate.

sat down. Perhaps the typewriter gave me the needed sign of respectability. It didn't take long for even the thought of coffee to disappear. I sat down. I fell asleep and stayed that way for an hour. Someday, if I ever develop a troublesome conscience, I'll figure out what I owe the Adlon and send them a check, if by that time my checks are any better than they are now.

Awake, I left my regards with the Adlon, found my way to the American Express Company, got my mail, and breakfast; then to look for a place to stay in temporarily. Ordinarily this would have been easy, but I had been up all night. Finally found a hotel that looked clean at the corner of Friedrichstrasse and Dorotheenstrasse. Didn't ask how much. Too tired and trusted to luck. Learned later that the price was 2 marks 50 and 25 pfennigs more for heat. Sixty-nine cents in all.

Gave bellboy my baggage tickets. Said he would bring my bags. I knew the station wasn't very far. Stretched out to get the tired feeling out of my bones. Third-class trains in Germany are not third-class trains in France. In France the seats are upholstered and soft. Here they are all boards, hard and smooth and shiny. Your bones ache from their hardness and their smoothness makes impossible any sort of settling down. The moment the car swerves one slides with the movement of the car. Was sound asleep when a banging on my door brought the news that instead of checking my bags until called for I had, through some error, sent them to Potsdam! Dressed and went chasing for my bags. Bellhop crazy. Found my bags at the Potsdam station in Berlin, exactly where I had left them. By that time all desire for sleep was gone.

Thought of Abramovitch[3] and called the office of the *Vorwärts*[4] to get his telephone number, and soon had him on the phone. Remembered me very well. Eager for news of America and I eager for news of Germany. Could I call on Thursday at four? Certainly. Good to know there is someone to talk to. Found myself more cheerful and decided that it was time to eat again. After dinner I walked the length of Friedrichstrasse. The crowds of men and

3. Rafael Abramovitch (pseudonym of Rafael Rein [1880–1963]). A Russian Social Democrat, former Bundist, one of the leading representatives of the Mensheviks in exile, and a member of the Executive Committee of the Labour and Socialist International (1923–40). In exile in Germany between 1920 and 1933, during the Nazi regime he found a second refuge in France (1933–40), and finally in the United States. Founder and editor of the *Sozialisticeskii Vestnik* (Socialist Messenger), the organ of the Menshevik Delegation Abroad, he wrote also for the *Jewish Daily Forward* (New York). Plotkin had met Abramovitch during a visit of the latter in the United States.

4. Daily newspaper, official organ of the SPD. Abramovitch was one of its regular contributors.

women packed the street. Most of them looked healthy and fairly well clad. They hide their poverty very well or else I am in the wrong part of Berlin. The same thing last night in Cologne. The streets were jammed, as were the restaurants, and to look at the people on the streets of Cologne was to see a happy prosperous people. The crowds here are not quite as boisterous, but from their appearances it would be hard to believe that the last unemployment figures show that 44 out of every hundred Germans are out of employment, and some of them for the last three years. One would not find it easy to believe that 23,000,000 out of 64,000,000 are living, in one form or another, on the aid that the state gives them! Why this is so I do not know. Neither do I know how the German state can carry such a terrific burden. Perhaps I'll know more before I leave. But I am impressed with the fact that on the streets there is no evidence of poverty.

◇ *Wednesday, November 23, 1932*

B4, F2

To bed early last night and slept until ten this morning. Didn't know how tired I was. Breakfast of coffee, rolls and butter. Coffee even worse than the coffee in Paris and the rolls very small. Paid seventy-two pfennigs—almost eighteen cents. More than it costs in the States. Started to look for a pension in earnest. American Express Co. gave me several addresses but too far out of the center of town. Walked north on Friedrichstrasse and decided that all of the places looked uninviting. Rain. Turned back.

Two thirty decided it was wise to start to see Dr. Abramovitch. The appointment was for four o'clock. Knew enough to give myself plenty of time. What ordinarily would take thirty minutes took exactly the time I allowed myself—and congratulated myself in the bargain on having arrived there at all.

Abramovitch was one of the leaders of the Bundists[5] in Russia both before and during the Russian revolution. As a Menshevik[6] he was driven

---

5. Members of the General Jewish Workers' Bund of Lithuania, Poland, and Russia, founded in Vilna in 1897. Also known as the Jewish Labor Bund. After the Russian revolution of 1905, many Bundist militants emigrated to the United States, where some of them, such as David Dubinsky and Sidney Hillman, played a key role in the development of the labor movement in the needle trades.

6. The Mensheviks were the minority faction of the Russian Social Democratic Workers' Party. At its London convention, in 1903, the party split into two factions, the Mensheviks and the Bolsheviks, which formed two separate political parties.

out. Perhaps he left of his own accord. I've never cared to go into the details enough to find out. Does it really matter? Since then he has organized an underground movement in Russia to help the political prisoners that are in the jails there,[7] and not infrequently in helping them to escape. A tired, gray-haired, little man of fifty, he looks at you through eyes that are harassed with the years of living in the fear of reprisal for his political activities, first against the Czar and for the last fifteen years against the Bolsheviks. Remember when I wasn't permitted to enter his meetings in Los Angeles because at the time my sympathies were wholly against him. He is the same Abramovitch whose meetings in the United States were turned into a series of riots by the members of the Communist Party.[8] I heard him speak at a later date and felt his warmth and sympathy. Wondered whether he really remembered me. He had been more than cordial during our brief telephone conversation.

Abramovitch's little sprite of a daughter opened the door. With the charming gesture of a girl of fifteen she asked whether I was Herr Plotkin? On learning that I was the one expected, she asked in what language I preferred to talk, German, Yiddish, English or French! With another perfectly charming gesture she indicated that it didn't really matter. A moment later she ushered me into the living room where Abramovitch, his wife, and a young Russian refugee were seated around the table having their afternoon tea. He remembered me very well and no formalities were needed. Mrs. Abramovitch, after the usual introductions, poured the tea and within a few minutes we were old comrades. He remembered me very well. After his meetings in Los Angeles, from which I had been excluded, Leavit, the editor of the *Forward* in Los Angeles,[9] arranged a meeting between the three of us. He recalled the incident and we both laughed good-naturedly over it. Since then we have developed many sympathies in common, and many new disagreements, naturally, but the latter, happily, is in a different frame of mind than the one in which we met in Los Angeles.

What was news from America? Was it true that Foster's campaign had

---

7. Abramovitch was also an active member of the Commission for Political Prisoners, set up in 1927 by the Labour and Socialist International.

8. Plotkin seems to suggest here that his sympathies were then in favor of the communists. Yet later, when asked about this ambiguity in his diary by oral interviewer Ethel Goldwasser, he simply replied that he was not allowed into the hall by the communists picketing Abramovitch's meeting (AP OH, B16, F3, pp. 845–46).

9. Most likely Julius Levitt, the Los Angeles editor of the *Jewish Daily Forward,* whose national editor was Abraham Cahan.

been canceled by the Communist Party and that there was war between Foster and Bill Dunne, the editor of the *Daily Worker*?[10] How many votes did the Communist Party get? Was it true that Foster really is ill? Or, was there more behind Foster's illness than was on the surface? As to Foster's illness, no one in our circles really knows. I told him so. That something was brewing in the Communist Party in the way of a fight was apparent. There was enough material lying about loose to start a dozen rows. Their trade union policy in America had been a keen disappointment. In other countries, as the unemployment figures rose, the Communist Party vote rose with it. Not so in America. And then there was the whole question of using tactics in America that sound as if they came out of a Russian boiler room. Even when an American worker reads the communist press, he finds it is so alien to him that he more often than otherwise finds that he doesn't understand their terms. There is enough for them to row about.

And what about the Socialist Party? Was the party membership growing, and had I seen the election returns? There was some growth in the party membership, how much I couldn't say. Moreover, I profoundly distrust party membership that is acquired during the heat of a campaign. As to the vote, the figures quoted were 1,300,000.[11] Not enough, was his answer. There were 42,000,000 votes cast and it is less than 5%. There is something wrong with the Socialist Party in the United States. What is it? I tried to explain to him that in the United States it will be difficult to build any political party representing the workers unless the American workers themselves want it and that both the Communist Party and the Socialist Party are regarded as foreign importations. But someone had to take the lead, he answered. Yes. Fitzpatrick of the Chicago Federation of Labor tried it, and found himself

10. William Zebulon Foster (1881–1961), a former organizer of the great steel strike in 1919, shared the general secretaryship of the Communist Party of the United States (CPUS) with Earl Browder. Foster was the CPUS candidate to the 1932 presidential election. At the highlight of the campaign, on September 12, he collapsed from a heart attack before delivering a speech in Chicago. In November, the Communist Party received 102,221 votes. The illness interrupted not only Foster's campaign but also his political activity for three years. As Abramovitch suspected, there was more to the crisis. The Comintern in Moscow clearly favored the line followed by Earl Browder, who had opposed Foster on trade union issues and was named general secretary at the 1934 convention. These party factions were reflected in William (Bill) Dunne's editorials in the *Daily Worker*, the CPUS organ.

11. Actually, the Socialist Party of America polled 883,990 votes in the November 1932 presidential elections.

double-crossed by the Communist Party.[12] Fitzpatrick brought the Farmers and Trade Unions together—enough to have made an excellent start—the Communists packed the meeting and took it out of their hands. Since then, even Fitzpatrick has turned his back on every effort to build a workers' political party. How long it will take to start something again I do not know. The depression and the unemployment may hasten it. I hope so.

But why had I come to Berlin? This was more difficult to answer. Personal problems always are harder to explain than the intricacies of political parties. For one thing, I was born in Europe and was curious about it. Another thing that made me want to come was the often expressed contempt that American trade unionists have of the trade union movement in Europe. Still, another reason yet was my suspicion that in spite of our independence and individualism and constant reiteration that the American Labor Movement would form its own patterns and structure, we eventually would have to adopt some of the European forms of organization and many of their political ideas as well. The most important reason of all, I suspect, is the possibility of real developments in Germany this winter. If anything happens, I want to be on the ground. I added that I was tired of reading about things that happened elsewhere.

And speaking of something that may happen—what, Dr. Abramovitch, is going to happen in Germany this winter? That depends. That depends on many things. Negotiations are on now between Hindenburg[13] and Hitler. I don't think he [Hitler] will take the Chancellorship. Not on the basis on which it has been offered to [him]. Either Hitler thinks it is too early and that he is being prepared as goat for the troubles that are expected this winter; or else he sees the utter impossibility of doing anything if he took office with the strings tied as Hindenburg proposes to tie them.

---

12. President of the Chicago Federation of Labor (AFL), John Fitzpatrick in 1923 had proposed a united front for a Labor Party, inviting the (Communist) Workers' Party to join his Illinois-based Farmer-Labor Party. Initially supported by Foster, the Workers' Party alliance with the Farmer-Labor Party was not approved by the Comintern in 1924. Once defeated, this attempt at a united front now further isolated the Communists from the mass of American workers.

13. Paul von Hindenburg (1847–1934), former field marshal, conservative politician, elected president of the republic in 1925, reelected in 1932. Played a crucial role in the final crisis of the Weimar Republic and in Hitler's accession to power. From November 21 to November 24, 1932, after von Papen's resignation, Hindenburg negotiated with Hitler in view of offering him the chancellorship, but he rescinded his offer upon the latter's all-or-nothing strategy.

What are the strings? The five strings are simple. Hindenburg is willing to appoint Hitler, whom he detests personally, provided Hitler agrees 1) to rule legally under the Constitution; 2) not to suspend the Constitution under article 48;[14] 3) not to attempt any financial experiments that may lead to inflation and drive Germany off the gold standard; 4) that the police force and the army remain in the hands of the President; and 5) that the von Papen[15] economic program be continued. I don't think he will agree to accept office unless he is given the power with which to carry through those plans of his that he has promised both to his followers and to his backers. If he takes office under the conditions proposed, his weakness would show itself in a very short time and what political strength he has will quickly be dissipated in the coming election.

Make no mistake. Hitler is dangerous. He is the most dangerous enemy of trade unionism, social democracy and the republic that there is in Germany today. And the trade union movement is quite right in believing that between communism and Hitlerism the latter, at the moment, is by far more dangerous. In a pinch, the army might swing to Hitler, it will never swing to communism.

It is simple enough. Germany has four alternatives. She may turn towards communism, although I think this is the least of the possibilities; fascism, of which there is every possibility, if not through Hitler then through someone else; a restoration of the monarchy, something that may seem remote but of which there is some probability; or a continuation of the republic. Anything is possible, but these are the four probabilities.

But these are political probabilities? They are contingent on what happens underneath. I understand that more than a third of the population

---

14. Article 48 of the Weimar Constitution granted the president special power to suspend civil liberties in case of trouble or imminent danger to the public safety. It was precisely by resorting to Article 48 that since 1930 Hindenburg had appointed "presidential governments" that did not spring from a majority in the Reichstag and governed by decrees.

15. Franz von Papen (1879–1969), an ultraconservative politician, one of the leaders of the right wing of the Zentrum, the Catholic Party, German chancellor from June to November 1932. Without any majority in the Reichstag, von Papen resigned on November 17, 1932. Two months later, he was to be vice chancellor in Hitler's first cabinet. In 1934, after being excluded from the government, he was assigned as an ambassador to Austria (1934–38), and later to Turkey (1939–44). Tried at Nuremberg in 1946, he was acquitted, but later condemned to eight years in prison in a denazification trial in 1949.

are living on various kinds of state aid. Who and what group can bring to Germany a program that will send her workers back into the factories and start the wheels of her industry humming once more? That, he answered sadly, is impossible. No one can supply a working plan for Germany today. Those who say they can are not telling the truth. Hitler has no real program beyond promising the industrialists that he will rule Germany as Mussolini rules Italy; and to the portion of the middle class that is out of employment he is promising a general overhauling of the political machine that will make vacancies for the outs and unemployment for the ins. He cannot overhaul international capitalism and make it work for the benefit of Germany. No one can do that, not even Mussolini.

The Communists, [in spite] of their noise and bluster, in my opinion, do not want a communist Germany today. They have troubles enough of their own at home. I could tell you a good deal about that but not now. A communist Germany at the present moment, for Russia, would only mean so many more mouths to feed. No. I can't see that they have a program either. As for the Social Democrats, I think that you know by this time that Social Democracy in Germany is not a socialist party. It is closer to liberalism than to Marx.

What the future will bring I do not know. All I know is that Germany and the other nations where capitalism has developed are in the worst crisis capitalism has ever known. So far, no one has brought forward a workable program. They cannot do anything for themselves, these other capitalist nations of the world, and Germany can do nothing for herself. And no one that I know, or any group that I know, at this time can do anything for either Germany or the reconstruction of international capitalism. This crisis, like every capitalist crisis before it, will have to wait for the operation of the blind laws that govern capitalism to revive it, if that is at all possible. Perhaps, and I am not too optimistic, before the next world crisis of capitalism comes, the workers will be better prepared to meet it.

Leaving Abramovitch, I took the bus to Potsdamerplatz where I met Mina and Herbert Kline. Kline is correspondent for the *Chicago Tribune*. He is certain that a communist uprising is due in Germany this winter. If only the Trade Unions will make a united front with the Communists—they could put anything over that they want to put over. So. It is as simple as that. The only difficulty, Kline explains, is that they will have nothing to do with each other; and blames the Social Democratic bureaucrats for their narrow-mindedness. I point out to Kline that in Russia the Bolsheviks were hanging and shooting Mensheviks long before the Social Democrats in Germany felt any antagonism toward them. That since 1919 the program of the Communists was not to work with any group except for the purpose of either capturing or destroying it and that it is understandable why the leader and the rank and file of the German trade unions don't want either to be captured or destroyed. The wrangling over this while drinking coffee in Aschinger's[16] was pleasant and good-natured, but at the end left both of us exactly where we started.

◇ *Thursday, November 24, 1932*

B4, F4

I am in the Alexanderplatz[17] district. This is somewhat like our old Hell's Kitchen in New York. The district, ever since reading Döblin's[18] novel of the same title, fascinates me. It is the district of the stockyard workers' homes, the small Jewish secondhand shops, pawnbrokers and brothels. I wander about and am fascinated by the ladies of the streets and their easy ways and the embarrassment of the men whom they approach. Crowds form and dissolve, but everywhere towering over the heads of the crowds one can see the hats of the *Polizei;* and they are needed in this district. It is the district that takes the foam from the other districts of the city and turns it into scum, not all of the district is in that category, but a considerable portion of it is pretty close to what the junction of the Bowery, Division Street and China Town were in the days before the Volstead Act in America.[19]

It is late in the afternoon and beginning to become quite dark. Out of the shadows I am approached and spoken to. A somewhat foreign voice, coming from a young man, wants to know whether I can direct him to Lehninerstrasse. I do my best, and as I direct him he becomes confiding and tells me why he wants to find Lehninerstrasse. He is Russian, a stranger

16. One of Berlin's popular beer houses.

17. A main square in the center of Berlin.

18. Alfred Döblin (1878–1957), author of *Berlin Alexanderplatz: Die Geschichte von Franz Biberkopf,* published in Berlin in 1929. Staged in this working-class, semi-industrial district, and written in typical expressionist style, the novel depicts life in Berlin in the 1920s. It was translated into English by Eugene Jolas as *Alexanderplaz, Berlin: The Story of Franz Biberkopf* (New York: Viking Press, 1931).

19. The Volstead Act (October 1919) enforced the Eighteenth Amendment to the Constitution, imposing prohibition of alcoholic beverages in the United States. It was repealed in March 1933.

in Berlin, and has some gold money that he wants to change into marks. Lehninerstrasse is in the Russian quarter.[20] I tell him that it is unnecessary for him to go to the other end of town—all he needs to do is to walk over to the nearest railway station. The station is only two blocks away and I offer to show him the way. While this conversation is going on another man joins us. This last arrival is very much interested and asks the Russian whether he will show him the coin that he wants to change. By this time I am beginning to see light. The teamwork is excellent. It is amusing. I say nothing and watch the byplay. The new arrival takes the coin that is handed to him, bites it, scratches it and then drops it to the ground to see if it gives the proper ring. It meets all tests. It really is gold. It is a gold piece with the head of the Czar on it, stamped in 1910 and worth about twenty marks. The new arrival wants to know what the Russian wants for it and the Russian answers that he needs ten marks. The new arrival promptly hands him the ten marks and our Russian friend for the moment disappears. The new arrival and I walk off together.

As we walk off together he becomes curious. American? I admit it. And you're Jewish also. I admit that too. Why didn't you buy that gold piece when you had the chance? I tell him that when it comes to business I am simply not there. Well. I am Jewish too, and when I get a chance to make easy money this way, I don't let it go. I noticed that. But tell me why didn't he want to go to the post office? I don't know. Sometimes, when here for a short time only, they think that the capitalists are out to kill every Bolshevik. I think he was scared. Suddenly here is our Russian friend again. Look here, and he opens his palm, I've got ten more of these. Will you buy these too? But I notice that by this time the Russian friend and the new arrival are not looking at each other but are looking at me. The bait had been prepared. Am I going to bite? I am looked at expectantly and hopefully. I ask the new arrival to let me see the coin that he bought. He wants to know what for? I tell him that I want to compare the faces of the coins. He produces the coin. Then I ask our Russian friend to let me see one of his coins and he promptly offers me one of them. I weigh the two and it is as I suspected. I return the two coins to their owners. I am not interested. Now the recent arrival loses patience. If you don't buy them, he tells me, I will. I smile and tell him the pleasure is his. I am not interested. But why not? This time I am more emphatic. I tell my Russian friend that I have seen better counter-

20. After the Bolshevik Revolution, Berlin had become one of the main centers of the Russian emigration.

feits and that he had better get out of sight before the *Polizei* gets interested in us. Then I tell the new arrival that in America we have much smoother craftsmen. By this time the Russian friend has disappeared from sight. My new friend doesn't take it hard at all. He smiles and invites me to drink a glass of schnapps with him, and I consent on condition that I choose the place to go to. I knew the Bowery in the old days and had no intention of letting myself get entangled in Berlin's replica of America's worst. We discuss "business" conditions in Germany, and as an expert economist he tells me that there is no hope for recovery and that all will go down together. I am not quite sure just what he means by all going down together but I surmise that as a phrase it expresses the last word in pessimism. Spengler[21] would have enjoyed the complete sense of despair that my friend put into it. We had a second glass of schnapps, wished each other better luck than we had been having, and parted the best of friends. Within a moment I am again swallowed by the crowds. Crowds that mill about you and suddenly disappear, reappear and vanish again. Perhaps I shall meet my two friends again. Since my pockets are chronically empty there isn't much they can get, but I'll keep my hands in my pockets anyway.

I wander back to Alexanderplatz. The tremendous circle of new buildings in the style of American factory buildings [is] both appalling and empty. Tenants these days are few and far between. In front of these buildings are many stands of street hawkers, quite similar to the street hawkers we have on 14th Street in New York. In front of Aschinger's restaurant stands a young woman of not more than twenty-five. She is selling small boxes of candy for ten pfennigs a box. I pass her, and as I pass her I notice that she is dressed in clothing altogether too thin for this climate. I walk on, but I can't forget her pinched face. I must go back to see her again. I walk up to her, pull out ten pfennigs and awkwardly hand it to her and she just as awkwardly hands me one of the small boxes that are her small stock in trade. It is obvious she is not a working girl. I notice that she is thin, blonde and has that pallor that speaks of hunger; and from her "thank you" I also gather that she doesn't belong in the community of Alexanderplatz. She looks at the ten pfennigs as if in wonder. I wonder too and before I realize it I hear myself asking her whether she has eaten today? She doesn't answer but swerves toward me and as she swerves toward me her assortment of small boxes go helter-

21. Oswald Spengler (1880–1936), a German philosopher and writer, presenting a pessimistic vision of culture, known for his work *The Decline of the West* (1918–22; reprint, New York: Alfred A. Knopf, 1926–28).

skelter all over the sidewalk. I catch her just before she falls and as I lift her I wonder at her lightness. Before the crowd gathers, I manage to carry her into Aschinger's—and I am made to feel that the intrusion is unwelcome. A moment later the *Polizei* enters and wants to know what happened. I explain to him that the woman fainted when I asked her whether she has eaten. In the meantime the woman comes to herself. She is too frightened to speak. I insist that she eat some hot soup—that is all she will eat. Then I insist that she must let me pay for the candy that by this time has disappeared from the sidewalk. It is only a mark. A whole mark. A whole mark between herself and the possibilities of starvation! I offer to see her home, but she is too frightened. One doesn't accept the help of strangers on Alexanderplatz.

I turn back from Alexanderplatz towards Elsasserstrasse. Elsasserstrasse is a long row of saloons and apartment brothels. The ladies of easy virtue are not permitted to speak to strangers, but are allowed to stand in the doorways. The regulations forbidding them to speak to strangers [are] honored only in the breach. Every doorway has its quota of the ladies who tap one on the arm and advise one of their willingness to accept favor, at a price. Most of them are pitiful creatures to look at. And I notice that all the side streets also are full of them. One approaches me, takes my arm, and tells me her price. I answer that I am not interested. To my surprise she asks me in English—"why not?" It is hard to tell her. I say nothing and pass on.

The noise from a saloon attracts me. Apparently they are having a gay time in there. The blaring of an orchestra and the shouts of laughter speak of some sort of a celebration. I enter and choose a table and order some *Bierwurst*[22] and a glass of beer. The place is crowded with women of the streets and their gentlemen friends. Opposite to me are four young ladies sitting together. Near them is a young soldier and at his side is a young woman. She rises in disgust and walks away from him. She joins the four young women and announces that she has been insulted. He offered her fifty pfennigs! One of the four speaks up—"Why doesn't he go to Wedding?"[23] I wonder about Wedding. Does this mean that they can go still further in the scale than in the Alexanderplatz section? I must find out later.

One of the five young women rises from the table and comes over to my table. Am I out for a good time? No. I am just drinking beer. Wouldn't I consider her at two marks? No. I am not interested. One of the other young women, perhaps? No. I am not interested. She looks at me and looks at the

22. A kind of sausage.

23. One of Berlin's working-class districts.

Bierwurst. I tell her to sit down and have some, and she accepts quite readily. When the *Bierwurst* comes I order a glass of beer for her. I tell her I am not interested in her but that I am interested in Wedding. Wedding! Faugh! The women in Wedding, she tells me, will sell themselves for a piece of bread! They are not professional and many of them are not registered, and a man takes awful chances staying with them. Well, why aren't they professionals? Because they don't know any better. When they get hungry they'll go on the street, stop the first man that comes along and go wherever they are taken. Professionals have standards. Two marks is the lowest. And why are you a professional? Because I like it! Are you telling me this because you take pride in your kind of life or simply because there is nothing else for you to do? No. Because I like the life. I could live as the other women like me in Berlin live who want to be respectable. How do they live? I can't tell you. Maybe I could show. I could show you, but not at night. And then you wouldn't understand. I did it as long as I could, and then changed to this. I slept in a bed during the night and had to get out so that someone else could sleep in it during the daytime. When I came home after work, when I had work, the room was cold and dark; coal was an extravagance and light, even when I was working I had to economize on light. When I lost my job it was walk the streets all day and come to a cold dark room, over a manure pit, at night. I like this life. I don't want ever again to see the other. Will you buy me a corn schnapps? I bought the corn schnapps. Will you come and stay with me tonight—the whole night—five marks, that's all? No. I am not interested in that. But tell me this? You came from a room over a stable. You are getting older every day. The lines in your face are already becoming hard. Within a year or two what you have now that appeals to men will be gone, and your body wasted with disease. Won't you have to go back to the room over the stable? Yeah—but I don't want to think about that now. I like this life and I am going to stay in it as long as I can. And when I can't—that will be my finish. Have you read Döblin's *Alexanderplatz?* I looked up startled. Yes—I have read it, and that is why I came down here. I wanted to see the district of which Döblin wrote. She turned to the table and shouted. The *Amerikaner* has read Döblin's *Alexanderplatz!* Think of that! So they read Döblin's *Alexanderplatz* in America! Well, she turned to me, do you remember that Döblin said that time is a butcher and that all of us are running away from the butcher's knife? Well that's me, and that's all of us. You too. I'll run until I fall. But until I fall I want to live. Will you buy me another schnapps? I decide that I've had enough for one day. Enough of con men, women who faint on the streets, and women whose view is so distorted by their lives that time to them is like a sword in midair. I pay my bill and once more refuse the lady's invitation to spend the night—at reduced price—and back to the *Bahnhof*[24] at Alexanderplatz.

◇ *Friday, November 25, 1932*

B4, F4

Settled at last. Fifty dollars a month to live on and three marks a day for rent alone will not work. Found a garret on Bahnhofstrasse. Since seeing garrets in Berlin I have learned to respect them. From my window, five feet wide and six feet high, I can see half of Berlin. Within walking distance are all the museums, the Kaiserschloss[25] and the University of Berlin.[26] My window overlooks the Hungarian Consulate gardens, while in the distance are the roofs of hundreds of buildings and the steeples of half the churches in the city, including that of the Dom,[27] the leading Lutheran church in the city. The rent is forty-eight marks per month, lights, sheets, towels and coffee in the morning are thrown in for good measure. Heating is twenty-five pfennigs extra. Good Germans are used to doing [without] it—but these foreigners are a soft lot and need more heating than a chicken's egg.

Having moved my things and settled down I started my search for the Gewerkschaftshaus[28] where I was to meet Fritz Fricke, editor of the *Aufbau,* but found a message from him instead. Called away on Party business. Fricke is editor of the inner Party paper of the Social Democratic Party. Also assigned a young German to guide me to the places where I wanted to go. Decent. Where did I want to go to first? I hadn't thought about that. Wouldn't it be inconvenient? What about his work? No—it wouldn't be inconvenient; and as to his work—he shrugged his shoulder. There was nothing more to be said. Could he take me to the Berlin office of Deutscher Bekleidungsarbeiterverband, the German Needle Trades Workers' Alliance? Yes—it is within walking distance. Would I mind walking? No, I like walking. And what was his name? Fritz Hintz. And what work did he do? He had learned

---

24. A railway station.
25. The Imperial Palace.
26. Humboldt University, on Unter den Linden.
27. The cathedral.
28. The Trade Unions' House, headquarters of the ADGB, situated in the Wallstrasse, in the center of Berlin. This imposing building was built in 1922–23 and enlarged in 1930–32. Another Trade Unions' House, situated on Engeldamm Embankment, served as the administrative center and meeting point for all Berlin unions.

the trade of a machinist. So. And now he wasn't working? No. Now he wasn't working. Obviously he did not want to talk about himself. I let the matter rest. Within five minutes we were at our destination.

The DBV of Berlin occupies an enormous building on Sebastianstrasse. The building, four stories high, is the office of the Berlin organization only. All of the branches, dressmakers, coat makers of both men and women's garments, underwear—in fact all of the organizations that have anything to do with the wearing apparel industry have their Berlin offices in this building. This economy may well be recommended to the needle trades workers in New York. Their national headquarters are elsewhere in Berlin also. Entering the building we climbed to the top story and here we met *Vertreter*[29] Willy Lehman—corresponding to the secretaryship of a central council of all of these affiliated needle trades unions in Berlin.

Lehman looked over my credentials. Yes—they were all right. What did I want to know? He was somewhat sullen. The truth was that I really didn't know what it was that I wanted to know. I wanted him to tell me what he knows—and finally said so. German thoroughness, I suppose, presupposes that everyone knows precisely what one wants to know. For a moment I felt terribly foolish. Then I explained that had I known beforehand what I was looking for, the probabilities are that I would learn only of the things that I wanted and nothing about the essential things of Germany. Suddenly the whole situation appeared funny to both of us. Even Hintz smiled. And in our laughter we became friendly.

I suppose, he asked, you've come to find out what it means to be unemployed? Not from you, I answered. You are working. But I would like to know how many you have that are not working, how long they have been out of work, and what is being done for them? This was more to the point. He could give me the statistics. Was that what I wanted? Yes. Well, the Berlin section has two hundred thousand workers in all of the garment factories and stores. One hundred and twenty thousand are completely unemployed and about half of the others are employed on part-time. Some get twenty hours, others less. Was this due to seasonal employment? He smiled, this time good-naturedly. Recalling our own experience in the United States I should have known better than to ask such a foolish question. No—the needle trades in Berlin have almost dropped the word out of their vocabulary. Last fall season the section manufacturing women's coats had a few weeks of work. The others had nothing. And how long has this condition

29. Trade union officer.

existed? Since the beginning of 1930. This more or less corresponds to the similar development of "slackness" in the garment industry in America.

[. . .] You tell me that you have one hundred and twenty thousand unemployed and eighty thousand on part-time. I assume that those who are not working are getting unemployment insurance. In America we have nothing like that. I know that, he answered. I understand that in America the workers have too much pride to ask for unemployment insurance. In Germany the workers are also proud. And we are not ashamed of unemployment insurance. If it were possible we would extend unemployment insurance to the point where it would be less expensive to give us steady employment than to pay us the insurance necessary to maintain us decently. But tell me, what do your people do when there is no work? I assumed that he was talking about the needle trades workers and told him about the system of dividing the work between all of the workers during slack time.[30] And what do you do when there isn't any work at all? Are the stories we read here in Germany of men and women sleeping on the streets of New York true? Having seen this in New York only quite recently I assured him that this part of what he had read was true. He shook his head in negation. No. In Germany that would be impossible.

As to dividing the work equally—he came back to this subject because it was of direct interest to him. We have our regulations too. But in the main equal division of work is possible only when there are large shops. Our factories are small compared to yours. And even in large shops we have to keep an eye on the conditions all the time. During times of unemployment there is a psychology of fear that grips the workers. Each one becomes suspicious of the other, and not infrequently, even when there is no real cause, each one suspects that the other is sneaking in a little more than the other worker. Fear becomes the main psychological current. Please do not misunderstand me, I see hundreds of cases of self-sacrifice that would be hard to describe. But it is the main current that I am talking about. And the main current at present is fear; fear that the little work that they are fortunate enough for the moment to have may disappear after a few days; fear that the workers in

30. Plotkin's own union, the ILGWU, was in no better shape than Lehman's. He alludes here to the shorter workweek advocated by some unions, especially in the slack seasons. In labor ranks, reduction of the working time became the most obvious solution to the economic depression. At its 1932 convention, the AFL demanded a reduction of the hours of labor "as a condition essential to the restoration and maintenance of prosperity"; the five-day and six-hour-per-day workweek was now advocated.

the shop may conspire against each other; fear that a section of the workers in the shop together with the employer will conspire to defeat the rules and regulations of the union and to cheat on the tariff—wages you call them. Of course we have rules governing the division of work in the shop during the slack period, but this we have learned to our sorrow, and that is that when there is not enough employment on which to base an equal distribution of work among all of the workers in a given shop, whatever machinery you may have for its enforcement breaks down. Do you not find it so in your country? I admit to him that the most difficult problem in the needle trades in the States is just that. Then perhaps your solution will be in just such provisions as our unemployment insurance provides.

Then again we have a problem that is absent in your country. A very large proportion of our industry in Germany is carried on in the homes of the workers. That is the hardest of all to control. You have a word for it. I mention the word sweatshops. That's it. Sweatshops. We try to control it. We have gone so far as to establish by law minimum wages for those engaged in home work. I like your word sweatshop better. I tell him that we have that problem too. Perhaps not as much—but enough of it to partially make necessary the perennial strikes that are the curse of the needle trades in America. And what regulations have you for this type of worker in your country? None. Occasionally the work that is done on power machines is forbidden in home dwellings—but this law is honored in the breach and is seldom enforced. You Americans should learn respect for the law and discipline. Nevertheless you are not very happy in Germany. True. But neither are you in America. Only you are rich. Your country can afford to do many things that Germany cannot do. To lift humans into the sunshine is perhaps harder than to build pyramids—particularly when they don't want to be lifted into the sunshine. That is why we are unhappy. Our people are so fear-driven today that they are content to stay where they are, and in the meantime the employers take advantage of every opportunity to exploit their fears and their differences. We have taken wage cut after wage cut—all in proper form and under the discipline of the organization. Why? Because the spirit of our people is weak and because we who are the responsible leaders, except in rare heroic cases, dare [not] accept the challenge. The fighting spirit, for the present, is too weak. At present we are concerned only with outwaiting the crisis. Later, when conditions become better then perhaps the fighting spirit will come back. In the meantime our people are afraid of their own shadows—not mentioning the other man's shadow.

But come. Let me show things of happier years. Have you seen our offices? The building you are in now belongs to us. Here you can see how we operate. All of the unions in the garment industry are together. We have only one union for all of them. I understand that in America all of the different branches have separate unions. We in Germany cannot understand that. We walk through the building together. I am struck by the modernity of the architecture and I can't help but admire the thoroughness of the equipment and was quite charmed with the dignity and the simplicity of the meeting chambers; but it was not what I particularly wanted to see. On his promise to invite me to the meetings where I can see the workers themselves and hear them discuss their common problems, we shook hands and parted.

Leaving the Berlin headquarters of the Needle Trades Workers' Union I suggested to Fritz that it was time for *Mittag*[31] lunch. Without looking at me he indicated that it would be preferable not to, but with a little urging he consented. Finding a little restaurant, we entered and ordered some beer and sausages, Fritz neither talking nor looking in my direction. The beer and sausage consumed, and not once did Fritz look at me, nor had he spoken one word. It was not sullenness. Something was bothering Fritz. Instead of looking at [me], I noticed that he would double up his fist until the skin on his knuckles [was] taut and almost white. How old are you Fritz? Twenty-two. Been out of work long? Three years. The skin on his knuckles got tighter and whiter. Three years. Well, it won't do any good worrying about it. Three years is a long time. But unemployment can't last forever. That's what worries me. In three years much can and has happened. If I were asked to go back to work tomorrow, I do not know whether I would still know my trade or whether the machinery on which I learned my trade is still the same. I may have to learn my trade all over again. And the fist bore more heavily down on the table and the fingers were clenched into the skin; and Fritz kept looking at his fist as though, if he could, he would find the answer to his agony through the use of it.

◇ *Saturday, November 26, 1932*

B4, F4

Bathing in Germany is not a right. It is a privilege based on two conditions: first that you are able to pay for it; and second that you don't mind going to considerable trouble in getting it. On asking my landlady this morning where the bathroom was, she looked at me in astonishment. The bathroom! Sure, it was the bathroom I wanted? Yes—it certainly was the

31. Midday.

bathroom I was looking for. The towel on my arm and the soap in my hand [were] indicative of determination and purpose. She stared at me, then at the towel and soap. Yes, I repeated, nothing else would do—I wanted a bath, and a bath I was determined to have. At this she left me cold. The lady was not in the humor for being trifled with. Strangers dressed only in pajamas, house slippers and bathrobe, looking for a bathroom either was a joke, and if not a joke cast serious reflections either on her or her house. She called her husband. In the meantime my teeth were chattering and my skin was turning blue from the cold. Finally her husband arrived. The American wanted a bathroom! Didn't he know? No. I didn't know whatever it was that there was to know. All I wanted to know was where in the name of all the saints on the calendar the bathroom was located. My landlady finally solved the problem. She called the lady on the floor below, and the two ladies called on the lady on the first *étage*. The three of them held a consultation that lasted ten minutes and at the end of the ten minutes my landlady came back in triumph. In her hand she held a note and on it was the address of the nearest public bath in Berlin. Thus ended my quest for the bathroom. I shall know better next time.

Had a short talk with Dr. Georg Stolz,[32] assistant secretary of the International Federation of Trade Unions.[33] Doesn't think anything startling will happen either in Germany or in any of the other European countries and that they will muddle through. Was very pleasant and gave me some letters to representative men in the labor movement here.

◇ *Sunday, November 27, 1932*

B4, F4

Yesterday my next-door neighbor, a young American named Pinson, introduced himself and invited me to go to the exhibit of contemporary

---

32. Georg Stolz (whose first name Plotkin generally anglicized as George), a Czechoslovakian trade union leader and socialist. Stolz was assistant secretary of the International Federation of Trade Unions from 1931 to 1940. In 1941 he became president of the Czechoslovak Trade Union Centre in exile in Great Britain.

33. The International Federation of Trade Unions was the main international trade union organization between the two world wars. In 1931 its headquarters was transferred from Amsterdam to Berlin, then to Paris in 1933 after the Nazi seizure of power, and in 1940 to London. In 1945 the IFTU was dissolved to be replaced by the World Federation of Trade Unions.

moderns at the Krohnprinzpalast.[34] May they live a long time, long enough to paint something worthwhile. Either my tastes are becoming conservative or the things I saw were really bad. On the way out we ran into four Van Goghs—and these were really worth seeing. From there we went to see the Pergamon. The Pergamon is the Greek section in the National Museum. I was so enchanted with this that Pinson and the friends who were with him had a difficult time getting me out. It is useless to attempt to describe it, as useless as trying to describe the Grand Canyon to Europeans. It was three o'clock—closing time—before they could get me out. I'll have to go back and see it again.

Leaving the group I went window-shopping. Clothing is amazingly cheap. I can buy a fair suit of clothes for ten dollars. A good hat can be bought for six marks, a hat that in the States would cost as many dollars. Shoes go for a song. The highest-priced shoe that I saw was twenty marks, a little less than five dollars—and shoes can be bought for as little as eight marks—shoes that look both durable and wearable. Shirts, however, are quite expensive, more expensive than in the States. That reminds me, laundry is even more expensive than in America. I paid seventeen cents a shirt for laundering. Restaurant food is as expensive as in the States, and some are even more expensive. The same meals that I can get in New York for fifty cents would cost as much here, while coffee is even more. Bread has to be ordered—and water has to be pleaded for. And so far I have not seen butter placed on the table in any of the restaurants which I have been in.

Amusements are comparatively cheap—except moving pictures. The cheapest price in the evening to a moving picture show is one mark—twenty-five cents. The first-run houses are even more expensive, about on a par with New York. Music concerts or the opera offer all sorts of prices but one can get a fair seat either at a concert or the opera for two marks, about fifty cents. In the theaters one can get in for less, passing the Odeon I noticed that they are giving a musical comedy—"Musik von Susie"—that had been highly praised. Walking over to the box office I read the price list and found that the cheapest price was fifty pfennigs, about twelve cents. Entering I found a modern theater, an excellent cast splendidly directed, and music

34. Crown Prince Palace, one of the main palaces on Unter den Linden. During the Weimar Republic it was a museum, holding the modern art collection of the National Gallery. It was closed after Hitler's seizure of power, modern art being considered "degenerated" by the Nazis. Wholly destroyed during World War II, it was reconstructed in 1969.

that was far superior to the run of Broadway shows. Leaving the theater I walked to Unter den Linden and within the two blocks between Unter den Linden and the theater I counted no less than thirty prostitutes—until I got tired of counting.

◇ *Monday, November 28, 1932*

B4, F4

Woke this morning to see, through my garret window, frost on the distant roofs. Frost, white, almost like snow. In the distance the white-green circular roof of the Dom and the tall steeple immediately behind it pointing into a sky of pink and rose sunrise. Washed in the cold water and wondered what it would be like when real cold weather comes along.

Walked Charlottenstrasse to the American Express Company. Called for my mail. Found it was still early and decided to walk to my appointment and enjoyed the frosty morning air. Arriving at the headquarters of the ADGB.[35] I presented my letters of introduction. I hadn't long to wait. A few minutes later a comparatively young man walked in and presented himself as Herr Dr. Franz Joseph [Furtwängler],[36] the directing head of the statistical and publishing departments of the Allgemeiner Deutscher Gewerkschaftsbund—the largest trade union group in Germany representing eighty percent of the working people here. The usual formalities were easily glossed over. He had heard of me through President Plettl[37] of the Garment Workers' Union and also through George Stolz, the assistant secretary of the International Federation of Trade Unions. Would I come to his private office where we could

---

35. ADGB, Allgemeiner Deutscher Gewerkschaftsbund, the General Federation of German Trade Unions.

36. Franz Joseph Furtwängler was head of the ADGB Department of Statistics and Publications. Plotkin misspelled his name as "Fuchwanger." Author of numerous publications on social and trade union issues, Furtwängler had been a member of the German trade union delegation that visited the United States in 1925.

37. Martin Plettl (1881–1963) was president of the German Clothing Workers' Union (Deutscher Verband der Bekleidungsarbeiter) from 1920 to 1933. He had also been part of the 1925 German trade union delegation to the United States. After the Nazi takeover in 1933, he was arrested by the Nazis in May 1933, and later escaped to Amsterdam. Through Plotkin's help, he was invited to the United States by the ILGWU and ACWA in the fall of the same year. He stayed in the United States until his death.

talk undisturbed? A moment later we were in his quiet den—surrounded by every publication published anywhere and in any language dealing with labor problems,

Dr. Franz Joseph Furtwängler is somewhere in his late thirties. Medium height, slim, blue-eyed, reddish hair rising in a pompadour, and a figure tense with nervous energy. When he speaks to you his eyes snap and the nervous tension within him expresses itself through the movement of the head and hands and the frequent shifting of his body. A tired nervous energy, too tired to rest, and too weighted with problems to rest without irritation, he had the harassed appearance of a slim trim young American businessman who was on the verge of losing a big deal. A metalworker by trade, he had come up out of the ranks, became an authority on labor conditions in Germany and already is the author of several books on labor conditions in Germany, one on labor conditions in India, and is now, in his spare time, writing on labor conditions in the Balkans![38]

I asked him whether he was related to [Feuchtwanger][39] the writer. No. There is no T in his name.[40] He knew his work and thought highly of it. Did I know Döblin? Fortunately I did. And what did I think of Feuchtwanger's and Döblin's work? Very highly indeed. Yes. They are good writers. There are other writers in Germany, writers who are much better. I admitted my interest and my ignorance. That is nothing. When I was in America some seven or eight years ago I got acquainted with the work of Sinclair Lewis—you must have other writers of whom we know nothing in Germany. The next half hour we forgot the purpose of my visit and discussed Upton Sinclair, Sinclair Lewis, Theodore Dreiser, and Sherwood Anderson.[41]

And how are conditions in America? I told him what I had seen. I told him of our bread lines, and our men sleeping in doorways, on courthouse

---

38. F. J. Furtwängler, *Arbeit und Volksklassen im Wandel der Geschichte* [Work and Classes in the Course of History] (Berlin: Verlagsgesellschaft des ADGB, 1928); *Die weltwirtschaftliche Konkurrenz des indischen Industriearbeiters* [Indian Industrial Workers and World Economic Competition] (Leipzig: Deutsche Wissenschaftliche Buchhandlung, 1929); *Indien* [India] (Berlin: Büchergilde Gutemberg, 1931).

39. Plotkin refers to the German writer Lion Feuchtwanger (1884–1958), whose name he incorrectly spelled as "Fuchtwanger," author of many historical novels, including *The Jew Süss* (1925; New York, 1930). During the Nazi regime Feuchtwanger had to live in exile in France and, after 1940, in the United States, where he died.

40. Plotkin's spelling confusion: there actually is a *t* in Furtwängler (see note 36).

41. Pioneering the schools of literary realism, naturalism, and social satire, these four writers were engaged in sharp criticism of American society.

steps, on park benches and on subway stairs. He looked at me in astonishment. In America! I nodded. Yes, in America. His fist came down on the table—In America! America and men sleeping on the streets! Why if Germany had the resources of the United States . . ., the rest he left unfinished. It was too much for him. Many times during the six hours we spent together he would come back to it. Bread lines and men sleeping in doorways in the cities of America—it was beyond belief and beyond his imagination. The America he had seen was altogether too rich, its prosperity was too amazing, its tall buildings, and its high standards—hadn't America through its own resources practically paid for the war?—it was incredible; and incredible it remained.[42]

So—you have come to Germany to study what we have done for our unemployed and what we are doing to solve our problems? How long do you intend to remain? And do you expect to know Germany after a short visit? And was I going to remain in Berlin all of the time? After all Berlin is not Germany. I answered that I came to see how similar their problems were to ours, and to see what solutions they had for problems that were very much like our own. How long I was going to remain I could not say exactly—but it would be at least several months—and that I intended to go into those districts where it is reported that unemployment insurance is breaking down because the communities are going bankrupt. What about the unemployment problem, and what about those districts where the workers may face starvation because the communities in which they live may go bankrupt?

That is our danger point, he answered. You see, there are three forms of help given to the unemployed. The first comes through the funds that are accumulated through contributions between the workers and their employers. The second comes from the state, that is, the state governments in which they live.[43] These two are limited. Then comes the help from the city—this is not really unemployment insurance. After twenty-six weeks when the state aid stops, the worker has to fall back on the city, and while this is official aid, it is nevertheless limited by the funds that the city has. When the city's funds are gone then we may expect desperation and rioting. It is here, at this point, that we will get much excitement this winter, excitement that in all likelihood may lead to a revolutionary movement. I

42. During the 1920s the United States was seen in Germany as the symbol of industrial modernity and wealth. See ADGB, *Amerikareise deutscher Gewerkschaftsführer* (Berlin: ADGB, 1926), partly written by Furtwängler.

43. The local governments of the *Länder.*

looked at him expectantly. Yes. I mean a revolutionary movement. I do not mean a revolution. A revolution in Germany is impossible. You speak as if you expected something of that nature to develop this winter. Yes. I can say to you that I shall be very much surprised if it does not come.

But who would lead such a revolutionary movement? Anyone who will promise them bread. Our people are desperate now. Any addition to their misery will bring them to the breaking point. I say a revolutionary movement because, I repeat, a revolution is impossible. Anyone who promises the masses bread is promising something that is impossible without a revival of international trade, and a revolution will not bring international trade to Germany one hour sooner, if anything it will postpone the revival of Germany for a good many years. We have to import forty percent of our food now—and who could promise to bring in food for Germany when conditions are such as to make it impossible for our country to function along industrial lines? But there is that danger. Hungry men do not listen to reason. Anyone who will come to them and promise them something to eat will carry them as the wind carries pollen. How else can you explain the enormous vote that the Communists and the Hitlerites have been getting? It is because the masses think that through some miracle these two groups can bring food to them. It is absurd, and the leaders of these two groups know that they are not telling the masses the truth when they promise them bread and better conditions at present, and both groups, confronted with the possibilities of taking power in order to solve the problem of food, would shrink, as you can see from Hitler's maneuvering. I tell you that unless Germany can exchange her goods for bread she will starve.

You say there is not enough bread in Germany. I have seen somewhere that the imports of foods in Germany have dropped enormously during the past two years. Yes—that is so. It has dropped—and so has the consumption of food. Our people are not eating as much as they did in 1928 and 1929. But isn't it possible that Germany could grow all of her food supply? He shook his head. No. That is not possible. Of course, he added, I speak as one who does not know much about this problem. You could speak to Dr. Bading, the agricultural expert for the Social Democratic Party. I will give you a note to him. But to me it is inconceivable. We have a very small area of ground—about the size of your state of Texas—and we have a population of sixty-four million. I know there is much waste in the manner in which we handle our soil. We have not used as much modern machinery perhaps, and have grown the wrong kind of crops, so much so that every time I speak to our agricultural experts they seem ready to go mad at the stupidity of our landowners, but I do not believe that we can come anywhere near growing all of the food we need. By this time it was noon. Would I have what is called in America a sandwich? We could talk in the restaurant. Within a few minutes we were seated in Aschinger's where sandwiches are only half clad and food is not intended to be eaten. I have seen Germans walk into Aschinger's, order a glass of beer, go to the magazine rack and read every one of the magazines and newspapers one after the other, all over this one glass of beer.

You say that you expect a revolution this winter, rather a revolutionary movement. What signs should one be looking for? I mean this. What would be the signal for such an uprising? Sporadic riots—they mean nothing. We have them in the United States, and no one in the United States seriously expects even a revolutionary movement. In Germany, he answered, riots are serious, especially at this time. But the danger comes not from riots alone. You will notice as you go along certain peculiarities in the similarity of the programs of both the Fascists and the Communists. Both say that whoever starts "plundering," the other will follow. That they do work together occasionally because of the similarity of their programs you would have seen, had you been here, during the streetcar strike.[44] Both wanted the strike so as to discredit the social democratic leadership of the streetcar men's union. And both of them joined hands for the time being to help make it a successful strike. That they were not successful is another story. The point is this, should a city like Cologne, a city that will probably go bankrupt, be unable to feed its unemployed, and the unemployed start plundering the stores, both the Communists and the Hitlerites will follow, and the sympathy of the population in the city will be with them. Once the movement in this direction starts there is no telling how far it will go. It will inevitably mean the *Polizei* and the soldiery and bloodshed. Then there is the danger of contagion. These things spread from city to city, and in Germany the cities are pretty close together, like wildfire. How far rings of isolation would work is problematic.

You speak of Cologne. That is not far from the Ruhr. It is quite close.

---

44. Furtwängler mentions the recent Berlin streetcar strike (November 3–7, 1932). The strike had jointly been organized by the Nazis and Communists to protest wage cuts in the Berlin public transportation system (BVG), but also to gain the workers' votes for the November 6 political elections. Several persons died or were wounded in the clashes with the police; the strike resulted in the laying off of about 10 percent of the 25,000 BVG employees.

Also quite close to France. What would France do, assuming that a revolution in that district were successful? Here you open a much larger field. The Hitlerites can do nothing. The Communists are promising bread from Russia—when they can't feed themselves—and the French promise stones whenever they get an opportunity to throw them. You think then that if an uprising in the Ruhr were successful France might walk into the Ruhr and give your industrialists the protection that your national government apparently would be unable to give them? He shook his head. I don't think so. Why not? The German industrialists would hardly dare accept such protection and they didn't during the last Ruhr invasion.[45] I was skeptical and he saw my skepticism. What makes you think that the Ruhr industrialists would fall in with the French in the event of an uprising in the Ruhr? How much did the Reichstag pay them the last time the French were in the Ruhr? Yes—that is so. But French domination of the Ruhr would lead to too many difficulties for her in spite of any traitorous activities, no matter from what source.

Having finished our sandwiches and beer we adjourned to the coffee shop next door. It wasn't long before we were at it again. Then tell me, after all the pessimism that you've expressed, what is the answer? The answer that I can see is this. And I hate to look forward to it. Hitlerism is rapidly going to pieces. And because of this the Hitlerites are becoming desperate and would be willing to try any measure possible to recuperate their dwindling strength. The Communists are now on the upgrade. Whenever a Hitlerite leaves the Nazis, he goes straight to the Communists, they are growing in strength. They too may face the same fate as the Hitlerites unless they keep their promises to the masses. In the meantime, conditions are becoming desperate and may ignite without the help of either one of the two. When it does, then both groups will be unable to restrain their followers from joining it. It will mean chaos. And I am afraid of it. But you've given me only half of the picture. What if these things that you expect to materialize fail to do so? What then is the program for the rehabilitation of German industry so that your millions of workers may return to their machines? Here again, I have little hope. Can't you see? We are an industrial nation. We depend on our exports. We need food. And we are answered with stones, first through tariffs, then through something worse than tariffs, what France calls hegemony. We are as blocked as if we were still in the war. Before we can come through, there must be a complete change of policy on the part of France and

45. The occupation of the Ruhr by French troops in 1923.

that I am afraid will be a long time in coming. *Ach*—France—she is asking the impossible. She is asking to be guaranteed a hegemony of her control of Europe when that is impossible. For the present she has all of us in her grip. [. . .]

He looked at his watch, it was almost four. We had talked for six hours, about everything under the sun, and had established a firm friendship. We stepped out into the dusk, shook hands, agreed to meet again and parted.

He was going back to his office to finish his work. I was on my way to meet friends and to hear the first performance of *Wozzeck*[46] given in Berlin. A magnificent performance and a magnificent audience—with all of fashionable Berlin in attendance. My seat in the gallery cost two marks fifty—sixty-two cents, seven loaves of bread. . . . There were no workers in the gallery. The workers were marked by their absence.

◇ *Tuesday, November 29, 1932*

B4, F4

All stores close promptly at seven o'clock. Aschinger's restaurant, a combination restaurant and bakery chain similar to Child's in America, is permitted to serve food at all hours, but the bakery department that sells goods to be taken out must close promptly at seven. When I tried to purchase a cake to go with my morning coffee after seven P.M., I was told that it was forbidden, although the same girl who was on the counter before seven was still dishing out cakes to the waiters to serve to the patrons. During the day I must watch my tobacco pouch, otherwise the evening will find me unable to get any tobacco at all. Imagine a United Cigar Store closing at seven!

The seven o'clock rule is general, and is part of the national agreement between the clerks and other affected groups and their employers in the retail trade. Department stores are open until seven in a good many instances, but the women have a two-hour rest period and lunchtime during the day—and their wages also are governed by law. This really amounts to a national control of hours and a national agreement on minimum wages to be paid to the women and white-collared workers in retail establishments.

---

46. The first full performance of this opera by Austrian composer Alban Berg (1885–1935) had actually taken place in Berlin in December 1925.

DECEMBER 1932

Thursday, December 1, 1932

B4, F4

The Berlin variety of grip is not to be trifled with, as I learned on Wednesday. Woke up with pains in my back, head dizzy, and feet unwilling to do anything else but rest in bed. Decided to obey my feet and let my landlady supply me with medicines and soups. Asked her what play she would like to see and was surprised to hear that she wanted to see an American picture called the "Chump." The mystery was solved when I noticed Wallace Beery advertised in the "Chump."[1] To see the "Chump" we will go with an extra supply of handkerchiefs on hand in case of emergency.

The League for Men's Rights,[2] to which Plettl, the President of the German Needle Trades Alliance, sent me an invitation, turned out to be a forum somewhat on the American order. The League itself is liberal and pacifist in its tendency but is willing to give anyone who has a message a hearing—provided he is willing at the same time to listen to such criticism as the audience or members of the audience may want to express. This meeting was addressed by Prof. Walter A. Berendsohn[3] of Hamburg on the menace

1. *The Champ*, an MGM melodrama, directed by King Vidor, released in November 1931, in which Walter Beery played the role of an alcoholic prizefighter, for which he won an Oscar.

2. The Deutsche Liga für Menschenrechte had been formed out of the Bund Neues Vaterland, a pacifist organization founded in November 1914. It was forced to dissolve in 1933 because of persecution by the Nazis.

3. Walter A. Berendsohn was a professor of Scandinavian literature at the University of Hamburg and active member of the League for Men's Rights. He emigrated to Sweden in 1933.

of the growing Nationalism. Somewhat accustomed to hearing professors in the States I was surprised at the feeling and heat that the professor put into his talk. The Hitlerites particularly were singled out and placed on the carpet, both for their unwarranted attacks on Internationalism and Judaism and for the support they are purported to have received from the Krupps[4] and other German industrialists. The Krupps, Berendsohn charged, during the war not only made profits out of the guns used by German soldiers, but another profit out of an understanding with Armstrong and Co., the English munitions manufacturers, whose guns and bullets shot German soldiers. He announced himself as a Social Democrat, and offered as a solution a program—a Marxist program—to be carried out along peaceful and democratic lines.

Berendsohn's talk concluded, the Chairman called on Professor Arthur Rosenberg[5] of the University of Berlin, whose book on Marx has just been published.[6] The substance of Rosenberg's book is that Marxism has its psychological roots in the feudal system. Nationalism, he said, is desirable and necessary. The restrictions of the feudal viewpoint in politics have as yet not been eliminated, and until that is done genuine democracy is impossible. Marxism is only an offshoot, a protest against feudalism in national life, in industry and in our entire economic order, and Marxism is certainly not the answer. I was waiting to hear his opinion on Hitlerism—and his answer to the charges against the Krupps and other industrialists who are supposed to be behind it. This however was prevented by the lack of time. After him others stepped forward, mostly young men with panaceas, each speaking in his turn; with Professor Berendsohn coming at the end to rebut all of the other speakers. But inasmuch as my head was beginning to travel in circles again and all of the bones to my body were in rebellion, I decided that for the time being even the growth of nationalism, Marxism, feudalism in politics and

4. The Krupps' major steel and manufacturing concerns financed Hitler and the NSDAP, and greatly benefited from the Third Reich regime. Most prominent in the family, Gustav Krupp von Bohlen (1870–1950) was president of the National Association of German Manufacturers from 1931 to 1934. Accused of war crimes at the 1946 Nuremberg trial, he was not sentenced because of his deteriorating health.

5. Arthur Rosenberg (1889–1943), a historian and one of the leaders of the KPD in the 1920s, left the party in 1927, while remaining an independent Marxist. He found refuge in England after 1933 and then in the United States. He wrote about the history of the Weimar Republic, Bolshevism, and democracy.

6. Probably *Geschichte des Bolschewismus: Von Marx bis zur Gegenwart* (Berlin: Rowohlt, 1932). Plotkin's account of this book, however, is questionable.

industry, and all the other panaceas, were unimportant. I quietly sneaked out of the hall, went to the nearest restaurant where I could get hot rum and drank almost a pint of it before leaving, and tied me home to revolutionize my own system before venturing out on larger undertakings.

◇ *Saturday, December 3, 1932*

B4, F5

I see that Leipart and Eggert,[7] your headmen of the trade unions, have been in a conference with General von Schleicher.[8] Is it true that they have come to an understanding? I was talking to Miss Heinrich, the young woman who officiates as secretary to Martin Plettl, President of the German Needle Trades Alliance. We were on our way, Plettl, Miss Heinrich, and a man who for obvious reasons had best remain unnamed, a principal of a school who told me that there is fifty percent more illness among the children in his school since the depression. No, Miss Heinrich answered. There is no understanding and no agreement. The trade union movement in Germany does not come to agreements with the von Schleichers. He called our headmen and they came. It is what in America you call a courtesy—on both sides; a courtesy that von Papen tried to dispense with. Our headmen, as you call them, took the opportunity to tell him a few things that would help Germany overcome the crisis. Is that not so Mr. Plettl?

Mr. Plettl agreed and elaborated. Since September 5th, when von Papen issued his decree that was to have revived Germany's industries, there has been an increase of unemployment amounting to 160,000. There are that

---

7. Theodor Leipart (1867–1947), ADGB president from 1921 to 1933. Leipart led a moderate reformist policy for the federation, steering it clear of communist or other radical factions. Emphasizing ADGB political independence, Leipart was not entirely averse to press labor demands to von Schleicher, but he was dissuaded from that course by SPD authorities. After Hitler's seizure of power, he tried in vain to save the unions from Nazi takeover by offering concessions. Arrested in May 1933, he remained in Germany after his release. Wilhelm Eggert (1880–1938), ADGB secretary and head of the ADGB economic policy section, was an expert in charge of the program for job creation *(Arbeitsbeschaffung)*.

8. General Kurt von Schleicher (1882–1934), chancellor from December 3, 1932, to January 28, 1933. Dissociating himself from von Papen's wage policy, he tried in vain to win the support of organized labor. That unlikely alliance would have involved the unions, the NSDAP left wing around Gregor Strasser, and the Reichswehr. Von Schleicher was assassinated by the Nazis in 1934.

many more out of work now than there were when von Papen formulated his famous economic program. To stimulate the revival of industry he asked that a subsidy of $175 million be given to the employers who would hire additional workers. Each employer was to be subsidized to the extent of 100 marks for each additional worker he hired and kept for three months, and 100 marks for every three months additional. At the same time, he announced that those employers who took advantage of this need not be bound by the tariffs, or wages, agreed on between the unions and their employers. It was provocative. It practically said to the employers to go ahead and break the unions, while you are doing this the state will pay you a subsidy. It did not say this openly, but the inference was as broad as daylight and many of the employers promptly proceeded along the lines suggested to them. Moreover, it was a form of intimidation to the labor arbitration courts, and the result was that many of the decisions that we had been expecting in our favor were suddenly turned against us.

You must know something of our judicial system as it affects labor relations in Germany to understand what this order of von Papen's meant. It practically told the representatives of the government in the labor and arbitration courts to side with the employers and to rule against us. It resulted in wages dropping far more rapidly than prices; and it also resulted in hundreds of strikes and lockouts. If you have seen the report in the *Gewerkschaftszeitung,* our official publication, then you know the deplorable results that followed von Papen's blundering. At a time when the whole German economy is dependent on the purchasing power of our internal market, von Papen proceeded to reduce it until the situation is bordering on the catastrophic.

Leipart and Eggert, in their talk with Schleicher, made these facts plain to him. They pointed out that under this subsidy, which was really a subsidy for cutting wages, only 40,000 men were put to work, and that in the corresponding period 160,000 were added to the total of the unemployed. They asked that the remaining funds of the $175 million created for this purpose be allocated to work creating agencies of a public character, that is, for public works of various sorts. They also insisted that the way out of the crisis was not through wage cutting but through the increase of the purchasing power of the workers. In addition, they insisted that there be no further tampering with the unemployment insurance funds; and that the 40-hour week be established nationally so as to absorb some of the unemployed. Leipart and Eggert talked practical economics to Schleicher. The same money that was to have been used as a subsidy to the employers, used for public works on a basis of the national government doing part of the financing could, for a short time, put to work 1,000,000 men. What the results of their talk with Schleicher will be, it is yet premature to say. But agreements and compacts between trade union leaders and the Schleichers, that is impossible. We are Social Democrats, and between Social Democracy and the frank representatives of a militaristic regime as embodied by von Schleicher, there can be no agreements. Plettl, who is medium height, somewhere in the early forties, ruddy-faced and bald-headed, crinkled up his little mustache until it bristled like a porcupine. No, Mr. Plotkin, between us and the von Schleichers, there can be no agreements.

By this time we had arrived in Zehlendorf, on the west end of Berlin, where one of the sections of the community housing buildings are located. Block after block of houses. One block patterned after another, strangely American, but an occasional breaking of the monotony with blocks of another pattern, it bore the stamp of regimentation and standardization, precisely as do the war-built strings of apartments and bungalows in any large American city. Nevertheless, they possess two qualities that are distinctly European. They are primarily built for workers' comforts and as far as modern architecture could achieve this object, within the range of building costs in which they had to work, it has been achieved. Trees and playgrounds are more than abundant. In fact, the occupants complain in one section that there are too many trees. During the short days of the winter months, they complain, they cannot get enough sunshine. This is not surprising. In fact, the buildings stand in the old communal forests, and except those trees which had to be chopped down to make room for the buildings, the forest remains intact.

After the war—as in the States—the housing shortage was so acute that the trade unions organized cooperatives to build housing quarters for their members. This they did so well, that the government recognized their initiative and their ability and proceeded to give them aid in the financing of their projects. Up to the present, there have been approximately one hundred thousand apartments built in Berlin alone, while in all of Germany the number of apartments that have been built since the war [reaches] one million eight hundred thousand. The buildings themselves fall in two classes in this district. The first class is a single family dwelling of either four or five rooms, while the second class is an apartment somewhat along the lines of modern apartment houses in America. The rents vary from $2.50 a month for two rooms all the way up to $14 dependent on size, transportation, whether there is a bath, central heating etc. The maximum rental for the largest apartments, 4 and a half rooms, is 120 marks—about $30—the lowest

$22. Plettl tells me that the rentals are somewhat higher than in the older sections of working-class districts in Berlin, but smilingly added—wait till you see them.

[. . .] As soon as twilight fell Plettl suggested that we go into the Wald. The Wald is the old communal forest that at one time surrounded Berlin. It is not hard to imagine that it was an excellent military buffer between Berlin and its enemies. After five minutes' walk we were right in the thick of the woods, mostly pine and birch, and quite a few silver birch scattered all through the forest. A few minutes later we came to what they called an inn. In front of the inn were hundreds of tables that during the summertime are doubtlessly occupied by the workers living in the cooperative buildings nearby. At the present time, however, it is too cold to sit outdoors. Entering the inn we found a glass-encased balcony running for hundreds of feet. Here we settled into comfortable seats, ordered pastry and coffee, and settled down to two hours of idling and talking.

◇ *Sunday, December 4, 1932*

B4, F4

The museum again. After the Louvre,[9] the museums in Berlin are paradisiacal. In the Louvre, if you want to see a picture you have to prepare yourself to march for miles—and then you may find that the day is too dark, or that the picture is hung too high, or that its place has been changed. The curator of the Louvre publicly announced that this policy seems to him to be the sensible policy to follow—to me it sounds like an outburst of resentment on the part of one who is too lazy to do anything else but keep the secret as to where, how and when a picture in the Louvre can be found. Not so in Berlin. Each room in the different museums I have been in, if [it] does not get the direct sunlight, is given a glass roof, so that a picture is visible at all times. And rooms are what they are represented to be. If the sign on the door is Rembrandt you can expect to find Rembrandts—and the door marked Dürer indicates that there are really Dürers in that room.

This time I went straight to the room in which the Rembrandts are. In spite of the lighting, the grayness of the day affected the pictures so that my first impression of them was not very strong. [Then I saw] a few examples of

---

9. During his one-week stay in Paris, Plotkin had visited the Louvre twice, November 13 and 15, 1932 (AP Coll., B4, F1).

the good-humored Hals—the examples here are excellent; both the father and son have in common a rough, good, hearty sense of living. This they have in common with Jordaens, whose work I first saw in Paris and enjoyed immensely. Like the specimens here even better.

By this time the fog had lifted and I wandered back again to the Rembrandts. With the sunlight on them the pictures became alive, and the colors gave out radiance that I did not believe possible.

Many more policemen on the streets today. Also, every corner has its quota of Nazis in uniforms with collection boxes. The first must be making preparations for the opening of Reichstag[10] on Tuesday. The latter seem to have run into difficulties of late. There are rumors abroad that the industrialists and the bankers have, for some reason as yet unknown, cut off their financial aid to Herr Hitler. Hitler's army,[11] variously estimated at between 6,000,000 and 600,000, is a paid army—and while the amount paid to them in American currency is laughable, nevertheless the $600,000 it costs each week is no easy sum to raise. To see uniformed men on the streets with collection boxes in their hands is something new—and to be seen only in Germany. Most of the men are young men—seldom over thirty.

◇ *Monday, December 5, 1932*

B4, F5

Herschel, he comes from America! First my pronunciation and then some inapt phrase gave me away. I was in a small grocery store, attracted by the obviously Jewish countenances of the owners, an elderly rabbinical Hebrew and his wife. The Herschel addressed was not her husband, but her son. Hearing his name called, he dutifully came forward. Meanwhile some others came into the store, and before I had realized it the store had turned into a community gathering. Why did I come to Germany? How long was I going to stay? Were there as many leaving America as were leaving Germany? One had a relative in America who wrote letters, and in one of them it said that all rich Americans were committing suicide and all the poor ones were dying of starvation. Was this true? And how were the Jews faring there? . . .

---

10. The German parliament, whose building was situated in the Tiergarten, near the Brandenburg Gate.

11. With this generic term, Plotkin meant the paramilitary Nazi groups: the SA (*Sturmabteilungen,* stormtroops) and the SS (*Schutzstaffel,* protection squads).

The son finally rescued me. Not all at once, he told them. In America they don't talk at the same time. But their questions had to be answered. I am in Germany because I wanted to see a bit of the old world. How long I will stay depends, perhaps two months, perhaps three. Yes, there were a good many leaving America, but not more than were coming in. Conditions in America are very bad, and there were some people who didn't have enough to eat—I saw no reason to alarm them—but it is not true that all rich Americans are committing suicide and that all the poor Americans were dying of hunger. I am not rich, on the contrary, I am like yourself, I have nothing, but I manage to stay alive. The physical evidence satisfied them. Now the son and I could talk quietly. Do you have a fascist party in America? No, not yet—we had the Ku Klux Klan for a while, but that's over with for the present.[12] Then the Jews in America are fortunate. Here we are cursed with anti-Semitism, the most bitter anti-Semitism that we have ever known. We have anti-Semitism in America too. I wanted to draw him out, and said this to him quietly, but the remark was overheard. Anti-Semitism in America? Impossible! I assured them that this was so. But surely the anti-Semitism in America can't be as bad as in Germany? The flock of questioners were at me again. Do they ever throw Jews out of subway cars in New York? Do they ever come into stores belonging to Jews and tear up all the stock and break up all the fixtures? Do they ever tell workingmen who are Jewish, who have lived their lives in Germany, that they ought to go back to Poland or wherever they came from when they ask for unemployment insurance? It was better not to tell them that in America we have no unemployment insurance—they wouldn't believe it possible. Do the Jews in America face boycotts? Why tell them about the thousands of small businessmen in the South who were run out of business by the Klan when it was in its heyday? The discussion would be endless. I looked at Herschel and Herschel understood. I would like to see your synagogue, will you show it to me? That is—if it is not too much trouble? It is nearby. Bidding my spontaneous hosts good-bye, I left with their questions ringing in my ears.

When we started, I noticed that the young man had no overcoat. Foolishly I asked him why—and regretted my question before I had completed it. You are in Germany now, he answered, and in Germany everything is

---

12. KKK membership is estimated to have ranged between three and five million in the mid-1920s, and then declined. The Klan was not a political party, but its new strategy influenced or captured the elections in the South as well as in the West and Midwest. Along with black people, Jews and Catholics were its new targets.

possible. We walked four long blocks to the synagogue. Identical with the orthodox synagogues I had seen everywhere through the States. We spent a few minutes and left. Taking his arm, on leaving the synagogue, I led him to the first *Konditorei,*[13] ordered coffee and cakes and then got my first square look at him. I had noticed that he was tall and gangly, as if the flesh and spirit wouldn't mingle and amalgamate, also that he had a very small head, the top of it sloping downward and closely cropped in the German style, but I hadn't noticed the enormous ears, ears so large that the sunlight came streaming through them. A thin mouth over a chin that almost curved into a semicircle, tensely embittered, small dark eyes that darted in suspicion at everything that came within their vision, a huge nose that quivered sensitively; physically it struck me as though he started growing feet first, and when it came to the head what it couldn't give him in size it gave him in intensity. Altogether a tensely constructed and an embittered personality.

Tell me something about the Jews in Germany? What is there to tell? The Jew in Germany is no different from Jews in other parts of the world. The same social stratums that Gentiles fall into equally absorb the Jews, not only here, but in America as well. What do you know about America? Not very much outside of what I have read. You are the first American Jew I have ever talked to. But from what I have read you have social and class divisions among the Jews in America as we have them here. If we are knitted together a little more tightly for the present it is not so much because of our Judaism but due to the peculiar position that we occupy in Germany today. The majority of the Jews in Germany are being driven into no one knows what. You saw the synagogue—well—there is hardly a Friday night that we pray without trembling; and for the first time in Germany, the Germans who thought they were part, parcel and baggage of German life, who thought that they had been "assimilated," are learning to their sorrow that a Jew is always a Jew, regardless of his class. That is why we are closer. His young, tense, eager face took on an entirely new appearance. He had something to tell, and really wanted to talk. I let him go on. In Germany we have three types of Jews. The first came here about one hundred and fifty years ago. They are the old aristocratic families, who except for their religious faith have integrated themselves into the German national life and have become part of it. Many intermarried, and there were also a considerable number who, rather than face the hardships of being forever regarded as strangers in a strange land, accepted the faith of the Nazarene. Marx's parents were

13. Pastry shop.

part of them. But the group as a group prospered, and as the years passed they became powerful in all of the economic enterprises of the nation. The Hitlerites say that they controlled the entire industrial, commercial and financial life of the nation. This, I do not believe, but they came very close to doing it. Don't look at me so strangely. I am telling you the truth. They not only took a position in the front ranks of finance, industry and commerce, but they and their children also came to the front in the cultural life of the nation. Quietly they subsidized artists, writers and publishers, created sustaining funds for musical development—that is, they spread into every field of art and science that was at the base of German culture. I could see nothing wrong in this and said so. No neither can I, he answered, except this. The first movement in modern times against the Jews was started in Austria in 1893.[14] This movement was intended to build up an international anti-Semitism against the Jew on purely cultural grounds. It was a protest on the part of cultured Germany and Austria against the trespassing of the Jew on ground that these men regarded as their own and therefore holy to them. Frankly, I countered, I don't understand. Would you have had these Jews ignore the cultural life of the land in which they live and confine themselves strictly to their own people? That's just it, he shot back; had he done just that, had he paid attention to his own people, had the German Jew stayed with his own, and prepared for problems that with the Jew [are] as old as history itself, the dilemma in which we find ourselves today would have been as sharp, and our suffering as bitter.

You raise an interesting angle, I parried, but I don't see where it is leading to. Suppose you tell me some of the things that the first group of Jews could have done. Perhaps I can then more easily understand your chain of logic. It led to this. The first German Jew was interested in making money only, and in getting his social and financial position in Germany consolidated. In establishing himself socially among the Gentiles he forgot the millions of other Jews. And when, immediately after the first Russian revolution in 1905, the exodus of Jews from Russia started, and later from Poland and the other countries East of Germany, the German Jew either didn't know or didn't want to know of their existence. You want to know what could have been done? I'll tell you. If they hadn't forgotten their birthright for a mess of pottage then instead of consolidating their own personal positions they would have fought for equality of the Jews with the other people in Germany.

---

14. Herschel probably alludes to Georg von Schönerer, Karl Lueger, or other Austrian nationalists who strongly advocated anti-Semitism in the late nineteenth century.

I am the second-class Jew that came here, rather I was brought here when still a child at my mother's breast in 1906. I cannot practice law without giving up those things that are sacred to me in spite of the fact that I was almost born here. I cannot teach in the public schools; and what is worse, I am paying for the crimes that have been committed by Jewry in Germany for which I have as little responsibility as you have. But I am not talking about myself. Did you hear that woman ask you whether in your country when a Jew asks aid they tell him to go back to the country from which he came? That woman and her husband have been in Germany for fifteen years. They are regarded as foreigners. They cannot be naturalized before twenty years! They are therefore shut out from all relief! Do you wonder that I am bitter?

Look here—you are brooding about something that is past and done. What about the present? He didn't give me a chance to go on. This is the present. At the present time our industrial workers are shut out. If you want to see how they live, come with me sometime and I'll show you. And not only are they shut out, but the thousands of young men in Berlin and many more thousands in Germany, like myself of Jewish extraction, who were trained in the nonmanual professions, as clerks in stores, or bookkeepers or whatever else requires the use of the mind in place of the hands, we are also shut out. Where are we to go? To the Communists who would deny us our religion? To the group of Jews who because of the Hitlerite propaganda are for the first time in the history of Germany pleading with us to come closer and to become active in their various brands of politics? What have they to offer us? Will they give us work? Charity? Faugh—I don't want their charity. Well, what do you want? I want, he answered, the right to live as a Jew with all the rights that other people around me have, not only for myself but for the other Jews around me, and the first group that offers it to me, with that group I will work. As to leading Jews that today cry from housetops that they have always loved us and offered us nothing but charity—to the devil with them. I'll go to the synagogue, but I'll go in my own way, and without their aid.

◇ *Tuesday, December 6, 1932*

B4, F4

A yank on the collar of my coat and a fist on the back of my ribs introduced me to the Berlin *Polizei*. At that they were in a playful mood. I'd hate to be around them when they really get rough. Today the Reichstag opened.[15] I did my best to get a ticket to get inside. But that was impossible. Unless you are a member of the diplomatic service or a newspaperman representing a world-famous newspaper, even in normal times it is very difficult to be admitted on the opening day. So I decided to try looking in from the outside. Some fifty thousand Berliners apparently were inspired to try it at the same time.

In the morning I became aware of an undercurrent of excitement. First, in passing the University of Berlin, I saw young Communists handing out copies of the *Die Rote Front*.[16] Then I became aware of the dozens of helmeted *Polizei* on horseback—my first glimpse of them since my arrival in Berlin. And everywhere I turned I saw the light-yellow-shirted Nazis with their light-yellow flour caps—poking collection boxes under the noses of all pedestrians.

At the same time I became aware that the crowds were larger than usual and largely moving towards the Brandenburg Gate along Unter den Linden. I had other things to do in the morning, but kept noticing throughout all of the morning that the *Polizei* on horseback were cruising about and covering every block of the streets leading to the Tiergarten in which the Reichstag is located. The Reichstag's building is just within the park about one hundred yards from the Brandenburg Gate. Unter den Linden, the eastern approach to the Brandenburg Gate, is a very wide street (300 feet in width) and runs east from the Tiergarten to the Dom, Opera, University and the Kaiserschloss, altogether about a mile in length.

About three o'clock I decided that it was time to go out and see how a Berlin crowd behaved. Two short blocks brought me to Unter den Linden where I turned west to the Brandenburg Gate and the Tiergarten. Here I noticed that the police were standing about fifty feet apart, usually in twos and threes, and in addition to them the *Polizei* on horseback quietly moving about on both sides of the Linden keeping an eye above the crowds to see if anything unusual was happening. The crowd, mostly young people of the working class, was good-natured and orderly. True, they were out to cheer their favorite political leader or party, and occasionally a few of them would exercise their vocal cords, but in the main they were quiet and well behaved.

---

15. The first meeting of the Reichstag after the November 6 elections. The session hardly lasted four days.

16. *Die Rote Front* (Red Front) was the organ of the Communist paramilitary organization Rotfrontkämpferbund (Red Front Fighters' League).

On reaching the Brandenburg Gate, I was surprised to see the large number of mounted police and truckloads of police kept in reserve and learned that the building South of the Gate was a local police station; and at the same time became aware of the huge crowds that were moving in the opposite direction. My first impression was that they had seen all they wanted to see and were returning and for the moment I debated with myself whether it was worth going in; but the crowd behind me was so thick that I decided it would be easier to move with it. Not until I passed through the Gate could I see what was going on. Every path leading to the Reichstag building was guarded by the blue-coated *Polizei* in their steel helmets, and in each path about fifty feet apart again in twos and threes, so that if a trespasser got through the first line he could easily be checked by any of the half-dozen other lines of police around the building. It certainly was an effective blockade. Breaking through the vaults of the Bank of France would have been easier.

The moment we passed through the Brandenburg Gate we were gently eased—I say eased advisedly—the rough stuff didn't come until later—across the streets. There was now between the Reichstag and the crowd not only the immediate garden (really a small strip of woods zigzagged with paths) and the continuation of the Linden through the Tiergarten. Tiergarten is really a miniature forest, in the heart of the city, about half as large as Prospect Park in Brooklyn. It is so heavily wooded that even now, in December, it is difficult to see the horizon for the trees. These woods are crisscrossed hundreds of times by boulevards, walking paths, for cyclists and horsemen. We were now on the heavily wooded side of the Tiergarten across from the Reich building. I tell all this because of the vividness of the experience, also because it seemed that there wasn't the slightest need for what followed—unless the police were inspired to give foreign visitors something to think about. The crowd, I thought, was even quieter than when it was on Unter den Linden.

As the crowd marched quietly and amiably I saw through the trees that the bypaths through the park were filling with people, and when I looked again I noticed that a larger crowd on a larger path was walking North, back to the main thoroughfare. It made little impression on me until I saw that a good many were running—then I began to wonder whether there was some disturbance there. At first my eyes followed the crowd that was running, then I did what thousands of others did, I turned around to watch them. Within a moment the crowd both in front and behind got so thick that one could hardly move either way. At the same time, one got the feeling that something unusual was going to happen. Everyone looked at the other and asked "What's wrong?"—*"Was ist los?"* There was something of the herd instinct that was terrifying, something as yet unseen and unheard, but of that peculiar psychological flavor that leads to a desire to stampede. I, for one, wanted to run. Anything to get out of the crowd. Then I became aware of shouting and yelling, and a roaring as of catastrophic thunder. It is the only way I can describe the bull-like thunderous tones of the German *Polizei* when yelling at a crowd. They were turning the crowd to the left and sending it into the interior of the park, and once in the interior of the park onto the first large path back to Unter den Linden. In the crush that followed, I was turned around several times when suddenly I felt as if a wild bull was thundering in my ear, a hand was tightened on the collar of my coat until my throat went dry and my eyes began to pop out of their sockets. I twisted and squirmed, while my first impulse was to put my hands in my pockets under some crazy notion that I was being held up. I was being held up. In truth, from the rear, by a policeman's hand turning my coat collar into a wringing machine and his fist in the small of my ribs pushing and yelling. When I finally did manage to turn somewhat I became aware that hundreds of people around me were running like mad, policemen after them yelling like hoarse Indians.

At this moment my good luck came to my aid. I yelled. I don't think I ever yelled as much, nor as vigorously, nor with as much feeling as I yelled this afternoon. And I hope never to have the need for yelling that way again. My tonsils are still sore. And I didn't yell in German. I yelled in good old Anglo-Saxon English. If ever that officer was made to feel that he was a novice in that sport he was made to feel it then and there. The yelling had its effect. Either it surprised him to hear such a volume of sound from so small and frail a body, or perhaps it was the sound of a strange language. That I will never know. All I know is that the louder I yelled the weaker grew the grip on my collar and the pressure of the fist against my ribs; and when these were sufficiently loosened, I turned about and to look at the huge officer whose bulging bloodshot eyes looked at me with complete astonishment. And such is the training of the German police that in a twinkling of an eyelash he was standing at attention, heels clicked together, explaining that he couldn't possibly know that I was a foreigner. What difference does that make?—I asked. The crowd was orderly! and they are your own people—had you told them quietly to move into the park they would have done so. He didn't answer but continued standing at attention. Then turning away from me he called another officer and asked him to see that I was safely escorted out of the crowd; he made certain that such an error wouldn't be made again. I was marched up to the [Brandenburg] Gate where my papers were looked into and warned to stay away from crowds in the future, and sent on my way.

Yes—I know the German *Polizei* now, I can't say that the introduction was a happy one, nor that I enjoyed it, or want particularly to meet them again. But I can say that I've met them, that I've seen them in action, and that I take peculiar pride in that knowledge that when put to the test I outshouted and outbellowed the best of them.

◇ *Wednesday, December 7, 1932*

B4, F4

Would I come and meet the General Secretary of the International Federation of Trade Unions, Walter Schevenels?[17] The note from George Stolz set today as the date, taking it for granted that I would come. The IFTU as it is commonly known throughout the world is the largest federation of trade unions in the world. Its membership, scattered into every country under the face of the sun, is close to 30,000,000 men and women. It is a curious sidelight that the two largest countries in the world, Soviet Russia and the United States, are not affiliated. The first because it is too radical, the second because it is too conservative.

Walter Schevenels is a young man in his early forties. Tall, compactly built with a physique that radiates power and energy, he is a commanding figure. One either likes or dislikes him, one either accepts him or quarrels with him immediately. To remain indifferent in his presence is impossible. I found myself liking him and at the same time wanting to draw swords. It wasn't long before I did both.

What is the IFTU doing to overcome unemployment?—was my first question. He gave me the stock socialist answer that under capitalism there is no solution for the unemployment problem. I agreed—with limitations. In the first place there have been periods within the capitalist system when there was employment for everyone. In the second place there were certain mitigations, certain programs formulated through which it was expected

---

17. Walter Schevenels (1887–1966), leader of the Belgian Metal Workers' Union and IFTU general secretary since 1930. See his *Forty-five Years: The International Federation of Trade Unions, 1901–1945* (Brussels: Board of Trustees, 1956).

that some relief would be found. Well, there was unemployment insurance. I nodded politely. Extending public works. Again I nodded. Increase of purchasing power on the part of labor and the consuming public. I shook my head again. Shortening of the workweek. All of these, I told him, were on the lists of the most conservative trade unions in America—All of them excepting unemployment insurance. Of all the countries in the world, the United States is the most likely place where the program, excepting unemployment insurance, may be carried through first. Provided, he countered, your workers want it. Whether our workers in America will want the things the program outlined by their trade unions—that is, will want it hard enough to want to fight—that is something else.

During unemployment periods, we call it crisis here, he went on, the willpower of the masses, for the time being becomes paralyzed. They may riot when they are hungry, but rioting is one thing and organizing to attain an object is another thing. Those things that labor has won during the past century were won when labor was employed and being employed had the will to power. When out of work their will to power ceases and instead there is a will to obtain food and shelter only. You are yourself a trade unionist. Tell me, when do you call strikes? When there is work—no? Why? Because as a practical trade unionist you know that hunger vitiates the hope and destroys the will to power of the members of the trade unions. The secret of the growth and permanence of the trade unions in Europe lies in this. During periods of prosperity we have made economic advances on the industrial field, and took the opportunity to consolidate our economic advances with political advances at the same time; and in periods of unemployment we used our political powers and apparatus won in more prosperous years to defend our previous gains. There is not a country in Europe that would dare to treat its unemployed as they are being treated in your country right now. Why? Why this difference in treatment of European workers as compared with the workers in your country? I think I can answer this for you. To me it is quite simple. You have learned to fight for wages and hours only. In Germany we say that you are wage conscious only. And the only time, therefore, that you can fight and win something is when the owner of the factory has work. And when the owner of the factory has no work and your people are idle, what happens? Your workers become demoralized and many of your unions disappear because you are completely and utterly at the mercy of your employers. I am not blaming you. Your trade unions are as much a historical product as the trade unions in Germany, France or England. The only difference between us really is in the point of time and experience.

When you have a little more of both, then you will come closer to us, both in your organization forms and in your political views.

In Europe we have trained and disciplined our members to know the meaning of their trade unions both in good times and in bad times. We cannot escape the weakness, the psychological weakness, that develops at a time like this, when we do not know how long the crisis will last, altogether. But we have taught our workers that they must hold together, suffer every setback if necessary, but not to let go of their will to power. For the time being, to keep them from becoming demoralized we propound measures that will keep them from suffering too much. Such measures as shorter hours, unemployment insurance, increased purchasing power etc., have two functions, first they have the power of cohesion, the power to hold our people together, and second, [their] more important [function] lies in the educational and propaganda value of these projects. The masses know that the Social Democratic Party, with whom we are closely bound, is the group that has, in the main, been the responsible agency through which they have obtained these measures in the past, and they also know that if there is any chance to defend these things that have been obtained for them, at a time like this, they can do so only through their trade unions with the help of the political party working at the other end of our social and legal structure. Our trade unions and the Social Democratic Party must go together—one without the other would be lost. It is the balancing wheel between the moments of strength and weakness of our people; and while our programs are on one hand limited by what we think we can achieve at the moment, we are never for one moment losing sight of the ultimate goal, socialism, with the least expenditure of human energy and human lives.

And now Mr. Plotkin, may I talk to you about something closer to practical matters and a little further away from the theoretical? From this you may perhaps get an idea of how we plan our work ahead. Has Mr. Stolz told you something about the international conference we are planning to hold next year, in Mexico?

No—Stolz hadn't mentioned the matter. Well, this is what we are planning. The substance of what followed was this. The International Office[18] of the League of Nations will take the initiative and ask all of the industrial nations to send delegates to Mexico to discuss a universal five-day, forty-hour week. I must have looked my astonishment when he asked me whether, in my opinion, there was any likelihood that the industrialists of Mexico and

18. The International Labour Office.

those of the United States would send representatives! Didn't I think it was at all possible? I told him that I assumed that the people in the International Office had already sounded out the governments whom they intended to invite; surely they had feelers out in those countries? Yes—but he wanted an opinion from someone who had just come from the States and who knows something of the mind of the American industrialists. What added to my astonishment was both the boldness and the hopefulness of the plan. He seemed to take it for granted that capital and labor would come together and discuss these matters. It was too much for me.

He saw both my astonishment and my incredulity. And when he laughed, through his eyes, I began to see what he was driving at, I felt that I could speak frankly. And I did. To me, I answered, the plan is absurd and impossible. There are countries, and you know it, that haven't as yet ratified the League of Nations agreement for a universal eight-hour day. He nodded in agreement. As to American labor and capital sitting across the table, discussing their troubles, in a foreign country, [when] we haven't even been able to get them to sit down together to discuss their domestic difficulties! [President] Wilson tried it and failed. I recalled to him instance after instance where, in major strikes, when the industry against which a strike had been declared had been completely tied up, and the owners' only answer was that they had nothing to negotiate and would not meet with the representatives of organized labor. He kept on nodding, and while he nodded a small smile played around his lip, and a small smile gleamed in his eyes. It finally grew on me that I was not telling him anything that he didn't already know. Suddenly the whole thing flashed on me. Whether the conference is successful does not really matter for the time being. The point he was developing was that unemployment would remain a long time and that long-range planning, and cumulative publicity, as well as propaganda focused on a single issue was the necessary program for the time being. It was long-range working-class politics in a world of hard realities, a program of developing political ramifications and political consciousness for a class that historically has never had political power before. This time I smiled and told him what the possibilities were in the way of publicity and what educational work could be built up on such a conference. I do not know whether it will work. The next few years will tell that. The point is that every weapon that can be used to hold the workers together, to hold them together so that the will to power, during periods of unemployment, will not be destroyed, must be used. Should the crisis, he concluded, destroy the workers' will to power, then the road is open to anarchy in Europe. We are confident that this will not happen. We have educated our masses too well and we have built up for them a thousand and one defenses that will hold them together. We have given them two traditions of the highest value, and through these traditions we hope to eventually bring them to where they are ready for socialism. The first is to will to defend what they have, and the second is to will themselves into power that will control their destinies for them—Now let us have some tea.

◇ *[Thursday, December 8, 1932]*

B4, F4

The entire afternoon[19] with [Valtin] Hartig[20] of the Transport and Municipal Workers. His group is the second largest federation in the German [trade unions]. Arriving at 4 Michaelplatz I was immediately taken to his office and found him with the secretary-treasurer of the organization. After the usual introduction I was taken to the office of the president where again the usual formalities and a few minutes' conversation about generalities. Then to see the building.

Most of the Federations of the trade unions in Germany, and there are thirty of them, own their own buildings. They are the last word in modern architecture, and contrast quite sharply with what we call modern architecture in America. The buildings in America are spoiled by their height. In the first place their height makes it almost impossible to see them. Then there is such need for space within the tall narrow lines that are built that beauty is often sacrificed for utility—or what is called utility. Here the lines are natural, the rooms spacious, and the decorations really bring out the beauty inherent in the materials used. It would be wise indeed for budding young architects to come here and see what can be done—and what has been done—and certainly no finer group of modern buildings exists anywhere in the States that will compare with those of Berlin. Among the most beautiful of these buildings are the Metal Workers' Building and the

---

19. The original date in the manuscript was Friday, December 9. But two other entries in B4, F5, reproduced below were also dated Friday, December 9. To keep the logical sequence between these meetings, it seemed to us that the conversation with Hartig had been held on Thursday, December 8.

20. Valtin Hartig, one of the leaders of the Transport and Municipal Workers' Union (Verband der Gemeinde- und Staatsarbeiter). After 1933, exiled in Paris, he worked for the International Federation of Employees in Public Services.

Municipal Workers' Building. I merely call attention to these buildings so that someone may, someone who has the technical knowledge to describe them properly, see them, and describe them properly. They are the modern temples of a modern movement.

Everyone in Germany who is in any way connected with any governmental department, or industry, from a member of the Reichstag to the women who scrub floors there; a doctor in a hospital, a nurse and even the barbers employed there; transport men, post office workers, policemen, tramway workers;—every group regardless of its profession, legal, or labor classification, in any way employed by the government, municipal, state or federal, is eligible for membership in the Municipal Workers' Union. This also takes in schoolteachers, state officials, administrative departments of various types of government departments, university professors—all of them members of the same union. I recommend this to the Building Trades in the United States where the plumbers and steamfitters are still snooty towards each other. Not that Germany is altogether free from this. There are still some state officials who are snooty and who maintain what they call a "neutral" organization of their own—but such is the power and prestige of the Municipal Employees' Union that even these state officials are beginning to waver and feelers are out for possible affiliation. The present membership of the organization is 680,000.

After seeing the building we adjourned to the Gewerkschaftshaus, a few doors from Hartig's office, for lunch. As we were sitting there we were joined by the secretary of the Nurses' department and the president of the Seamen's Union. The latter, a rough sea tar, immediately became friendly, and within a few minutes became quite outspoken. Apparently he doesn't think much of the Seamen's Union in America. Nor of Andy Furuseth,[21] its president. William Green[22] he called a Sunday School teacher. At first I was sorely tempted to argue, but quarreling with him was like bucking sea waves on a stormy day. His voice had that rich booming quality, and within a few minutes I

---

21. Andrew Furuseth (1854–1938), president of the International Seamen's Union of America from 1908 to 1938. He secured the passage of the 1915 Seamen's Act that improved the conditions of maritime workers in the United States. In the 1920s he was challenged by radical dissidents (Communists and Industrial Workers of the World).

22. William Green (1873–1952), president of the American Federation of Labor from 1924 to his death, succeeding Samuel Gompers in this capacity. He participated in the 1919 Paris peace talks as AFL vice president. His "Sunday school" appearance may have come from his Protestant culture and soft manners.

was drawn into his circle of persuasiveness—as though I was listening to an old sea tar's adventures.

On returning to Hartig's office I pounced on him and asked him to give me the details of the [street]car strike in Berlin.[23] He told me nothing I hadn't already known about the strike itself. Because of the crisis the income of the company had dropped to a very low level. There had been a number of wage cuts, and in September the company came with a demand for another cut—asking fourteen pfennigs an hour. This demand was so extravagant that the trade union leaders took it for what it was meant to be, a point of bargaining in order to get some kind of a reduction. The men, however, took it otherwise and were infuriated. In reply the trade union leaders issued a strike ballot—the last resort of a trade union in Germany—and a final warning to the employers—and usually recognized as such. The German trade unions are not in the habit of bluffing.

Had the matter taken its usual course the difficulties probably would have been ironed out through the usual channels, but suddenly a new factor entered the field. The Communists and the Hitlerites entered the field and demanded a strike. When the strike ballots showed that there was not a legal majority to order a strike—although in all fairness it should be stated that three-fourths of those who voted, voted to strike—the Communists and the Hitlerites joined in issuing a strike call. In the meantime the leaders of the [trade] Union and the company, a quasi-government institution, got together and settled the demands of the company for one-seventh of what the company demanded, and refused to sanction a strike movement. Going over the social democratic leadership of the union, the Communists and Hitlerites called the strike and were successful in tying up transportation for a few days. However, when the men realized that their leaders had refused to sanction the strike movement, and had made a settlement far better than the one they expected, most of them promptly deserted the Communist-Hitlerite alliance and returned to their posts. Those who did not were given several days' notice, and on failing to report were replaced. Legally these men—about twenty-five hundred were victimized by this Communist-Hitlerite fiasco—have no chance of getting their posts back again. Quietly, however, the SPD leadership is trying to get many of them reinstated.

According to Hartig the strike itself was purely a political maneuver on the part of the two parties that are opposed to the SPD leadership of the

---

23. That is the Berlin public transportation (BVG) strike of November 3–7, 1932. See chapter 1, November 28.

trade unions in Germany. The time factor certainly indicates this to be the case. The strike was called one week before the election, and was timed so as to affect the general elections set for a week after the strike was called. Had the tactics of the "alliance" been successful it would assuredly have been followed by hundreds of illegal strikes throughout the nation—with a tremendous demoralization of the ranks of labor in the offing. The trade union [leadership] of Germany could not afford to do otherwise than take the challenge of its power and discipline over its followers. And in the face of it the cabal of the Communist-Hitler combination broke down; and while the SPD doubtlessly was hurt at the election, the result of the strike has tended to strengthen its control over the trade union movement. The lesson taught by the failure of the last combination will free the movement, at least for the time being, from such "conspirative" movements. To me, personally, it was hard to believe that such an alliance really had been formed. Communism and fascism are so bitterly antagonistic that it hardly seemed possible; but to whomever I speak, the moment I mention a doubt I am laughed at. No one doubts it. At the same time it is not hard to understand the political motivation behind the scenes of such a cabal. The SPD in Germany is the one barrier both communism and fascism must break down, if they ever hope to get anywhere. At the moment it does not seem likely that they ever will. In every one of these communities you will find our representatives sitting alongside of the employers' representatives and the governmental officials to take up the cases and to see that the laws are enforced even for the agricultural workers.

At this point I explained to him that getting the theoretical background was one thing, and extremely interesting, but that seeing unions operate was even more so. He promptly invited me to attend several meetings of his national committee and of the district meetings of the workers themselves. Would I have time this week? I said I would. He promptly called Robert Schultz, organizer of East Prussia, and asked him when and where his next meeting would be. Schultz was very kind. Would I have time on Friday? There is to be a meeting in Schoneberg, about forty kilometers from Berlin. If you will join me, say at six o'clock, we can get there in an hour. Time and place settled, I left, all set for tomorrow night.

In the evening walking through Wedding. Walked two hours. Noticed for the first time cards in the windows announcing that this or that store had to sell to the unemployed at reduced prices. The discount, I understand, amounts in some cases to 20%. No mean item when the budget is small.

This district is harder hit than any district in Berlin. Will have to see it from the inside—and that too is arranged for Saturday.

◇ *Friday, December 9, 1932*

B4, F5

A long talk with Dr. H. [Bading], agricultural expert for both the Social Democratic Party and the Trade Unions. Asked him for data on the food resources in Germany. Gave me a mass of statistics; but more from his positive assertions. There is enough food, and enough food can be grown in Germany to feed every man, woman and child. Can they be fed, let us say, as they were fed in 1928 and 1929? The answer was an unhesitating yes. Excepting such commodities as citrus fruits, coffee, tea, etc . . . There is every reason to believe, he went on, that Germany can and will, in time, if she has not already done so, make herself independent of food imports. [. . .]

The terrible thing in Germany, he continued, lies in this. While we are producing more than ever before, and are producing almost enough today to feed our population, Germans do not get enough to eat. If you will come several weeks later we will have the charts ready so that you can see for yourself the drop in food consumption per individual in Germany. And they will show you [. . .] the changes that have taken place in the diet during the past fifteen years. We are working on the charts now, when you come again I shall be glad to show them to you. We made a tentative appointment for sometime immediately after the first of the coming year, shook hands and parted with the usual *Aufwiedersehen.*

Otto Engel, secretary of the Agricultural Workers' Union for all Germany, to whom I went immediately after leaving Dr. Bading, was even more emphatic on the possibilities of German agriculture. However, as secretary of the agricultural workers' union, he is interested primarily in seeing to it that his people are permanently employed. Realizing this, I turned the subject towards general conditions for farmworkers and this led inevitably to the unemployment problem. In July, he said, 150,000 agricultural workers were out of work. July is the most important and the busiest month on the farms during the entire year. Last February they had 313,000 out of work. Coming February, he estimated, there would be no less than 350,000. Out of how many? Three million, he answered. And what is done for those who are out of work? That depends. They come, with some exceptions, under the unemployment insurance provisions, dependent on whether they have made their contributions, or under the *Wohlfahrt,* the local community social agency. [. . .]

The Deutscher Landsarbeiterverband, as Otto Engel explained, represented only a small portion of the land workers (150,000 members). But its benefits extended to all agricultural workers: minimum wage, paid legal holidays, maximum number of working hours, and bonus pay for extra time. Proud of these achievements, Otto Engel explained that his union had elevated the German agricultural workers out of feudalism. He pointedly remarked to Plotkin that feudalism continued to exist in the United States in the form of the peonage system in the southern states, a system by which some workers, never receiving any cash payment, were permanently indebted and therefore tied to the land.

◇ *Friday, December 9, 1932 (evening)*

B4, F4

Plotkin met Robert Schultz, the secretary of the Agricultural Workers' Union, the Landsarbeiterverband for Prussia. The meeting took place in Schoneberg, a small town twenty-five miles from Berlin. There Plotkin was made to understand that farmers in Prussia were not farmers in the American sense of the word: they did not own their land and were employed as farmhands on estates belonging to large landowners, the Junkers. As organizer for the entire state of Prussia, Robert Schultz's role ranged from settling family disputes among disgruntled peasants to visiting the sick in the hospital and seeing that they received the union sickness benefits and dealing with the unemployment problem. A program of house building to provide work to the unemployed farmers had been enacted by the Social Democrats. A resolution was pending in the Reichstag to extend this program, but, as Robert Schultz explained, the Junkers' opposition as well as that of the Communists made it unlikely that it would pass. That day, Robert Schultz was speaking to the workers about the new negotiations on wages and working time.

Our agreements will soon expire and new agreements will have to be negotiated. The landowners are demanding a return to the old conditions. You younger men present do not know what the conditions in the old days were. You were in your swaddling clothes when we were making our fights for you. But you, older men, know. Following von Papen's suggestion, the landowners are demanding a return to the days when there was no minimum tariff for land workers; when there was no time limit how long a farmworker could be worked; they have even demanded that the minimums for the women and the young ones be abolished. One of them in a moment of frankness already has stated that the least they would be satisfied with would be a reduction of twelve pfennigs on the minimum for the men. One of the men very quietly interrupted. They wouldn't dare! The very quietness of it was effective. It was greeted with a storm of applause. Schultz laughed. They wouldn't dare, you say. Tell me what the Junkers don't dare and I'll tell you the impossible. He was forceful, direct, he spoke their language and he knows his peasants. What followed was not a meeting in the ordinary sense. There were very few speeches. There were a few expressions of unbelief in the possibility of such a program as Schultz had outlined to them. [. . .] Twelve pfennigs an hour! Translated in purchasing power it would mean a reduction of twelve cents an hour.

Schultz turned to me. It is always so. They will not believe until they are confronted with either take it or leave it. Aren't you warming them up for organization purposes? I have done exactly that myself. No. It is not needed in this district. They are well organized here. These will stick through thick and thin. In this district we do not have to tell them to strike, we are more often faced with strikes that are not sanctioned than otherwise. But you see the most intelligent of the land workers, in Germany. The others have a strong faith in what their landowners tell them. And when their landowners show their workers that the things they raise can't be sold for profit, that the market is glutted, and then tell them the reason they are unemployed is because their wages are too high, they not only believe them, but will not have anything to do with us. That is why our legal machinery is so important to us.

Do you really mean to say, I asked him as we were driving home, that there is a glutted market in food commodities in Germany? I not only am saying it, but if you will spend the time with me I'll give you the physical answer to your question. I am saying even more, I am saying that our landowners are doing just what your landowners are doing, they are destroying crops rather than selling them at the low prices that are offered to them.[24] You have complained of restaurant prices in Berlin. The prices to you are high. The production costs are really high. We are making the most stupid use of our land imaginable. But that is not the fault of the workers. It is the

24. Robert Schultz's comparison with American farmers is ironic in historical perspective. A few months later, under the New Deal Agricultural Adjustment Act, to restore a higher level of prices and wages, American landowners were encouraged to destroy parts of their crops rather than sell them at a low price.

fault of the landowners, many of them are still working their land as their forefathers worked it, and many of them are using their land for crops wholly unsuited to their soil. That is not our fault. But even so. Our soil produces enormous quantities of food and can produce more, if scientifically managed. Correlate this with the dropping standard of living in Germany and you will understand why the agricultural market in our country is glutted with food commodities that can't be sold. To protect this market, our landowners demanded and got a tariff. And to sell their goods, these same landowners, through their von Papens and their Schleichers, cut the consuming power of the nation so that their crops are rotting in their warehouses. If this is not insanity I want to know what it is.

We are in a ring of stupidities that will take years to get out of. Our first problem was to get rid of von Papen. This we did so effectively that not even the Hindenburg prestige can bring him back. Hitler is on the way. Schleicher, I hope, is next. If, in the meantime, we can hold on without sacrificing the very foundation of our organization, then, and not until then, will the road be clear.

◇ *Saturday, December 10, 1932*

B4, F4

So, this is Köslinerstrasse. The name was familiar, I asked Hans about it. Yes. This is the famous Köslinerstrasse, Wedding. Had I heard about it in America? No. Someone in Berlin told me something about it. [. . .]

The Köslinerstrasse incident is quite recent. It goes back to May 1, 1929.[25] Barricades and all that sort of thing. Fifteen were killed by the "Tanz" machines[26]—as Hans calls the machine guns. This time it wasn't blue blood that was shed, fifteen workers' souls shot over the river Styx—Hans was quite

---

25. Bloody May (*Blutmai*) 1929. On May 1, 1929, the KPD organized a demonstration in Berlin, thus openly defying the December 1928 ban on demonstrations in the capital. Under the command of Social Democratic chief of police Karl Zörgiebel, the police most severely repressed the protest march, causing some thirty-one deaths among the participants. More than twelve hundred were arrested. This episode contributed to making the relations between Communists and Social Democrats even more bitter. See Thomas Kurz, *"Blutmai": Sozialdemokraten und Kommunisten im Brennpunkt der Berliner Ereignisse von 1929* (Berlin and Bonn: Dietz, 1988); and Léon Schirmann, *Blutmai Berlin 1929: Dichtungen und Wahrheit* (Berlin: Dietz Verlag, 1991).

26. "Dance" machines.

proud that a few of those killed were members of the Social Democratic Party. Hans also belongs. Hans is only twenty, and is not unlike boys of his own age in America, only sadder and wiser. Already he has confided [to] me that he is in love, but on account of unemployment can't get married. The girl is also on the dole and if they should marry she would lose the dole and he doesn't get enough, etc.

We would go first to 2 Köslinerstrasse. Had I been there before? No. The houses all looked alike. Huge tenements—tenements far larger than East Side tenements, all of them built around narrow courts so that the inside apartments never get the light. The usual swarm of gaunt children—this is my introduction to 2 Köslinerstrasse. How many tenants in the house? We were talking to the janitor. Eighty. How many *Arbeitslos?*[27] Five are working. The others? All the others are on the *Wohlfahrt*—the city poor law. The poor law? Yes. They have been out of employment too long to be on the insurance dole. And how are they getting along? He shrugged his shoulder and passed on. Life has closer problems for him. Besides it isn't good policy for a janitor to express too much sympathy, occasionally these tenants have to be dispossessed. Now we enter a dark narrow hallway. Hans took out his cigarette lighter and showed the way. A rat came scurrying down the hallway. Hans knocked on a door. The door opened and a woman greeted us. She knew Hans. Hans occasionally served food at the *Gemeinschafsküche*—a sort of communal kitchen based on the philanthropy of the industrialists in the Wedding district. He was therefore a person of some importance. That was where I met Hans. Had lentil soup there. Lentil soup for fifteen pfennigs to the unemployed only. She greeted Hans cordially. It was two o'clock in the afternoon, but the darkness inside was something to get used to. By the time I had been introduced I could make out things and people quite clearly. First I was introduced to Frau Schoner, then to her mother, then to her daughter aged eleven who curtsied to me with that springy dip of the knees that is taught to all German children. Her husband was out. He was trying to find the janitor. The rats were becoming unbearable. They were eating the little food they had; and such things oughtn't to be allowed. I agreed, they certainly oughtn't to be allowed.

There were two rooms. We were in the "sitting" room. The "sitting" room was ten by eight. A table, a chair, a bed, the peculiar house stove that is built into every apartment in Germany, a cupboard and a box on the floor comprised the entire house furnishing. On the table were dozens of coppers,

27. Jobless.

the last weekly donation from the *Wohlfahrt.* The walls were literally wet with dampness, and one portion of it had tar paper tacked on to keep the dampness from dripping through. Frau Schoner turned to Hans. Hans for the moment was the messiah. Do you think it ought to be allowed? First the dampness, and then the disappearing of the food and now the rats. I am going frantic. Let me show you. She stooped over and opened the cupboard. Rats must have strong constitutions to survive on so little. An American social worker would have sent in an emergency call at once—that is, in the old days. What an American social worker would do now I do not know. By this time I was beginning to have a strange feeling of nausea. The atmosphere seemed polluted with a strong sour smell of warm urine. For fear of offending I kept a distinct silence and said nothing about it.

How many in the family? Four. And how much help comes to them from the *Wohlfahrt?* Sixty marks a month. And rent? No. That has to be paid out of the sixty marks. And how much was the rent? The rent was 23 marks for the two rooms. She was apologetic. On account of the child and the grandmother. The child was out of the room and she could talk frankly. It is not nice for the child to sleep in the same room with the parents. Others in the house do it, but I do not think it is good. And her husband? He was taking it very hard. When one is out of work for three years and begins to lose hope—he had been in the *Krankenhaus*[28] where they said there was something wrong with the food he had been eating. As if he could help that. The child walked in. Well, the *Krankenhaus* had not been so bad for him, or for the family. Everyone got an additional allowance. It would pay for them to take turns getting sick and getting the additional allowance from the *Krankenhaus.* Hans persisted in getting his question answered. Was there something wrong with the food her husband had been eating? She glanced at the child. It was no use saying in front of the child that her father wasn't getting enough to eat. The child got little enough—that was only too obvious. Besides, what kind of food could one buy? One had to buy what one's allowance permitted. The smell of cabbage answered Hans's question—plus a slight pressure on his arm. Cabbage soup was being cooked for the evening meal, and cabbage soup only. The big *Mittag* meal was either potatoes with herring on some days, and when that became tiresome then the herring was changed to margarine; the inevitable potatoes remain. Butter is never mentioned. Meat is served on Sunday—one pound for four people; milk a luxury that is occasionally indulged in for the child; and clothes came from

28. Hospital.

the *Wohlfahrt*. There was a time when one could get clothing without much difficulty, but now even those who at one time could afford to donate their old clothes, either are unwilling to, or can't. I asked Hans what her husband's trade was and was told that he is a machinist.

The unbearable smell of warm urine became stronger than ever. I began to feel a slight uneasiness at the pit of my stomach. I looked at Hans in mute appeal and he understood. We bade Frau Schoner and her family farewell and left. As we walked into the daylight again Hans asked—did you notice the smell? Had I? Well—come with me and you'll see what caused it. We swung into the rear of the tenement house, and as we entered I saw two huge dung pits filled with fresh cow manure, and two men with pitchforks loading it on a dray cart. Behind the pits was a stable, and in the stable a number of cows. In Berlin one mustn't look behind people's coattails, someone told me—neither should one look behind their courtyards. This is December. What does it smell like in July? And in August? Had anyone told me, I would not have believed it possible—seeing it was believing. Also clarified some things I had heard about Wedding; and certainly helped to explain certain districts in Wedding that are not usually mentioned in polite society.

Again we climb stairs. This time I am introduced to a little man of perhaps forty-five. A charming little man who at forty-five looks ten years older. With him are Rudolph aged five, Edward aged seven and Hans aged nine. This time the mother is out. I notice many toys made of wood. A complete railway engine built out of wood, finished this morning, fascinates the boys. Hans asks me whether I know anything about engines. As it happens I know enough about engines to talk glibly, and promptly the boys gather around me to listen and to establish a comradeship based on boilers and pistons and exhausts. Father Gehring looks on and smiles. He has some secret, but I surmise it's largely the secret joy that comes out of having done something that he knows had pleased his boys.

The matter of engines exhausted, we turn to other matters. How long has Herr Gehring been out of work? Something over two years. I tell him that my impression is that he is a woodworker. No. Hans answers for him and tells me that he is an expert mechanic on organs. The toys, some of which were excellently carved, were done for the amusement of the boys, and his own. His dole, for himself, his wife, and his three boys, is ninety-three marks per month. The one room they occupy costs eighteen marks, and serves for everything, kitchen, bedroom, playroom, and workshop where Gehring manages to make the toys that amuse his boys. Food? Three days each week they have salt pork and potatoes and three days each week they have sauerkraut and potatoes. Meat—on Sundays—one pound for five people. Occasionally they had food from the community kitchen. Amusements such as moving picture shows, or what to the German is even more beloved, a trip to the favorite café for coffee or a glass of beer, whole family tagging along—long since forgotten. It is more important, explains Gehring, to buy writing paper for the two older boys so that they may not have hardships in their school attendance. Hans inadvertently brings up May 1, 1929.[29] Herr Gehring's face changes from a kindly fatherly look to something of bitterness and determination, but he refrains from saying anything. One doesn't talk about these things in the presence of strangers.

We climb still higher. This time we meet Frau Fluchalt and her seven children. Five boys and two girls. Her husband is an ironworker. Four years out of work. Frau Fluchalt doesn't want to talk and doesn't take kindly to Hans's questions. Just then a neighbor enters. The neighbor is more kindly disposed to us and at the same time is quite indignant with Frau Fluchalt. Frau Fluchalt is advised that it doesn't pay to be too proud. Not in this world. Certainly not on Köslinerstrasse. Frau Fluchalt answers her neighbor that she isn't proud—as if pride were a luxury—only she didn't want to talk in the presence of the children. Then she warmed up. She pays twenty-two marks for the two small rooms she occupies and doesn't know what to do. If she pays the rent then there won't be enough left for food, and if she buys food then there won't be anything left for rent and they may be thrown out. How much does she get from the *Wohlfahrt?* For nine in the family they receive 115 marks per month—less than a dollar a day—out of which rent, clothing, writing materials for school purposes for the children, somehow had to be squeezed. Yes, food also had to be bought. Well, how much food was necessary for a family of nine? This she doesn't know. She only knows the minimum that has kept her brood alive until the present and is concerned only with continuing the same amount for the present. At least until her husband could find work. Well—what kind of food do you get now—what do you and your children eat? The *Mittag* meal—breakfast is ignored—we have three liters of soup from the *Gemeinschafstküche.* I recall the soup that I had there. Good thick soup it was. Hans had served it to me with pride. Soup thick with lentils and occasional pieces of *Einlage*—meat—and coming in out of the cold the liter of soup had both warmed and nourished me. I said so, and Frau Fluchalt was pleased. It complimented her on her management—and it saved the fire too—and really was cheaper than she could

29. See note 25.

cook it at home. My mind works in terms of costs. For half a mark—twelve and a half cents—she provides the main meal of the day for nine people. Then it occurred to me to ask how much is a liter? Hans looks startled. It hadn't occurred to him to ask. He had been serving liters of soup to some six hundred people each day. They are bowls of soup, thick, very thick soup. I know. I had a liter of it only a few hours ago. One liter for one man and one liter for one woman—that was how it went. A liter is a quart. No, it is a little less than a quart. The problem becomes all-absorbing. Just how much is a quart and how much is a liter I try to recall some vague figures. Instead I see the patterns of the dampness, the walls and burning staring eyes of the children. Well, it isn't so important after all. A liter is somewhere close to a quart—why bother? Three quarts roughly for nine people. Now it comes to me that somewhere I recall reading that a liter is eight-tenths of a quart. Perhaps it is all wrong. Suddenly I turn sick. The whole weight of meaning bears down—nine people living on less than three quarts of soup—one-third of what I ate only a few hours ago; and this repeated day after day until strength and vitality were gone. I turn sick and want to get out. I can't. It is like a torturous dream from which I want to escape and can't.

I come back to the soup and the liters and the problem of how much food, etc. Yes—Frau Fluchalt tells me—to the liters of soup she adds a slice of rye bread, and sometimes two slices, when they can afford it. And in the evening? In the evening she tells me, again the three liters, but this time the three liters of soup are cooked at home. Some milk, some water and some flour, mixed together and cooked. Once in a while they have potatoes with it. Last Sunday they had a pound of meat with it. One pound of meat for nine people—this time she didn't think she could. I looked at Hans and Hans's face was stone-cold. In Germany they have their trade unions and their party and their meetings and their programs. I must not offend these people. I didn't. My hands remained in my pocket. Hans's face was stone cold, even in the gathering darkness I could see the rigid determined lines. I rose, Frau Fluchalt rose with us. We shook hands and, as I felt Frau Fluchalt's wasted hand in mine, I knew that not very much of the three liters of soup, thick soup, went into her thin frame. Then I shook hands with the solemn-faced children of Frau Fluchalt, and they curtsied in their German fashion and were polite as German children are taught to be in the presence of strangers. And their eyes followed me until the two holes they know as home were behind me.

Can you stand one more? Hans wants to show me everything. It is as if for the first time he has been able to show something [that one must] show.

It is getting late, the street lamps are already lit. But Hans insists. Well, one more. That will be the last. We walk to the ground floor of the adjacent building. How many unemployed in this tenement house? One hundred and eight out of one hundred and twenty—exactly ninety percent. Again Hans's cigarette lighter shows the way. This time we enter a one-room apartment, not larger than a fair-sized room in an East Side tenement. Into this one room are crowded cooking stove, two beds, an eating table at the foot of the beds and two chairs. I am introduced to the Shuler family, father, mother, two boys and two girls. Shuler is a cement worker and has been out of work since 1928. He is short, stocky, about thirty-five and very active in the trade unions. The unions, he tells me, are very active in the fight to see that unemployment insurance and *Wohlfahrt* aid are maintained. There are many communities where the cities will not be able to keep the *Wohlfahrt* aid going much longer. Perhaps Berlin itself? He doesn't think so, and intimates that Köslinerstrasse in that event might be turned into another charnel house all over again. Conditions were bad enough now—it would not be wise to drive the workers any further; between bullets and empty stomachs, he added, there isn't much choice. He turned to Hans: have you shown him the workers who live like rats in cellars? No? You should. Then he would have something to tell the American workers about Germany. Why haven't you taken him there? You must show him how these people live. It is enough to drive one crazy. Hans apologized. It is not good, he answered, to show strangers the worst—I had been on the point of asking whether what I had been shown wasn't the worst there is in Berlin. Here was the answer: there are those who live still lower than those whom I have seen today. But why don't you show him those who are completely *ausgeschlossen*[30]—those who are refused aid even by the *Wohlfahrt?* Hans was embarrassed. I interceded for him. I see you have only one room—have you another? No. This is the room we live in; sleep in; and eat in—and often die in. Let me show you how we live. You Americans have a bathroom in every apartment—is it not so? There are a hundred and twenty tenants in this building and not a single bath. They tell me that in New York every apartment has a toilet. Come. I'll show you what we have. We walk to the head of the basement stairs through the dark, Shuler lights a match and opens a door. I see before me an old-fashioned wooden toilet made of wooden boards. Do you know how many families use this toilet? Nine families. The pots in the rooms in the morning would choke you. Go to America and tell them you saw this.

30. Excluded.

Hans—did you show him the cow stables in the rear? You should be here in the summertime. Then you would know what it means to be a worker in Germany. I promised that I would certainly tell the American workers. He has a strange faith in them. He forgets that only fifteen years ago they were shooting at German workers with *tanzing* machines similar to the ones the police used on them on May 1, 1929.

I walk down the street with Hans. He tells me of other places that are worse. I ask him about the cellars and he promises to take me some other time. I walk down the street with Hans and as I walk I keep thinking of Dr. Bading, the agricultural expert of the Social Democratic Party and the trade unions, of Herr Engel, the secretary of the Agricultural Workers Union, and Robert Schultz, the organizer of East Prussia, also of the Agricultural Workers' Union. It was only yesterday and the day before that we had talked about food conditions in Germany. I had asked dozens of questions, but we always came back to the same question—is there enough food in Germany to feed the population and to feed it as well as it ought to be fed? All of them assured me that not only was there enough food to feed the population of Germany at least as it had been fed in 1928 and 1929, but that there was a surplus on hand that is rotting. They had made my head whirl with figures and statistical tables. Then why, in the name of all I have seen today, is what I have seen necessary? Here are cement workers, and ironworkers, and carpenters, and building craftsmen of all sorts, the latter I am told [are] ninety percent idle, and here they are starving and living like rats in traps. Why can't they be put to work building decent homes, and fed while they are working? Are the Schoners, the Gehrings, the Fluchalts, and the Shulers destined to die in their holes, or are they likely to turn in their desperation and repeat over and over again their occasional barricades and their dances to the death measures and rhythm of the *Tanz* machines? Something Hans said brought me back to amenities and polite conversation. We shook hands under a lamppost under the watchful eye of a member of the blue-coated, black-helmeted, sword-, gun- and club-carrying *Polizei,* and went our different ways.

◇ *Sunday, December 11, 1932*

B4, F4

I confess I am not convinced. Everyone tells me that the middle class in Germany is ruined. But what I see with my own eyes is hard to contradict. Every district in Berlin, [whether] it is the old or the newer sections, everywhere I go, the stores are occupied and the vacancies are rare and far between. I have seen far more store vacancies in the States in normal times than I see here when conditions are abnormal.

Whenever I approach the subject of the middle class I am promptly reminded of what happened to the middle class in Germany during the inflation. True, the bondholders who had government securities were ruined. But bondholders alone do not make up the middle class. I am never told of the millions of property holders who were enriched during the inflation because they could, and did, pay off their mortgages with the equivalent of postage stamps. So much so that the government taxed them up to forty percent of the value of their gains, and, I am told, applied the money on the new housing schemes.

For definitive purposes the middle class here is defined as all those who do not work with their hands or have had the benefits of an education beyond that [which] workers' children get. The result is endless confusion. Culture does not make a class, rather have I found the opposite to be true. Certainly I will have to be shown considerably more before I take the supposed ruin of the German middle class as a fact. True it is that during the inflation millions lost their savings and other millions lost their stocks and bonds, but at the same time a new group was enriched through the juggling of the financial bookkeeping of that period. But the evidence of the demise of the German middle class as a class will have to be made clearer to me than it is now. The shops, in the main, seem well stocked, and seem to be getting along. The sights one sees in American cities, one store after another vacant, is something that I haven't seen here.

◇ *Monday, December 12, 1932*

B4, F4

One of the responsible labor officials who doesn't want to be quoted gave me what purports to be the inside story of Brüning's downfall.[31] He puts it

31. Heinrich Brüning (1885–1970). Leader of the Zentrum, chancellor since March 1930, he was dismissed in May 1932. His dismissal was more the consequence of intrigues on the Right (especially by the East Prussian landowners, irritated by his projects of agrarian policy) than of his deflationary policy of wage and unemployment-benefit cuts. However unpopular, his policy was "tolerated" as a "lesser evil" by the SPD. After the Nazi takeover, Brüning went into exile in the United States in 1934, where he stayed, teaching at Harvard University, until his death, except for a brief return to Germany between 1952 and 1954.

squarely up to Hindenburg's hatred of the Catholics. I have no reason to question the veracity of the man, on the contrary, I have every reason to believe him. At any rate, I pass it along for what it is worth.

Brüning is a Catholic and represents the Catholic Center Party,[32] whose main strength is in the West and South of Germany, and great weakness lies in the East and Center of Germany. The Center, as it is known, gathers considerable strength from the impoverished peasants in those sections, and has repeatedly promised that when they obtain power they will make it possible for them to obtain land. Brüning therefore developed the idea of purchasing the lands of the East Prussian landowners who for one reason or another have not been able to run them profitably, divide these lands into small peasant holdings, and sell them to the peasants on long-term contracts. To make this plan feasible he planned to organize a bank with the help of state subsidies and to handle the transaction through this newly created bank.

The East Prussia Junkers, or large landowners and noblemen of the former *kaiserlichen*[33] days, did not like the idea. [So] they reached the ear of Hindenburg, who by the way also owns a large estate in East Prussia. [It is then] that Brüning planned to settle East Prussia with Catholics and thus break the political power of the landowners in that section. Thereon Hindenburg called in Brüning and dismissed him. Prejudice in politics, it is also not wanting in Germany.

◇ *[Wednesday], December 14, 1932*

B4, F4

Those who control the police powers of Germany are the real masters of it. To imagine that a revolution is possible in Germany, a successful revolution, is counting without its costs.

The police powers of the state are of two kinds. The ordinary police one sees on the streets are state employees. Although they are dressed similarly in all of the cities in Germany, they are really in the employ of the state and not of the cities. Thus the *Polizei* of Berlin are employed by the state of

---

32. The Zentrum, the Catholic Party founded in 1870. During the Weimar Republic, five chancellors (Konstantin Fehrenbach, Joseph Wirth, Wilhelm Marx, Heinrich Brüning, and Franz von Papen) belonged to this party. Their political persuasion ranged from left of center (Wirth) to the extreme nationalist right (von Papen).

33. Imperial.

Prussia, and so on.[34] They will remain loyal to whoever really controls the political strings. They have too much at stake to do otherwise. While their wages are nothing for them to brag about—from a minimum of 125 marks a month up to 300—there are so many other rights that they acquire in the service that to expect them to go along with any movement that may make their status uncertain is like trying to swim up the Niagara. In addition to their wages, comfortable wages for Germans, they get their uniforms, and a uniform in Germany is an honor not to be taken lightly, pensions, sickness insurance, and all the other insurances, excepting one, and that they do not need—unemployment insurance. They can resign at any time, but if they stay in the service twelve years they are entitled to one of two things, either a flat sum of money, between two and three thousand marks, enough to establish themselves in some small business, or preference in state employment where the work is easier. I am told that most government "functionaries" are recruited from their ranks. A "functionary" occupies a special rank in Germany—both in the monetary returns and in prestige. The "functionary" may be nothing more than a doorkeeper guarding the entrance to a courtroom, but they had better not be trifled with. Once a functionary, always a functionary, runs the proverb—and all the rights and privileges that go with the position. The police will not give these things up with any bellwether movement that springs up over night.

◇ *Friday, December 16, 1932*

B4, F5

Noticed this morning that the Nazis were advertising a mass meeting and concert to be held tonight at the Sportpalast.[35] The speaker announced was none other than Dr. Goebbels,[36] the propaganda director for the entire Nazi

---

34. Since von Papen's "coup" in Prussia in July 1932, the Prussian (and therefore the Berlin) police were under a conservative government. On the Berlin police, see Hsi-huey Liang, *The Berlin Police Force in the Weimar Republic* (Berkeley and Los Angeles: University of California Press, 1970).

35. Mass meetings were held in the Sports Palace throughout the Weimar Republic and the Nazi regime. It had been built in 1910–11, and was destroyed in January 1944 by the Allied bombings. The Sports Palace was located in Schöneberg on Potsdamerstrasse. It was rebuilt in the early 1950s and razed in 1973.

36. Joseph Goebbels (1897–1945), Nazi gauleiter of Berlin in 1932 and Hitler's minister of propaganda from 1933 until his death.

movement. I therefore decided to go. On mentioning it to Herbert Kline he advised me to get there early. The notice stated that the doors would open at six. The meeting was slated for eight. I got there promptly at seven.

As I got off the bus, I noticed dozens of *Polizei* supplemented by dozens more of Nazis in black trousers and light, almost fawn-colored, shirts. From the massing of the *Polizei* and Nazis I was almost certain that I was too late. Therefore, when a Nazi approached me and offered to sell me a ticket I wondered whether they hadn't gone in for ticket speculation. I asked the price and was told it was one mark, and he explained to me at the same time that his group was given so many tickets to sell and that I would be helping his particular group if I bought my ticket from him. Since its price corresponded with the box office price and made it unnecessary for me to stand in line in front of the box office, I purchased his ticket and started to walk in. As I passed the box office there was comparatively no line. I decided that either it was too late, or that the sale of tickets through the organizations made it unnecessary to stand in line altogether.

The meeting was held in the Sportpalast. The building is shaped like an O. The rear was curtained off and a platform raised in front of the curtain for the orchestra and the speakers. The main floor, I judge, has a seating capacity of five thousand. Three balconies hold an additional seating capacity of ten thousand, about fifteen thousand in all. When I entered the hall there were only about two thousand people in the entire hall. The young Nazis, in spite of their uniforms, looked disheartened and disappointed. What preparations had been made can, perhaps, be [derived] from the fact that the section roped off for press correspondents contained five hundred seats. Later I noticed that the chairs were filled, but I doubt whether they were filled by press correspondents. By eight o'clock the orchestra or ground floor was two-thirds filled, and about half of the next two balconies filled, the top balcony was entirely vacant. I doubt whether there were more than seven thousand people in the hall, including what I should estimate at about one thousand Nazis in uniform. Promptly at eight o'clock, the orchestra, two hundred strong, broke into martial air. The outburst of applause that greeted it however was weak. One felt as if the spirit had taken flight. Perhaps the internal dissension among the Nazis had something to do with it, or perhaps it was due to the fact that political meetings were forbidden, or it may have been due to the fact of Christmas being so near, at any rate I felt that something was wrong. The music continued for half an hour, in the meantime I had the opportunity to walk around the hall and to gather what impressions I could of the audience itself.

The audience was about equally divided between men and women—if anything, more women than men. The crowd was, aside from the young Nazis in uniform, somewhat middle-aged—although most of them seemed to take the meeting as a lark. There was much saluting, but I noticed that the saluting mostly came from the younger men and women. The raising of the hand above the head, that constitutes the salute, when done sloppily resembles very much an old lady signaling a streetcar. Many of the young girls present, to be in the spirit of the gathering I suppose, were dressed in suede jackets, almost of the same color of the light-brown shirts of the Nazi troops. This uniform business is a great thing in German politics. The moment a movement gathers momentum, up pops the uniform. And when the finances will stand the burden the uniforms are turned into an army. Somehow the Nazis turned the trick—and dame rumor has it that the number of uniforms among them is not less than 800,000. Others, more conservative, say that the number is closer to 400,000. Whether 4 or 8 doesn't really matter—when seen marching into a hall with their banners flying, they look formidable enough.

To recruit this army Hitler had to raise enormous funds. It meant not only purchasing uniforms, it meant also an allowance to the boys for wearing them and for accepting the discipline that a military uniform carries with it; and a certain amount of "sports," a polite term for military training. When Schleicher accepted the Chancellorship, the industrialists in the Ruhr, so it is said, decided that Schleicher would serve their purposes as well as Hitler. Whether Schleicher will or can deliver to the Ruhr industrialists remains to be seen. In the meantime, with Christmas approaching, Herr Hitler has not the funds with which to maintain this huge private army. To raise the daily expense of 600,000 marks is becoming more and more difficult. Moreover there is mutiny in the ranks, of which at present there is only the vaguest rumor. It is therefore no wonder that either the crowd was small or that the enthusiasm seemed lacking.

I had been told that Goebbels is the best political showman in Germany, and for showmanship I must hand it to him. At eight thirty, I noticed a craning of necks towards the entrance and on turning my own I beheld in the aisle a fife and drum corps, behind them, a double file of uniforms headed by a Nazi carrying the swastika banner—an enormous flag. At a signal the fife and drum corps broke into a martial flare of music and slowly marched forward. As they moved everyone raised his or her hand in the Nazi salute. Had the enthusiasm been there at this moment it would have been quite stirring. My neighbor turned to me and said something about calling meetings just before holidays. That may account for it. Or is it that the fires of enthusiasm, as with our own KKK—after reaching their peak when they controlled thirty-four governors[37]—suddenly turned to ashes? Certainly, standing on street corners all day, tin can in hand, to raise funds, when the weather isn't exactly California sunshine, doesn't add to one's enthusiasm. As the drum and fife corps approached the platform, with the double file of Nazi uniforms behind them, the band took up the martial air and the hall was filled with a volume of music that made every rafter in the huge building shake. It was the only moment in the entire evening when the audience was completely carried away.

When the fife and drum corps finally reached the platform it swerved from the center of the aisle to the right side and then up the stairs and to the rear of the band. The carrier of the swastika banner stood exactly in the middle of the stage right behind the band and held his flag aloft, presumably for the rest of the evening. The two hundred troops that had marched up the aisle behind the banner separated, one hundred troops on the right side of the stage and the other on the left side of the stage, no doubt to guard the platform against outside attacks. They stood at attention the rest of the evening. It made an impressive show of force and gave the meeting a picturesqueness that was out of the ordinary; but added nothing to the enthusiasm of the meeting.

This was followed by another blare of military music, lasting till 9 o'clock. An officer in military uniform, very much resembling the uniforms of our motorcycle cops, except that the uniforms here are black, stepped up to the microphone. He was promptly greeted with a flock of hail hails. The hail hail seems to take the place of applause. The hail hails and the raising of the hands were premature. There was something wrong. For a moment he stood wavering. Apparently he had bad news and didn't know how to start. At last he raised his hand for silence. In a moment the crowd grew quiet and tense. The crowd also sensed that the news wasn't cheerful—one could feel it. It didn't have long to wait.

After a few preliminary remarks, during which he gathered his military courage, he finally announced that there was a political truce in Germany, a truce to which the Hitlerites had agreed. The Nazis, he went on, never break their word. The word of a Nazi was the most precious thing in Germany. This was met with some cheering, but mostly in silence. The concert

---

37. In the 1924 elections the Klan surely contributed to the election of many U.S. congressmen and some governors in the South, but thirty-four is too high a number.

would go on, he announced, and Dr. Goebbels would speak, but they must not expect anything of a political nature tonight. A woman yelled that this wasn't right, and she was loudly applauded. The officer drew himself erect, saluted the Nazi salute, and left the platform.

So this was the famous menace to Germany and to the world. I confess my disappointment. At the same time I realize that the time for a real whacking meeting was not propitious. I'll have to see more of their meetings. But I had come to see a whale and found a minnow. The answer itself may be in these meetings. The answer may be in the control of this movement by big businessmen who for the moment have decided against fascism in the Hitler form. At any rate, since Goebbels would not discuss the political situation and my ears were beginning to feel the strain of too much martial music, I decided to leave. A prizefight would have been much more exciting.

◇ *Saturday, December 17, 1932*

B4, F5

Am on my way to Plauer. On Tuesday, at the social gathering at the Gewerkschaftshaus, the secretary of the Berlin Trade Unions told us of two meetings he was going to hold today and invited a group of Berlin trade unionists, George Stolz, Dr. Hartig and myself to come as his guests. Now we are on our way. Plauer is a few miles out of Brandenburg, the old capital of Prussia. On the way we pass through Potsdam, but have no time to see Sans Souci.[38] Reserved for another date.

We pass through Brandenburg and I notice it is an industrial city. I ask George about it and he tells me that the population is almost wholly dependent on a steel mill and bicycle manufacturing. Eleven thousand are being taken care [of] on the dole or charity. He goes on to say that the city has a socialist administration and that the administration is going frantic because it is faced with bankruptcy. We stop for a cup of coffee and for the four of us, whom I treat, I pay fifty-five cents for the equivalent of one American sweet roll, divided into four portions, and four cups of coffee. Again I am confirmed that restaurant prices in Germany are as high if not higher than American prices.

We leave Brandenburg and within half an hour we are in Plauer. The

---

38. Royal residence built by Frederick II, situated in the outskirts of Potsdam, not far from Berlin.

town originally was a farming village. During the war the government built a munitions plant there and employed 8,000 workers. One tenth of that number are working there now. I notice the separate living quarters as we drive around the plant to our destination.

On the way I asked George to tell me something about [. . .] the *Freiwillegearbeitnehmer*[39] camp where we are going. [He explains] that all over Germany camps have been established for boys between 16 and 25 who are employed on roadwork, on community parks and in the repair work that has to do with the maintaining of community sport stadiums etc. There are approximately two hundred and fifty thousand boys in these camps at the present time. If properly managed it would not be a bad thing for the young men. [. . .]

Arriving on the grounds, [Vomerhaus],[40] the secretary of the Brandenburg district council of the trade unions, takes charge of the party. He leads us through some wooded land until we see a series of what looks to me like barracks. I comment on the looks of the buildings and Hartig smiles but says nothing. We are led into the kitchen where we find the leader of the camp and six women of various ages preparing the *Mittag* meal. Vomerhaus explains that [. . .] the boys in many cases had grown flabby from the lack of work, and many of them were starved. In some cases they gained from two to three pounds a week. I ask about their hours of work and he explains that they work six hours and four hours are devoted to "sports." I then ask why they are called "volunteer workers." This, he explains, is due to their receiving but little compensation. The state appropriates two marks a day for each of the boys. Out of these two marks must come for their food and clothing. Shelter is already provided by the community in which they work. This also applies to the women who do the cooking. The only compensation that the boys get in cash is thirty pfennigs, about six cents a day. We are then led to the house where the boys sleep and again I notice the barrack-like atmosphere, army cots, etc. Again I comment on the military aspect of the rooms, the arrangement of the army cots and the uniforms. Vomerhaus tells me that this phase will be explained to me later. In the meantime, what do I think of the way the young men are being in care? I tell him—in America we undoubtedly would oppose it. [. . .] This is work that should be done by

39. Voluntary workers.

40. Unable to ascertain this name, spelled "Vollmeshaus" in this diary entry, we adopted the spelling used by Plotkin in the printed *American Federationist* article where spelling seems more certain.

men and paid for in wages that would make it possible for men to support their families. [. . .]

[*Vomerhaus later explains that*] when the Volunteer Work for the Young was established the trade unions first felt that it was competition against their members. We fought it on that basis for five months. During that time, the Hitlerites and the other groups organized approximately two hundred and fifty thousand boys in these camps. We watched them grow in size and remained unaltered in our opposition. But when we saw what these camps were developing into, we decided to take a hand and organize our own camps. In organizing them we have two objects: first to set an example before the other camps where already a number of strikes have taken place because of bad food, too rigid discipline, bad sleeping quarters and inhuman treatment; and second to prevent if possible the militarization of these boys. Most of us at the present feel that the whole has evolved not so much with the idea of getting work for the young men, but as an undercover method of again militarizing the youth in Germany. [. . .]

We are not only protesting against these practices but as far as possible we will try and prevent them. In our own camps they will not be tolerated. So. The rumors spread in America about the militarization of the German youth were not altogether unfounded. I sat back and watched the faces of the men before me. Once before, Germany had been completely militarized. At that time they also saw the menace of militarism, but had no idea that it would lead to the loss of their loved ones—two million men, mostly boys, killed outright. Were they really determined not to permit it again? They were silent. But their silence spoke both of their bitterness and their determination; and I feel that, if it is left in their hands to prevent the remilitarization of German youth and another war, they will not sit silently as they did the last time. [. . .]

I can't say that I saw a single boy's face, however coarse, that wasn't softened by something composed both of suffering and worry. Mostly they ate their food in silence. Their life's problem was altogether before them. Twenty weeks of respite . . . then the street and the daily search for work again. Time is a butcher and the twenty weeks will soon be over . . . what then?

Meal over they sang. Sixty young voices singing. Sixty young boys facing problems too old for them. Sixty young bodies getting a respite in their search for food. Will they escape the hardships they have faced once before or will they be stricken down, either one by one or in mass, by an industrial and military system over which they have no control and which they do not understand? Time will answer. In the meantime I rode back to Brandenburg with the faces of the sixty boys before me.

◇ *Sunday, December 18, 1932*

B4, F5

Ran into Furtwängler today and had a short chat with him. Asked me why I hadn't called on Leipart. Explained to him, as I explained to Stolz the evening he introduced me to Leipart, that I regarded the invitation to call on him as a courtesy not to be taken seriously. The sort of thing that is said to anyone and promptly forgotten. Furtwängler looked surprised, and then said that in Germany an invitation from Leipart is equivalent to a command. I was surprised in turn and assured Furtwängler that I would write immediately asking for an appointment. At the same time we were both amused at what it was that made an impression on the president of the labor movement in Germany. On being introduced to him, Leipart asked me what industry I was associated with. On being told that I had been associated with the Ladies' Garment Workers' Union he wanted to know how it was that a man could represent them? When it was explained to him that the name indicated the industry and not the workers he simply couldn't get over it. Furtwängler tells me that he spoke of it several times. Also met Eggert the same evening. It was an evening devoted to wishing each other a merry Christmas and happy new year over a game of cards and a glass of beer—politics and trade unionism for the moment forgotten. I will have to write to Leipart in the morning.

◇ *Monday, December 19, 1932*

B4, F5

Returning from the American Express Co., I found a note in my room from Dr. Hartig. The letter was sent by special delivery, an extravagance seldom resorted to by Germans. I promptly opened it and found that he had arranged, much to my surprise, an interview with Dr. Loewenstein, head of the Berlin-Lichtenberg health department. One appointment already had been made—and broken through no fault of my own. I dropped everything else and promptly took the *Bahnhof* to the section of town where Dr. Loewenstein has his modest apartment.

Arriving there I was shown into his study and was told that he was delayed for a few minutes. A moment later Dr. . . . walked in and greeted me in excellent English. She is a woman of middle age, teaching I suppose in one of the schools in Berlin. She told me that she was born on 52nd

Street in New York, was taken to England at an early age, and then brought to Germany where she was educated and where she has lived ever since. She explained her presence—she had come at Dr. Loewenstein's request to act as an interpreter. The Herr Doctor did not speak a word of English and thought that perhaps it would be better if there was someone there to interpret what he said. I expressed my pleasure but did not indicate that I had a slight familiarity with the language. A few minutes later, we were joined by one whom I at first took to be the daughter of Dr. Loewenstein but who really was his wife and the mother of his two children. Mrs. Loewenstein is by far the most charming woman I have yet met in Germany. As we were being introduced, Dr. Loewenstein himself walked in. After a few minutes' preliminary conversation, with Dr. . . . translating, Mrs. Loewenstein led us to a tea table next to the tile stove—in Germany tile stoves can be made quite ornamental—and promptly made me feel completely at home. So much so that even [our interpreter] forgave me for confessing that I understand quite a bit of German. Up to now I was afraid of offending her. The warmth and charm of this household is one that I shan't forget for a long time.

Loewenstein himself is perhaps in his late thirties. Slight, thin, long head, quite bald, very large brown eyes and slightly sunk cheeks, his face has almost a Hebraic mold. When he speaks it is as a medical man, choosing each word for the subtle differences in the meaning that it will give to the idea that he is trying to develop. While I made no inquiries I gathered that he is not affiliated with any political party, yet he believes sincerely in the need for socializing the practice and treatment of medicine. He would, were it in his power, have the state take over the medication of the sick; and complained rather bitterly that, while the Hitlerites were attacking him for his views, the Social Democrats were lukewarm.

We finally got to the reason for my visit. I told him of my visit to Wedding and what I had seen there; families in one room; walls in apartments that just oozed with slime; of houses built over cow sheds and horse stables and dung pits in courtyards. Also of the talks I had had with Dr. Bading who pointed out to me the decreased consumption of food in Germany. What effect was all this going to have on the people? Dr. Miller, one of the superintendents of one of the local schools, told me that since the depression the amount of sickness among the children had doubled. It was inconceivable to me that a protracted condition of this sort would fail to leave its mark on the German people as a whole. What could he tell me about it?

For the next hour Loewenstein spoke. He spoke without heat or indignation. It was a health problem and the facts spoke for themselves. Fact after fact, analysis after analysis, pyramided themselves into a story of the physical and mental decay of a nation. When he got through I was exhausted. It seemed as if I had passed through a nightmare, and I realized that what I had seen in Wedding was only the surface, the ulcers on the surface, not the cancers hidden deep within.

Generally speaking, he started, our experiments are comparatively meager, but they indicate definite tendencies. Here is a report of one of my assistants, Dr. H. W. Bansi of Berlin. Briefly this report indicates that while on the surface the majority of the unemployed are healthy there is nevertheless a loss in resistance power. To put it another way. There has been no increase in the death rate; but those who, for instance, have a tendency to tuberculosis when stricken with it will die more rapidly. We see that already. Not only in tuberculosis but in many other diseases. When they come to the hospital, their chances of recovery are much slimmer than they were before the crisis because the resistance to disease has been lost in the years of denial.

An outsider cannot understand what Germany is living through. You walk on the streets and you see great crowds. I said that this had been a source of wonder to me. You need not wonder, he said drily. The crowds on the streets are not there because they enjoy walking. Most of them, particularly the single people, have no money for either lighting or coal. It is pleasanter on the streets than in their miserably cold, dark rooms. [. . .]

Infectious diseases are spreading rapidly. In those houses where there are bathrooms, in order to save coal bills for heating, many families use the same tub, somewhat like the toilet you mentioned in Wedding that is used by nine families; not only that, but they have also to economize on their laundry bills. Many people therefore use the same towels. The result is a steady growth of scarlet fever and such other diseases that come from either infection or contagion. In connection with that let me call your attention to one fact that tells its own story. The public baths in Berlin have lost two-thirds of their patrons. The people simply cannot afford to pay the extra pfennigs for what was to them at one time an absolute necessity. When you see our people on the streets you see them comparatively clean and fairly well groomed, as well as their great pride will induce them to keep their hands and faces clean. Speak to any physician in the city and ask him how much scabrous scalps and eczema cases he is treating. It is exactly twice as much today as it was two years ago.

What applies to the physical applies to the mental. Since the crisis we have had an enormous increase of consumption in spirituous liquors. It eats their stomachs out. They drink to forget. This was not the case in the past.

Or take the matter of abortions. We have one million abortions every year! And in addition we have thirty thousand women who die at the hands of illegal practitioners, either unlicensed physicians or midwives. [. . .]

But these are surface symptoms. They are not the cancer underneath which is the gradual wearing away of the physical and moral resistance of a nation of 64 million people. It is my opinion that we have a condition that may have tragic consequences for the whole country. The first epidemic that will come will wipe out huge sections of the population as if they were flies. I tell you this as a medical man, and not as a propagandist. As you can see I have little faith in propaganda. I am concerned only with what the facts show and the facts that may lighten the tension. I suggest that perhaps conditions will change. [. . .] There is hope, but I cannot see from what source help can come. Only in the matter of taking care of the newborn are we still exercising care. Outside of that, we are losing sound mental perspectives. The other nations, even France, are rapidly sinking to our level. Your own country too. International diplomacy is a hopeless muddle. From our Babel of political parties? Less yet. Hitler has lost forty percent of his following. Communism? Impossible. It would mean war, with the police and the military on the side of the authorities. They have their pension at the end of twelve years' service and many other rights as well which they will not endanger. A monarchy is possible, much more probable than any other form—it will be fought hard and bitterly but I think it will come. And then? He was almost savage in his answer. It was the first show of feeling during the entire afternoon. More chaos in Europe. More prewar conditions that many of us had hoped were gone forever, and who knows perhaps more battlefields for our young to die on. I can hope—but I cannot see the way out.

◇ *Tuesday, December 20, 1932*

B4, F5

Invited by Dr. Kahn-Freund,[41] judge of one of the labor courts in Berlin, Plotkin attended a series of cases dealing with industrial disputes. He was interested to

41. Otto Kahn-Freund (1900–1979), a specialist in labor law. Exiled in England from 1933, he was appointed professor at the London School of Economics and Political Science (1951–64) and then at Oxford University (1964–70). A specialist of labor law of international reputation, he became a member of the British Academy and the House of Lords.

learn that in these courts of initial jurisdiction, where both parties had to appear, workers' unions and employers' associations were equally represented. Plotkin was impressed with the court's respect of the workers' rights.[42] *But the case of some transportation workers who had participated in the recent Berlin streetcar strike was not ruled in their favor.*

The strike had not been sanctioned by the union, on the contrary the union had denounced it as a political maneuver on the part of the Communists and Hitlerites to break the control of the union by the Social Democrats. The calling of the strike just a few days before the last election certainly lends color to the charge. More than two thousand men were victimized and left without employment when the strike was called off. In America these men would have no chance of returning to their employment. Here they could apply to the court for their reinstatement. But here the court reversed the rules of evidence and demanded of the workers that they prove that they had offered their services when receiving the announcement from their official leaders that the strike was over. Many have refused to accept what they regard as a stigma on their class consciousness. Those who applied were judged and either sent back to work on producing evidence that they had applied for employment, or were denied employment if their case was found faulty. [. . .]

◇ *Wednesday, December 21, 1932*

B4, F5

Visited Mr. [Hochgelerer], connected with the Jewish organization to prevent anti-Semitism. Found him cordial but chary about talking. Called his attention to my talk with Herschel and he promised, after the holidays, to get me in touch with a Dr. Lutman who is the authority in this field.

He does not know Herschel, but assumes that he is an excitable young man and insists that conditions are not as they have been painted by him. As we talked about Herschel I asked about Wertheim, one of the largest department store chains in Germany, and he promptly replied that while Wertheim

42. After 1919, unions had put pressure on the government to reform the court system handling labor disputes between individual workers and management. In these labor courts, the judge was appointed by the government, and two assessors, one nominated by the unions and one by the employer associations, represented community interests. In 1931 alone, the ADGB delegated ten thousand personnel to the courts.

came from a Jewish family he was no longer a Jew. Neither was Marx, but his Jewish ancestry was never forgiven nor forgotten. Israel, whose stores I have seen in other cities, is Jewish, while the stores that are the largest, or seem so to me, [those] of Hermann Tietz, belong to a Jew whose religious leanings leave no doubt. I am told that on Jewish holidays he closes his store so as to strictly observe them.

In industry, Hochgelerer tells me, the largest of the Jewish industrialists since the war have been forced out. This also applies to the Jewish bankers, most of whose holdings in the larger banks were taken over when the larger banks were nationalized. There are some who are still acting, and influentially so, as bank directors. He gave me their names but did not know what banks they officiate in. Best leave the whole matter until I reach someone who can tell me the whole story.

◇ *Thursday, December 22, 1932*

B4, F5

The whole city is in a ferment of Christmas shopping. The stores are stocked with Christmas goods, and every wurst shopwindow is filled with delicatessen enough to make the mouth water. Roast *Gans*[43] seems to be the favorite, while candied products abound on every side. Every other corner seems to have its layers of Christmas trees, although some of the trees are awfully small. I stepped into Wertheim's and found the store crowded. The store is really a series of stores that would put many of our department stores to shame. It is simply enormous.

Monday there was a news report of demonstrations in the Kurfürstendamm district. This [area] is the middle and international section of the city and has an enormous shopping district. To cater to the Christmas trade they applied to the authorities for permission to open their stores on Sunday afternoon. This gave the Communists an opportunity for a double protest and demonstration. They demonstrated against opening the shops on Sunday, and also against Christmas. Their logic, in this instance, is rather hard for me to follow. Perhaps I am stupid; but I really can't see that anything was gained by them. Perhaps they have other reasons that are not so clear to an outsider.

---

43. Goose.

◇ *Friday, December 23, 1932*

B4, F5

Everyone is going home. Practically all of the officials in the labor movement, and in other national organizations whose offices are in Berlin, are heading for the different parts of Germany to spend Christmas and New Year there. The only ones who will remain will be Plettl, Hartig and George Stolz.

One reads much of the desire of the industrialists to avoid another election because of the fear that excitement may hurt the slow beginnings of a revival in industry. One may regard this as so much blarney. An election at this time will undoubtedly increase the communist vote. While the figures up to the end of October show a slight drop in unemployment, the total since July 30 [1931] to October [1932], 14 months, has increased from 3,990,000 to 5,109,000. The maximum of unemployment came in July of this year when 5,392,000 were out of work. These figures are official, they come from the Labor Exchanges where the unemployed register. But they do not tell the entire story because there are many hundreds of thousands who are not registered, and it is a certainty that unemployment since October 30 has increased rather than decreased. How much we will [not] know for some time.

The figures on unemployment are an index to the danger points in the German economy. A million more and Germany may face a complete economic collapse.

◇ *Saturday, December 24, 1932*

B4, F5

Spent the day in Wedding, mostly at the community kitchen for the unemployed. In addition to a double portion of food, for weeks the woodworkers have been working making toys to give to the children. When I told them that I wanted to buy a gift for a child I know, I was told that I couldn't buy the particular doll's head I wanted. But I could contribute to the Christmas fund. I got my doll's head, only it really isn't a doll's head. It really is a long narrow head with wide mouth, flat nose, bulging eyes, flat ears and short powerful horns on his head. A head that Perry Dilley[44] the puppeteer will delight in when he sees it.

The individual craftsmanship that went into the making not only of the toys, but into the articles that are used in the house made me feel the terrific waste of modern civilization. Small chests of drawers, perfectly fitted for a child, without a nail in them, miniature tables and chairs and stools, horses and dogs whose legs actually move, and above all hundreds of dolls. On the other hand, every bit of work in the basement where the supplies are kept and the four rooms on the first floor, all of it has been done by the unemployed themselves. Even the books in the library have been rebound; and their library is not to be sneezed at. Between Goethe and Schiller and Heine, without which no German library is complete, there is Thomas and Heinrich Mann, translations of Dostoyevsky, Dickens, Upton Sinclair and Sinclair Lewis.

As I walked to the place, I saw—it was raining—a youngster not more than five years old, playing with other youngsters, in place of shoes he wore house slippers! Coming back to the subway was another youngster, whom I had seen there before, standing in front of a bakery. I asked him why he had been standing there so long, but either he couldn't tell or was frightened, or was it that the sight of cookies was too tempting to leave?

◇ *Tuesday, December 27, 1932*

B4, F5

Fritz Kummer[45] is the Schriftleiter of the *Metallarbeiterzeitung*. That means that he is editor of all publications of the Metal Workers' Federation in Germany. When Hartig took me into his office in the Metal Workers' Building this afternoon, I saw a giant get out of a chair and then an arm reach out to me clear across the width of his desk and behind was the lovable, kindly face of old Judge Ryckman of Los Angeles.[46] He greeted both Hartig and myself

---

44. Perry Dilley, one of the earliest puppet performers on the Pacific Coast. He started performing in Los Angeles in 1915 and had a large repertory of burlesque plays.

45. Fritz Kummer (1875–?) traveled to the United States, Japan, China, and Palestine between 1907 and 1911. He reported this journey in his *Eines Arbeiters Weltreise* [A Worker's World Tour] (Stuttgart: Schlicke-Verlag, 1913). The book was reprinted in 1924 (Jena: Thüringer Verlagsanstalt) and 1986 (Leipzig: Kiepenheuer). Kummer contributed several papers in trade union journals, especially in *Die Arbeit* (the ADGB organ).

46. A judge Plotkin had known when he was a labor organizer in Los Angeles.

in perfectly good English, and to my surprise told me that he had worked thirteen months for the Otis Elevator Company in San Francisco. In my youth, he added, I spent three years in America studying their methods. I worked in San Francisco before the earthquake—by the way have they rebuilt all of it? . . . Then I worked in Pittsburgh, and my last job was for an inventor whose name now escapes me. He had a couple of rooms in the Flatiron building in New York, and we all thought he was crazy. He was working on a flying motor. I never found out whether it worked. I had to leave before it was finished.

Hartig, having matters to look after, left the two of us together, after the usual showing of the building to foreign visitors, then the two of us adjourned to the Excelsior for coffee and a bite. In the States I thought I was a heavy coffee drinker. Here I have learned the meaning of the term coffee addict. Without either coffee or beer conversation is impossible, and since people, particularly Germans, must talk, coffee is the one medium around which one can discuss, quarrel, argue and fight, and do it good-naturedly enough, provided it is around a table with either the usual *Tasse* coffee or glass of beer within easy reach. When the argument gets too warm one takes a sip and cools off. I find that is a habit worth cultivating.

After talking about the building in which the Metal Workers have their headquarters, the most modern building in Germany, I asked him to tell me something about the form of organization of the trade union movement in Germany. This, he answered, is very simple, and yet entirely different from the trade unions in your country. You are organized along trade union lines. We are organized more along industrial union lines.

Our own organization can be used as a pattern. The Metal Workers' Federation has in it forty-two different industries. I will name only a few of them to you. Machine workers, iron- and steelworkers, electrical workers, cutlery workers, gold- and silversmiths, these are a few. The last two by the way are still guilds of the old school, but they come under our jurisdiction. Our membership today is 870,000. We are the largest trade union in Germany and in the world. When you saw our printing presses this afternoon, he said with pride, I told you that we have to turn out three magazines each week, one for each of our members. In addition, we have also to print millions of propaganda leaflets, special magazines for the women, in our industries, for the apprentices; from that you can get an idea of how far-reaching our organization is.

Now, you are organized according to trades. We are organized according to the industry. The steel industry is an example. Every man working in the steel plants belongs to us. When they meet, they meet as steelworkers who are members of the metalworkers' union. And [they do so] in one of two ways. They meet in the factory to discuss their factory problems; or in the districts where they live. The district organization is the official organization. The shop or other meetings are subordinate.

The district organizations are hard to define to you. Take Berlin as an illustration. We have eighty thousand metalworkers in Berlin. To call them all to a business meeting would be an impossibility. We would need six Sportpalast. Therefore, for administrative purposes, they need to be decentralized. The unit with you is the trade they happen to be in. With us it is the factory. Sometime next week I have to speak at two large factory meetings. Come along with me and see how we carry on our work. The meetings are held in the factories? Certainly, where else would they be held? In my mind's eye, I could see some of our American employers having everything short of paralysis at the mere suggestion of such an idea. A union meeting on their premises! On the other hand, I am not sure that our trade union leaders would like the idea. I told him so and he expressed his surprise. Why? In America, I explained, we think that while the workers are in the factory they can't help but feel the influence of the employer's control. Here we do not feel that so much, he smiled. Here it is just the other way around. A meeting in the factory strengthens the worker in the belief that he has power. [. . .]

The districts have thousands of "functionaries" whose duty it is to keep the members in touch with their union. They distribute the trades papers we send, they see that committees visit the sick and that the sick are given the proper state and social aid, whether it is hospital service or at home; they organize the meetings, and in general look after the details that keep up the contact between each individual member and the union; they also attend to his complaints in the shop. [. . .]

We have six different kinds of insurance, and it's as if we handled five million insurance policies alone. [. . .]

The districts have no property of their own. Everything belongs to the national body. We have 52 buildings in the different cities in Germany. Then we have all sorts of printing plants, and we are tied up with shareholding in many cooperative projects. [. . .]

What about strikes? Strikes, he answered, are unlawful. Only at one point are we permitted to strike. When the agreement has expired, then we have a right to strike until a new one is agreed and is negotiated. Once the agreement is concluded then strikes become unlawful. The penalty for strikes is the damage that has been done by either party. Whichever party is to blame has to pay the damages.

When an agreement for a certain branch of the metal industry is about to expire our representatives and those of the industry come together and try to adjust their differences. Frequently that happens and that of course closes the matter. But suppose we can't come to an agreement and we see that the firms are not willing to give us what we think is justice. Then the government steps in, calls both parties to a conference, and then arbitrates their differences. But supposing the employers or the workers refuse to come? They have to come. That is the law. And if in the meantime, as it sometimes happens, a strike has been called, because the old agreement has expired and there is no agreement to take its place, the moment the decision of the arbitrator is handed down, it becomes the law for the industry for the time being. We can appeal to the Minister of Labor against the decision of the arbitrator, but in the meantime we are forbidden to strike.

But I read constantly of strikes that have broken out. There hardly seems a week that the newspapers don't record some labor disturbance. True. In many cases the strike is legal because it is taking place between agreement and arbitration. At other times we authorize strikes because the employer has broken his agreement, or refuses to abide by a court order in which he is ordered to make restitution of wages to employees whom he has underpaid. These strikes must first be ordered by our national office. [. . .] Once in a while the workers will take things into their own hands and walk out. When that happens it is hard to make them see that their national union may face tremendous difficulties if they do not permit us to settle matters through usual channels, but, as a rule, they soon see that their national headquarters is trying to adjust matters in their interest and obey the instructions of their official leaders.

By this time Hartig and Plettl joined us. Aronovici[47] had expressed a desire to meet a group of labor men. Inasmuch as I had no place to invite them to, and inasmuch as both Carol and his wife are charming hosts, we adjourned to Carol's for dinner, about which more some other time.

◇ *Thursday, December 29, 1932*

B4, F5

A national congress of the factory councils! This is news. Hartig phoned me today. The national congress meets only once in two years. Luck is therefore with me. The problem now is how to get an invitation. However,

---

47. Plotkin's friend from Los Angeles. See Introduction, note 32.

I'll worry about that later. The congress does not meet until the 22nd of January.

Hartig then proceeded to explain the history of the factory councils (Betriebsräte). *He noted that the idea of workers' committees had existed for decades in the German labor movement before they were finally established, in factories employing at least fifty persons, by the November 1918 agreement between employers and trade unions. The function of these councils was to check the application of collective agreements within the factories. Later, factory councils were extended to establishments with a minimum of five employees.*

The Communists immediately attempted to turn these councils into revolutionary factory Soviets. A struggle ensued between Socialists and Communists as to the role of the councils. In 1925, ADGB president Theodor Leipart obtained a vote upholding the factory councils as organs of the trade unions subordinated to the will of the trade union community. Since then, however, the role of the councils continued to be the object of much contention. The Communists tried to turn the councils into a weapon that would supersede the unions, while the employers, on the other hand, attempted to separate the councils from the trade unions by pleading that they had authority to make separate agreements. Up to the present time, according to Hartig, the trade unions had succeeded in warding off both factions. The unions had maintained a majority in the factory council elections, thus holding back the employers from interpreting the powers of the councils independently from the unions.[48]

---

48. In the 1931 factory council elections, 116,000 Socialist, 11,000 Christian Union, 4,700 Communist, and 700 Nazi representatives were elected.

JANUARY 1933

◇ *Sunday, January 1, 1933*

B4, F5

To Plettl, the President of the German Needle Trades Unions, the American trade union movement seems very strange and archaic. As strange as the trades unions here seem to Americans. He is, by the way, well acquainted with America, both by way of correspondence and through personal visit.[1] We have formed the habit of taking Saturday afternoons, hopping on a train, and spending the afternoon in the forest. His home is in Bavaria, and since he has to spend most of his time in Berlin, [he enjoys] the weekend trips to the forest. Usually winding up at some inn for dinner where, over the dinner table, we can discuss different movements and points of view to our hearts' content. This time we took the train to the Schoneberg road, walked to the lake where for a time we watched boys skating, crossed over to the island where the forest proper is located, climbed to the top of the hill where the inn is, and settled down to a feast of sandwiches, conversation and coffee. It isn't easy to argue with Plettl. He has spent so many years negotiating the broader needs of his people, and in settling their national problems, and has so immersed himself in questions involving the need of a national and an international point of view, that frequently he becomes impatient with what to him seems narrow and provincial. At the same time, there is an impatience with details

---

1. As already noted, Martin Plettl had been part of the 1925 ADGB delegation to the United States.

that often makes impossible the building up of explanations so that they take on the force of logic coming from the pyramiding of facts. He likes to cut right through when it is possible to do so and more [than] once I have had to stop in my narratives and insist that he stop interrupting me so that I could give, at least to myself, a sense of coherence. Nevertheless, he is a charming companion, forceful, direct, and it is easy to understand why he wields the enormous influence that he does, both with his own people and with the employers as well.

Your President of the American Federation of Labor, he started, is a great man, and a great leader, but your political as well as your trade union ideas are old, very old, and so is your idea of what constitutes practical organization. Here in Germany we are far advanced. How far [I rejoined]? Is your Socialist Party so far in advance of, let us say, the English Labour Party before MacDonald turned it into a fiasco?[2] Isn't it closer to liberalism than to socialism? And is there such close coordination between your trade union movement and your political party? And is your industrial unionism in Germany so far advanced in time that we may not very soon come up to you? How long since your labor congress met and settled this issue and, in settling it, had to compromise with the natural craft instinct within the different trades?

Hold on—he answered. Not all at once. In time we are not so far in advance of you—at least on the issue of industrial unionism. Those things were finally settled in 1924—and as you say on a compromise—but the compromise works very well.[3] We were able to absorb and through absorbing to strengthen, and what takes one hundred and fourteen internationals in your country to do, and certainly not as well because the number of men you have organized is a fraction of what we have, we are able to do with thirty unions.

Our political ideas are really far in advance of yours. Our trade unions are today recognized as a part of the administrative powers of the state, with

---

2. James Ramsay MacDonald (1866–1937), prime minister in the first Labour government of Great Britain in 1924 and again in the second, in 1929. In 1931, his proposed cuts in unemployment benefits split the Labour government, and MacDonald agreed to lead a new cabinet with Conservative support. Considered a traitor by the Labour Party, he led a so-called National government with the Conservative Party until 1935.

3. By 1924, the ADGB executive had required its constituent unions to adopt the principle of industrial unionism. Because of the die-hard resistance of some craft unions, some were allowed to survive, provided that they would organize a concentration process among them.

legal rights and powers that capitalists and their associations cannot ignore. Since we have won these industrial and these political rights, our employers have repeatedly tried to break them down, even going to the point of attempting to organize company unions—is that what you call them?[4]—until the government, of which we are a part, ruled that only the recognized trade unions have the right to negotiate and to be a party to the settlement of workers' problems and demands.[5] But wait a minute, I broke in, is it not true that even your standards of working hours have been broken during the past five years and your legal eight-hour day so encumbered with legal restrictions as to make it almost useless? The blood mounted to his head and his face grew almost purple. Yeah. What you mean, he answered, is that we have surrounded ourselves with legal rights until our legal rights under present conditions choke us. I couldn't help grinning. But it is the specific economic crisis that makes you right and not the general political history of labor and its achievements in Germany. It would take the whole night to explain it to you. I said that I was born in pain and raised in patience. It would be hard to understand it otherwise he retorted. Pleased with himself, he returned to the subject.

Our trade unions, he started, were organized by the Socialists. Again I interrupted—and Bebel[6] fought tooth and nail to separate their functions and to make the unions free from political domination. Moreover, you don't like political domination any more than we do. Your "free" unions indicate that, even by their name. You complain because we refuse to become the tail of a political kite, but you make no effort to understand our position and our logic. In our country [the United States], until 1886, we had no real trade union movement precisely because every time a trade union was organized so much of political action was brought into it that the real issues escaped them.[7] In a country without foundations that were stable, trade unionists

---

4. Organized by employers to combat independent labor organizations, company unions had flourished in the United States in the 1920s.

5. The Stinnes-Legien agreement signed on November 15, 1918 (Hugo Stinnes representing the employers and Carl Legien representing labor), recognized organized labor as the sole representative of the wage earners. Employers thus accepted not to support company unions any longer. These decisions were later enacted into labor laws.

6. August Bebel (1840–1913), one of the founders of German Social Democracy and its revered historical leader before 1914.

7. Plotkin is developing here the classic description of American labor as "pure and simple trade unionism," according to the words of Samuel Gompers, who founded the American Federation of Labor in 1886 and presided over it until 1924. The ex-

fought among themselves whether they ought to follow the German pattern or the British pattern. They still do, only today it's the Russian pattern. They fought among themselves over political questions infinitely more bitterly than they fought their employers. What was the result? The result was that every trade union up to 1886 either fell of its own weight or was smashed by the first blow the employers gave them. Their eyes were on the millennium and not on the hard realities of the day. Haven't you that force to contend with now? How many of the Communists have you permitted to remain in your trade unions? How many have you expelled? I am not questioning the wisdom of your policy. I am simply asserting that for the historical position in which we found ourselves we could permit neither religion nor politics to enter our trade unions. I am also asserting that you cannot measure trade unions in America with a yardstick made in Germany.

There, my friend, he shot back, is where you are all wrong. You separate the workers into different psychological and historical categories. The truth is that they have nothing of the sort. Workers are workers the world over. The only difference that comes in lies in the development of capitalism in their respective countries. And what I can't understand is why in your country, where capitalism is so [much more] advanced than in Germany, your trade unions are so far behind us and have learned nothing from us during our periods of transition.

Exactly. How much was there really to learn from you? I asked. We started with capitalism. You started with feudalism. You started with guilds, and we started with embryonic trade unions with a political pattern. You started with insurance schemes long before we even knew the meaning of the word; and when your unions were made illegal in the days of Bismarck,[8] you made your insurance schemes the starting point for reorganization.

---

pression meant that labor political allegiances or activism divided the rank and file instead of uniting it, and that trade unionism in America had to limit its goals to economic improvements—higher wages and a reduction of the working time—gains to be made through direct confrontations with employers but not through political or legislative action. In other words, the "pure and simple" doctrine also meant that without independent political action, the American Federation of Labor supported the two-party system as it was and renounced the eventuality of a labor party.

8. Bismarck's antisocialist law in 1878 *(Sozialistengesetz)* ruled out all the Social Democratic Party's organizations and its press as well as the unions created by Social Democrats. The law did not, however, exclude the party's parliamentary representation, nor could it prevent the party's growth, which had tripled in popular suffrage by 1890. While persecuting the Social Democrats, Bismarck introduced the creation of social insurance programs in part to beat back the Socialists on their own territory.

More than that, was his answer. We even provided a Journeymen's travelling fund so that we could send our bright young apprentices, like Bebel,[9] on organizing trips through Germany, while they were learning their trade. But you completely fail to grasp what I mean.

That we started with a different background is true. That we built our trade unions along different lines is also true. But that capitalism is developing along different lines in different countries is not true. The phenomenon that results from capitalism is the same the world over, and has now become so linked up that one country can't suffer without compelling the other countries to suffer in the same way. You speak of the crisis—and you speak not of Germany alone—you speak of the whole world. This is what the Americans have failed to learn. We had large beneficent unions,[10] protecting our workers, long before we were legalized into trade unions. Our political ideas developed even before capitalism developed. Take unemployment insurance as an example. We paid out millions in unemployment insurance long before the government would listen to us. When the emergency came the government had to turn to us to help in broadening and expanding unemployment insurance to take in the entire working class in Germany. Inseparably linked up with the unemployment insurance is the labor exchange where the workers have to register for employment. Where and how are you preparing yourself to become part of this machinery that sooner or later is bound to become part of the national economy of your country? That is what you have to learn. Always to have the foresight and to know the emergencies that under capitalism will afflict the workers is the first need of any labor movement in any part of the world where there is capitalism. In that you have to come and learn. No, my friend, it is well that you came to Germany. We may be able to make ourselves understood to American workers through you. I liked the compliment but denied the inference that the workers in America would listen to me. Then, he answered, they will have to listen to capitalism, a much harder teacher. You know, he smiled, you will think me cruel. I really am not. But I honestly think that it would be a good thing for America to have to live through unemployment another two years. At the end they will come much closer to us than through twenty years of theorizing. When you get back to America tell them that. If they are still unemployed they will believe you. We paid our check—Dutch fashion—and rode home together.

---

9. Bebel was a wood turner by trade.

10. Here Plettl meant mutual-aid societies.

◇ *Monday, January 2, 1933*

B4, F5

The Bund der Technischen Angestellten und Beamten is simply the German name for the Union of Technicians in Germany. I did not know there was such an organization in existence until I saw their representative sitting in Judge Kahn-Freund's court. Returning to George Stolz's office I asked him about this group and he promptly phoned their president Otto [Schweizer][11] to make an appointment for me. Entering their five-story headquarters I was shown to a private waiting room and told that Schweizer would come very soon. Ten minutes later, I was seated in his office.

The president of the Technicians' Union is a tall, powerful figure, broad-chested and -shouldered, with a fine long but powerful head capped by straight black hair parted in the middle, giving his face the appearance of a fine athlete ready to spring into combat. We weren't long in getting at the things we wanted to know.

Why aren't the technicians in America organized? I told him that they were. That is, if I understand the word technicians correctly as meaning engineers and architects, etc. I thought it best to understand each other's terms before we got into serious difficulties. Yes, he answered, engineers, architects, draftsmen, and there are all sorts of categories within these groups. You have what we in Germany call cultural and scientific organizations among these groups but trade unions among technicians in North America are unknown—that is, if they exist we know nothing about them. The stress put on the pronunciation of North America for a moment halted me. Why do you lay stress on the northern continent only? I thought you know, he answered, we have organizations in most South American countries that have technicians working for them. We have today trade unions in 19 countries, composed entirely of technicians. [. . .]

It is surprising to me that America, so far ahead in everything else, should be so far behind in matters of social organization. We went through exactly the same period that your technicians are going through. Let me give a little of our history. In the late eighties of the last century, when technology developed into a profession, feelers were put out for organization. This resulted in much the same type of organization as you now have in America. Meetings concerned themselves with developing the social and cultural level of their

11. Plotkin spelled this name in different manners: Schwitzer, Sweitzer, or Schweizer.

members, and exchanged their views on scientific matters dealing with their professions. A number of the young men in the professions imbued with the ideas of Marx and Liebknecht[12] began to propagate the idea that these groups were valuable in an abstract sort of way, but utterly useless when problems involving their economic and political interests arose. It was in 1904 that we made the first move. Here is the 25-year jubilee publication, published in 1929.[13] [. . .]

You see, we had been fed long enough on nice words. We were engineers, architects, men of intelligence and education, often making terrific sacrifices to raise ourselves in the industrial and economic world; instead, when we entered industry we found that outside of the honors that in Germany go to men of education, we got nothing but honeyed words, long hours and wages such as American bricklayers or steamfitters would laugh at. [. . .] So when the crisis came, in the early part of the century, and thousands upon thousands of our people found themselves on the streets with no more protection than say an immigrant who had just landed in Germany, and on the other hand we saw thousands of trade unionists go to their unions, receive their unemployment insurance—the lesson was vivid. Not to realize that our interests and our activities were bound up with those of the workers would have given proof to the world that we were utter fools. [. . .]

I wish that I could speak to your technical men in America. It is strange indeed that the most advanced country in the world, the most efficient group of technicians the world has ever seen, should be so far behind in its social thinking. In Germany we cannot understand it.

◇ *Tuesday, January 3, 1933*

B4, F5

Ask any German a question arising out of a labor problem and he will promptly refer you to the *Arbeitsamt.* As I learned quickly, this is the equivalent for the Labor Exchange. The Labor Exchange in Germany is a very important institution. So important that without it today the nation would not know how to get along, while the average German would be lost. It does

12. Wilhelm Liebknecht (1826–1900), one of the founders and main leaders of German Social Democracy.

13. *25 Jahre Technikergewerkschaft, 10 Jahre BUTAB* (Berlin: Industriebeamten-Verlag, [1929]).

exactly what its name implies, it is the labor office through which ninety-five percent of the employment is secured and distributed. And more than that. It actually creates workers for the employers. Thirty different trades are taught to young workers as part of their vocational guidance, and many more in reeducational work, when workers who are inefficient must be brought up to the standard or lose their jobs, or in extreme cases, reeducation of the worker into another trade when his own, because of invention or rationalization, is destroyed. But of more interest to me at the moment is the fact that the labor exchanges are the sieves through which all of the unemployed workers must pass in order to either obtain employment or relief. Without the authorization of the labor exchange, the worker who is out of a job is simply out of luck. [. . .]

◇ *Wednesday, January 4, 1933*

B4, F5

This morning the kiosk was rather ominous. On the same wine-colored paper announcing both the Nazis' and the Communists' mass meetings was another announcement from the *Polizei* offering 500 marks reward to anyone supplying information that will lead to the murderer of Walter Wagnitz. Wagnitz, a young Hitlerite, was stabbed to death on New Year's night—the first political murder of the year, according to the Nazis. Other rumors are that he was killed in a drunken brawl. Since my arrival in Berlin, there have been but few killings of that nature, except in Bavaria, where some of the *Ausgeschlossenen,*[14] ex-Nazis, have announced their intention of seeking asylum in Italy. . . .

Five o'clock, approaching Charlottenstrasse, I thought I heard some singing. I wasn't certain, but I commented on it to the several friends who were with me, but neither of them could confirm my sense of sound. A moment later I was quite certain that I was hearing human voices in song, but was still uncertain as to where it came from. Turning the corner of Jägerstrasse into Charlotten, I noticed through the eerie light of the lamps in the Staatstheater Square a thin line of human beings winding their way along the walls of the buildings on the other side of the square. The next moment, the singing became quite audible. My first reaction is that the students from the University of Berlin are out on some new year jamboree, but my companions who

14. Excluded.

are Berlin-wise tell me that those shadowy figures moving along the walls of the buildings on the other side of the square are not students, that they are workers on their way to the Communist demonstration, singing their revolutionary songs. My two companions were impatient and ran ahead of me. I went on to the American Express Co. where I was to meet several other friends. Ten minutes later they were back, marveling at the steady stream of marchers and the number of *Polizei* that accompanied them.

Five thirty, we also were on our way. And as we walk we join the steady throng that is marching, while here and there an occasional band appears. All keep to one side of the street, thus permitting traffic to pass on the other side, while alongside of the stream of people and marchers going to the meeting are hundreds of *Polizei*—some on foot directing the line that is moving forward, others on horseback overlooking the crowd to look ahead and to move rapidly in case of need; and the usual truckloads of *Polizei* seated on their benches on their car, mean-looking fellows, and the followers whom I suspect of being prepared for those emergencies that require real action. Their machine guns are not visible, but their high-powered searchlights are. They move silently and efficiently, and there is no telling what may happen when they get into action.

As we approach the Lustgarten, I am suddenly shaken with the thought that the place, in case of a row with the police, is a perfect trap, and I wonder whether the place was granted to them for a meeting with the thought in mind that if anything started in this square it could be closed tighter than a drum in less than two minutes. The Lustgarten is the open space facing the Dom, while on the north is the old Kaiserschloss and facing the Schloss on the other side of the square are the different art museums of Berlin. The whole square is on an island, and except for one entrance is approachable only by crossing the bridge over the canal on one side and the river Spree on the other.

Every building therefore, every statue and every cornice of the buildings, in case of emergency could, if the police needed to, be turned into a machine-gun nest; while at the same time, as I saw later, five men on horseback could close each of the bridges and approaches to the place. A riot inside the Lustgarten could have been completely isolated so rapidly that not a sound nor a groan could be heard in any other part of the city and the *Polizei* or the other enemies of the Communists could easily have turned it into a charnel house. The *Polizei* standing in groups on the upper levels of the statues to the approaches indicated that they did not intend to stand any disturbance.

As we marched into the square, which is about the size of Washington Square in New York, I became aware of the strange lighting. In the fog, the lights of Berlin are different from any other city I have ever been in. The lamps are a light yellow with some pink, and the result is a rose-colored light that accentuates and marks every approaching face and figure. And since there are no trees, every part of the square showed the lines of marchers moving at first like queer lines of shadows to the rhythm of their songs and their bands, and later to become sharply discernible in form and features as they came closer. At the head of each column, coming in from the separate entrance, were the red-colored banners announcing the districts from which they came, whether from Wedding, Neukölln or Tempelhof. In addition to the banner indicating the district from which they came were a multitude of other banners with slogans of various sorts, all uniformly red. Later, it seemed as if there were almost as many banners as there were people.

By this time, the individual faces of the people became discernible. Mostly young people. Everywhere I looked I saw young people. Youth—in all its bitterness and frustration. Faces that spoke of gaunt hunger and pinched circumscribed lives. I thought of Fritz Hintz and his doubled fist[15] . . . and didn't realize that within a few moments I would see a forest of them. Young faces with eyes of bitterness coupled with disciplined determination. Easily eighty percent were under thirty, and the great majority far less than that. The middle-aged men or women were noticeable only because of their scarcity. From their clothes and their haggard faces it was easily seen that the great majority were among the unemployed—and it was as such that the chairman of the meeting greeted them through the loudspeaker that reverberated through every part of the huge Lustgarten, with the walls of the museums and the Dom throwing the sound back so that it sounded as though two meetings with two speakers saying identically the same thing [were] in progress.

The chairman, whose name I could not catch, after greeting the assemblage announced that the huge band at the base of the elevated platform would lead the meeting in singing the Russian national anthem[16]—every head uncovered and every voice was raised in song, song as deep and ritual as the rolling sound of an organ in a cathedral. Every head uncovered in the fog and every throat voicing its hope and faith in the promised system of a workers' control of human destiny. Then the chairman asked the huge

15. See November 25, 1932.

16. Plotkin refers to "The International."

throng, one hundred thousand he said, to remember that they were responsible for the meeting, that there were enemies within their ranks who would try to create disorder, and it was for them to remember that communism was discipline and order. He announced [that] the song [was] for the dead martyrs, Rosa Luxemburg and Karl Liebknecht[17] and thousands of others who, in the various struggles between communism and the other sects in Germany, particularly with the Hitlerites, have been killed. Again heads were uncovered, and again throats gave vent to their feelings through song, this time pledging themselves to the dead martyrs to carry on in their names the work of propaganda and education and struggles to achieve the philosophy for which the martyrs had given their lives. At the conclusion, the chairman called for three cheers for the *Rote Front*[18] and every voice shouted and every right fist moved upward in unison, three times repeated until the cry was thunderous and the fists with Fritz Hintz's white knuckles looked like white forests of human fists trying to batter down the doors and vaults of capitalism.

Following the hymn for the dead, the chairman introduced Florin,[19] the communist member of the Reichstag. He also greeted the *Arbeitslosen*.[20] Was the meeting to be entirely devoted to a protest against unemployment? I wondered. The communist meetings I have attended elsewhere were never really devoted to one subject. This was no exception. Florin started by denouncing the inadequacy of the unemployment relief and stated the program of the Communists—obviously impossible under capitalism—and admitted this to be the case. The real cure for unemployment lies in the communization of Germany. At this point he waited. A second's pause and three cheers greeted this statement of principle; the same formula of shouting *Rote Front* and the raising of the right fist halfway towards the sky. It lacked the spark of spontaneity. However, since none of the meetings I have seen in Germany

17. Rosa Luxemburg (1871–1919) and Karl Liebknecht (1871–1919, son of Wilhelm Liebknecht), Marxist revolutionary leaders and founding members of the German Communist Party in 1918. They were murdered in January 1919 by the Freikorps (right-wing militia) mobilized by SPD minister Gustav Noske to repress the Spartacist insurrection in Berlin. This event did not ease relations between Communists and Social Democrats.

18. Red Front, one of the KPD's main slogans.

19. Wilhelm Florin (1894–1944), Communist leader and member of the KPD's political bureau since 1929. After Hitler's seizure of power, he escaped to France and then to the Soviet Union, where he died.

20. Unemployed.

so far have indicated more than a passing enthusiasm, I take it that this is usual and not out of the ordinary.

Schleicher, he continued, is a fascist dictator, dictating with a bloody fist supported by the still bloodier arm of the reformists in the Social Democratic Party.[21] Witness the men who are in jail for their loyalty to the Communist Party—and the martyrs who have given their lives for the cause. But neither Schleicher nor any other figure in Germany could save the proletariat from sinking still further into the slough of unemployment, poverty and hunger, and as the crisis grows the Schleichers and those supporting him would seek to further cut the unemployment insurance given to the workers. The reformers and others who were supporting the Schleichers will have to go. It is the workers' task to carry on the propaganda and educational work among the workers in the trade unions and in the Social Democratic Party to overthrow their reformistic leaders and to join hands with the Communist Party in the sovietizing of Germany. Again he paused and again the ritualized three cheers and lifting of tight fists. Was it discipline? Or was the crowd, in spite of its temporary numerical strength, unconvinced? It was impossible to tell. It may have been that the fog which was turning into a slight drizzle was having its effects. Not even the most stimulating statement of principles will take the place of thin jackets and worn-out soles through which the skin can feel the wet pavement.

The Nazis, he continued, have voted against the opening of the Reichstag. A long echo of booing worked its way through the crowd as the significance of this statement was grasped by the crowd. I turned to Kline of the *Chicago Tribune* and asked him what this meant. It means, he answered, that the Nazis are afraid of another election and therefore do not want to take a chance of meeting and being dissolved, as is probable, and if the Reichstag is dissolved, then an election is inevitable under the German constitution. Florin's next statement confirmed Kline.

None of the parties want an election he shouted. An election would give the Communist Party an overwhelming majority. This again was greeted with the usual three cheers and uplifting of fists. There was something automatic about it. It was as if some phrase or signal were prearranged and the crowd followed the signal to cheer and to lift their fists. Cheers over and fists down, he started again.

Until such time as we are in the majority, we will remain a party of revo-

---

21. In these years, the KPD designated as "fascist" all nonrevolutionary political organizations, especially the Social Democrats.

lution and of protest. We are a party of revolution and of protest throughout the entire world today. Do not let the left phrases of the Social Democrat reformers mislead you. Wherever there are workers we, the KPD, are leading the workers towards the revolution against their capitalist exploiters. Witness China; we greet Soviet China tonight and welcome her into the ranks of the communist world. Witness the strike in Czechoslovakia. Who is leading it? We are. Witness the rebellion of the Swiss military. Who carried on the propaganda that led to the upheaval there? None other than the members of the Communist Party. Everywhere the Communist Party is carrying on its fight against the capitalist system, and throughout the whole world, we will not rest until the reformers and the capitalist system are in the same grave. Long live the KPD. Long live the Third International, and long live the Soviet Union. Again the ritualized cheers and methodical raising of fists. Florin was through.

By this time, the drizzle had turned into a steady downpour. The chairman again called attention to the need for discipline and order. Again he called attention to the enemies in and out of the Communist Party. This time he lay particular stress on the efforts of the militarists in Germany and the militarists in France to combine and make war against the Soviet Union. Against this the Communist Party would fight with all its power. Communists would know how to meet that issue when confronted with it. In the meantime the struggle was on both fronts. On one side the struggle was on for bread and work and on the other side against the enemies of communism and the Soviet Union. It will take the sacrifices and if necessary the lives of many of the members of the KPD before these objectives were achieved, but there was no compromising with the enemy. The struggle will have to go on to the end; until communism in Germany joined hands with communism in Russia. Again the cheers and the fists. Calling for the *Marseillaise* sung bareheaded in the rain, the lines formed themselves again, faced the entrances through which they had come in and slowly began to wind their way out.

Undoubtedly the meeting, judged by American standards, was cold and lacked enthusiasm. Nevertheless there must have been extraordinarily strong motivation. In order to attend the meeting, many of the groups coming from outer sections had marched the better part of the afternoon to get there. Certainly those from Tempelhof had walked for hours and would have to walk back again. We followed this group, as slowly it wound its way to Franzosenstrasse. It was here that I saw the remarkable discipline that governed the crowd. Five policemen on horseback simply closed the street.

No one knew exactly why, although it probably was to give the street traffic a chance to ease. In any American city the crowd would have been restless within thirty seconds and thirty seconds later the crush behind those in front would have been so severe that a conflict with the police and the clubbing of heads would have been inevitable. Instead the line stood perfectly still, a song was started, and when the first was finished a second song was started, until the police on horseback drew their horses aside—not until then was there the slight move to shove either through the line or ahead of it.

Down through Franzosenstrasse to the street facing the Staatstheater and then north towards Leipzigerstrasse they marched, and we marched with them. And as they marched they sang. They sang on their way in and they sang on their way out. I stood at the corner of Leipzigerstrasse watching them on their way out. Mostly young men, mostly ill-clad. Mostly hungry most of the time. But singing—and singing with discipline so that their voices were raised in unison. Is this the real Germany? The Germany that can ritualize itself into a revolution? From all those to whom I have spoken I am told that this is not the real thing. And certainly I know that within their hands today there is nothing resembling real power. I stood watching them and listening to them as they marched and sang—and wondered.

◇ *Wednesday, January 4, 1933*

B4, F6.2

When you see the straps under the chins of the *Polizei,* that means there is an emergency. Dozens of them are standing along the blocks leading to the Sportpalast, as Plettl was doing the right thing and taking me to the door. He, of course, as a sworn enemy of Fascism in any form, would under no consideration enter any of their meetings. But I am an American, and what one does not do at home, one may do when one reaches foreign shores. At that he tried to dissuade me from going. But the more I thought about the matter, the more I felt inclined to think that perhaps the first meeting of the Nazis that I saw was not a typical meeting.[22] Leaving him at the door, I purchased my ticket and walked in.

As I walked in, I looked at the clock again. It was exactly 28 minutes to 8. I saw then that the place was filled. The orchestra was filled, and the

---

22. Plotkin refers to the December 16 meeting.

first two balconies were entirely filled as well. So I walked to the top of the gallery, where only through good fortune was I able to find a seat. Better yet, the seat was so placed that I could see the entire house from where I was sitting. Infinitely better than if I had found a seat downstairs. The arrangement of seats was the same as at the first meeting, except that the platform was removed, the orchestra had been placed at the left side, and a small speaker's stand with a mike in front of a series of press tables, this time placed behind the speaker. Behind the press tables, there was ample room for the Nazi troops to move in and out, room for about five hundred of them. To balance the pageant of soldiers in the middle, the band on the left side, the right side was given over to young people in uniforms of black trousers and white jumpers—or so they seemed from where I was sitting. The speaker's stand had two quartets, one on each side, of standard-bearers, and two sets of husky guards, both of whom were changed at intervals of ten minutes. Standing at attention for ten minutes at a stretch is no easy task for anyone.

The preliminaries, up to the parade of the standard-bearers, were the same as at the first meeting, except that at one point a small group of four people walked in. When these four people walked in the entire house stood up and gave the fascist salute. Among the four was a woman in black. I asked my neighbor who they were and he answered that they were the parents of the boy Wagnitz who had been stabbed to death on New Year's evening. After they sat down, I noticed a figure get up from behind the platform, walk over to the mother and present [himself] to the mother. I was told that this man is Dr. Goebbels.

When the standard-bearers' parade came it was different from the one at the previous meeting. No fife and drum corps this time, and no band playing martial airs. Only the slow roll of drums and the slow measured steps of the March for the Dead. Double file, halfway down to the two aisles they marched and stopped, while the standard-bearers forming a line between the double file of soldiers marched through to the platform, one platoon on each side, and waited until soldiers behind them passed; all to the slow roll of drums.

I was too far from the stand to see Goebbels' face clearly. Even good opera glasses failed to give any fair picture of the man. Dark hair, dark features, strong features, never in repose, always contorted with emotion, it was impossible from where I was sitting to get a good mental image of him. Whether his voice would have carried without the mike I do not know, but I suspect that it would. His is a powerful voice, a voice strong enough, I think, to be heard in Madison Square Garden.[23]

The political truce, he started, is over. The *Kampf*,[24] he announced, is starting all over again. It is therefore time to take stock, and to do what is necessary to reconstruct the history of Germany during the last fifteen years.

When the war was on, [President] Wilson made his famous announcement that the war was not against the German people. It was against the Kaiser. And when the Kaiser was overthrown what happened? Germany was sold hand and foot to the Allies by the Social Democratic Party. The Social Democrats were traitors to the German people and the quicker they were driven out, the better for the German people. They not only permitted the Allies to humiliate it before the world, but had permitted them to fasten reparations on the German republic that drained the lifeblood of the republic out of it. Not until the National Socialist Party was organized was there an awakening of the German national spirit and this spirit was determined to break all of the chains that had been fastened on the nation through the cowardice and treasonable attitude of the Social Democratic Party. Having reached a climax, he waited for the applause. It came, but rather weakly. The appeal for nationalism for the moment fell flat.

What is National Socialism, and what do the Nazis represent? A regenerated nation, free from the domination of its outside enemies; the right of Germans to conduct their own affairs; the elimination of all groups within the state who placed internationalism above their loyalty to Germany; and the right of every German to make a living. I didn't quite get the reference to christianity being at the base of National Socialism, but at the reference to Christ and christianity he was applauded, still somewhat lukewarmly.

Schleicher, he called their attention, says that he is neither socialist nor capitalist, neither catholic nor protestant. The man isn't anything. He has no principles. He is ruling by force and force only. He has no plans for Germany, and when he goes the way of von Papen, we will be ready to step in and rule Germany as she should be ruled. Neither with von Papen nor with Schleicher have we anything in common. When we rule, we will rule alone. Principles cannot be divided, and the principles of National Socialism cannot be divided by giving us only a shadow of power. This time the

23. The covered stadium in New York City that often harbored political meetings. It could seat a crowd of ten thousand.

24. Struggle.

applause was somewhat warmer. The crowd was gradually beginning to feel the accumulation of feeling, slowly disintegrating itself into a mass psychology in which individuals forget themselves and swing with the emotions of the speaker.

Hitler has been denounced. By whom? At the mention of Hitler's name the building shook with applause. By the enemies within the Nazi movement, and the enemies outside. They try to separate Hitler from the Nazis and it can't be done. At the head of each movement there is an individual who symbolizes the entire movement. Remove Hitler and you destroy the whole Nazi movement. Again cheering. And no one knows this better than Hitler. He knows that when he accepts power without real power to rule, he will betray those whose loyalty to him and his principles have made us the strongest political party in Germany. Twice he has refused power, and because he has refused power we have lost two million votes, very well. We can do without them. The crowd by this time was integrated. It swerved with the speaker, listened to the intonations and caught his evangelical spirit. They say, he went on, that Hitler has made himself unpopular. Perhaps this is true for the time being. But mark this. In his refusal to accept power and betray his followers he has sunk deeper the roots of a newer and stronger popularity to come, and in February—the hint was taken and a storm of cheering broke out, it was a hint of an election to come in February—he will come back as the greatest national figure in Germany to whom the nation will give the mandate to rule, and to rule alone.

We have our enemies who are denouncing Hitler. There are some within our ranks who would have Hitler accept power at any price. With them we will have to part company. They have not the strength to combat the evils afflicting Germany. As for Hitler and those who are with him we will go on. We will go on even if it takes a century. We have the strength of the old Romans who year after year fought their battles against Carthage until Carthage was destroyed. We will not stop working day and night until our battle is won. To that end we consecrate our lives. The storm of hails greeting this declaration of war swept the hall. I looked down on a mass of cheering men and women whose hands were in the air, and the lights danced before my eyes with the intensity of the excitement.

Who else? Who else can be counted as our enemies? The Social Democratic Party I have already named. The Communists and their murderous gangs who have been murdering our members? A hush fell. With them we will have our day of reckoning. But let this be known. You cannot kill the Nazi movement. When they kill one of us, fifty spring up to take his place.

Our lives are nothing compared to the movement. And now he came to the most effective part of his speech. And who is responsible for the death of young Wagnitz? Who? I notice he has the trick of repeating the phrase to make it effective. Who? None other than the Jews. None but the Jews. Read their press. You will [find] nothing in it about the murder. Why? When anyone has nothing to say it means they have something they want to keep to themselves. I say to you that the Jews are responsible for the murder of our beloved young comrade Wagnitz! By this time the mass was as if it had been charged with electricity. Men and women were cheering themselves hoarse, and others whose pent-up prejudice could spend itself in no other way were shrieking curses and anathema. For a moment, I was certain that he would lose control of his audience and that in every part of the house spontaneous meetings would break out, but gradually these dissolved themselves into the mass, and Goebbels had the upper hand.

The Jews, he shrieked at the top of his lungs, the Jews have dominated our national life, our national economy, newspapers and our politics until we no longer have a German people. We have a nation of slaves dominated by a handful of Jews. It is to rescue Germany from the hands of the Jews that the National Socialist Party was organized, and until we do we are slaves!

So I have seen a meeting of the Nazis and their real atmosphere. Nationalism evolving through prejudice and dictatorship; hatred directed against a group that historically has been the butt of every movement that needed prejudice and intensity of feeling to mask its real program. And, as I walked out, I recalled the history of our Ku Klux Klan. Was it in 1924 or 1925 that they controlled thirty-four of the governors in the United States, and then suddenly collapsed? I am told that in Germany it will not be so easy for the Hitlerites to collapse, but it strikes me that any movement that depends on the intensity of emotion such as I saw tonight must either win power quickly or its foundations of hatred and feeling will collapse. At any rate, it is the movement most feared by those who know Germany and will bear watching.

◇ *Thursday, January 5, 1933*

B4, F6.1

Now that I have seen three major political meetings I am satisfied that nothing exciting will happen in Germany unless it comes in the cities where unemployment relief breaks down. The Nazi meetings are dispirited, as if beaten and know it. Dr. Goebbels, their leading platform orator in Berlin, aroused but little enthusiasm except when he denounced the Jews. A loss of two million votes in the last election, a refusal on the part of a good many of the industrialists to support them because they expect to get from Schleicher the same things they expected from Hitler, and the revolt of [Gregor] Strasser[25] because of Hitler's refusal to go into the cabinet except on his own terms make the future lose its brightness. The meetings, except for Goebbels' dramatic oratory when he denounced the Jews, were quite dead. The Communists on the other hand seem to handle their meetings with an iron discipline. Florin, their main speaker at the Lustgarten meeting where he spoke to close to 100,000 people, aroused no particular enthusiasm, and it struck me that he didn't particularly want to. The Social Democratic party, so far, has not announced any demonstrations. Perhaps they are waiting for the others to shoot their guns.

The only disquieting factor is the number of killings that are political in their origin. The fifth political killing since the political truce was ended, rather since New Year's eve, is reported from Breslau, where a member of the young people's branch of the Social Democratic Party was stabbed to death in a fight with the Nazis. Fights were also reported in Hamburg, Erfurt and Aachen. Here Communists and Nazis had it out and a number of them were hurt.

◇ *[Friday], January 6, 1933*

B4, F6.1

Hitler and von Papen conferred today in Cologne and the papers are full of it.[26] On the other hand Schleicher today conferred with Herr Braun,[27] the titular minister of Prussia. The two seem to balance each other. Hitler and von Papen issued a joint statement stating that they had talked about the

---

25. Gregor Strasser (1892–1934), Nazi leader. In December 1932, while Hitler had refused to participate in the government, which Schleicher eventually led, Strasser had negotiated separately. Isolated in 1933, Strasser withdrew from politics. Considered a traitor by Hitler, he was assassinated in June 1934 along with Ernst Röhm and Kurt von Schleicher.

26. The meeting had in fact taken place on January 4.

27. Otto Braun (1872–1955), a Social Democratic leader and prime minister of Prussia (1920–32), whose government was deposed by von Papen in July 1932. After the Nazi seizure of power, he lived in exile in Switzerland from 1933 until his death.

possibility of forming a great united national front. Both the trade unionists and the Social Democrats deride the possibility of a united front between Hitler and von Papen. On the other hand, there is considerable dissatisfaction expressed among the groups representing heavy industries with the new turn of von Schleicher's policy. It seems that he countermanded von Papen's orders on matters appertaining to the labor laws in Germany. It seems that von Papen issued a number of decrees which canceled many of the provisions of the labor code. Now the industrialists are dissatisfied. Apparently Schleicher is not giving the industrialists what they wanted.

◇ *[Friday], January 6, 1933*

B4, F6.2

Kummer and I have taken to each other like a pair of ducks in need of shelter. The old man has very fond recollections of America and wants sometime to be able to go back and see it again. I would like, he tells me, to go back and compare the things that were America when I was a boy and the things that are America now. I am not sure that I would like them as much. But I would like to see San Francisco and Pittsburgh and New York once more. So would I. On the other hand, Kummer is such a lovable old soul, and such an encyclopedia of information, that I am constantly reaching out for the phone to ask him this and to ask him that; and never once has he disappointed me.

This time we are sitting in the Pschorr Haus, reputed for its beer and excellent sausages. Fritz's bald head is almost inside his glass when he hears me hold forth on the lack of information on the background of unemployment insurance in Germany. His head comes out of his glass, he wipes the foam off his lips, chuckles and leans back. I know that I am in for a lecture and gladly so. I also sit back and wait.

Unemployment insurance in Germany, he starts, is as old as your great-grandfather! When I was a boy we had it. Not in its present forms, but it was unemployment insurance. Neither was it anywhere near as extensive as it is today, and it was mostly based on other principles, but provision against unemployment and hunger, Germany has always had. [. . .]

Tracing the roots of the notions of relief or social insurance to feudal times when local communities were in charge of their paupers, Kummer enumerated the steps by which guilds and then craftsmen's unions provided travel allowances to their members in search of work. According to Kummer, even Bismarck's law forc-

ing the unions underground did not prevent them from devising unemployment benefits for their "traveling" journeymen, who used them to keep organizing. By the turn of the century most unions had unemployment insurance plans, which were supplemented with the financial help of the city when socialists had enough influence over their councils. By the time of World War I, Germany, before Britain, had proved that widespread compensation to the jobless was possible. The problem of joblessness was made more acute by the postwar demobilization of German soldiers. Yet Social Democrats and the trade unions used the labor movement's experience to generalize unemployment insurance. Funds were to be raised at all levels, communal, state, and federal. And the constitution of the Weimar Republic recognized that the "victims of capitalism" deserved special status and adopted a new status for labor.

It is this principle and new status that von Papen and the reactionaries have been trying to break down. [. . .]

Kummer was getting tired. It was past one and I had egged him on since nine o'clock. But he stuck quite gamely. During those eight years,[28] he went on, we had alternated bad years and good years. Contrary to your ideas, the bad years were not the worst for us. The year of inflation [1923] was really the worst. That year everybody both worked and starved. But in the main, after we settled down we had no really extraordinary unemployment periods. The highest before 1932, I think, was a little over 2,000,000. In the meantime, the Social Democrats and the trade unionists learned that what the constitution says and actual realities are two different things. Whenever we tried to pass a bill on federal unemployment insurance, immediately there would spring up opposition from every quarter. The employers didn't want it. The communities, except where we controlled, did not want it either. Then the higher-salaried brackets came in with complaints that if a flat rate would be established they would be treated unfairly. Year after year, the unemployment insurance bill would be brought into the Reichstag and at once everyone fell on it and tried to tear it to pieces. Not until 1927 were we able to swing it. In that year we placed unemployment insurance on a federal basis controlled by the Reich.[29] It is not the best bill in the world. It

28. Kummer was referring to the 1918–27 years of the Weimar Republic.

29. Unemployment insurance was made compulsory by the 1927 law of Employment Service and Unemployment Insurance *(Arbeitslosenversicherungsgesetz)*. Yet what had been planned to cover the needs of a maximum of 1.1 million workers in 1927 proved vastly insufficient after 1929 with the economic crisis.

could have been made much better. You call it scientific. To me it is just plain common sense verifying the experience of the whole labor movement for the last century. Whether you spend your time making fine distinctions between unemployment insurance and legal relief, giving someone the semblance of a right and the other charity, no longer interests me. In Germany we have three forms of unemployment relief, and all three of them are based on the legal right of the worker to support when there is no employment for him. The first is unemployment insurance, the second is emergency relief due to the crisis, and the third is communal relief. All three function side by side, and all three of them are the answer to the workers' legal right to them. To us this quarrel is settled. Settled so long ago that it seems almost forgotten. It is only when I read an article by an American or run into someone like you that I am reminded of it.

◇ *Saturday, January 7, 1933*

B4, F6.1

A report comes from Munich announcing the dissolution of the Nazi stormtroops in Franconia. I am told that a considerable number of Nazi detachments have been similarly dissolved. One would not think so when one sees them on parade. [. . .]

◇ *Saturday, January 7, 1933*

B4, F6.2

I do not speak to Jews! The answer was as startling as it was direct. Attracted by the noise of a military band as we were leaving the Deutsches Museum this afternoon, we came across a parade of Nazis. Fifteen thousand men in uniform marching to the funeral of the young boy Wagnitz who was stabbed to death a week ago. As they passed, some of the troops, to break the monotony of marching, started to sing. My companion turned to a woman and asked her the name of the song. I do not speak to Jews, was the answer. We refrained from asking further questions. But on noticing an announcement that there would be a mass meeting in the Lustgarten in the evening, and gathering the impression from the announcement that Hitler himself would speak, we decided to go.

Arriving just in time, we noticed that the fifteen thousand troops, aside from a few contingents along the canal fence, were gathered in front of the speakers' stand. The same atmosphere prevailed here and the same program, except that this was a memorial meeting and was therefore limited to twenty minutes only. The crowd was easily the number announced as 100,000. They filled every bit of standing room up to the palace in front of the Dom where we were standing, fortunately on the steps of the statue so that we could see above the heads of the crowd.

The song for the dead over, a representative of the Nazis took the stand and read a short prayer for the boy who was killed. Following him came another song, then came Goebbels again. Hitler was elsewhere.

The more I see and hear of the Nazis the more I am impressed with how little either of truth or fact is necessary to set a huge mass aflame. This man Goebbels hasn't, in either of the two meetings, produced a single fact to corroborate his charges. His appeal is to the emotions and to the emotions only. This time he wasted no time in getting down to the arguments that would stir his audience. *Soldaten* and Friends—his voice carried into every section of the Lustgarten—we are here to pledge ourselves to revenge the murder of our young Comrade Wagnitz! As we stood at the grave of our beloved comrade thousands marched by; *Soldaten* who knew him as one of their own; leaders in the National Socialist Party who expected great things from him because he was not without certain abilities; intellectuals who understand the significance of this boy's murder; friends who loved him for the lovable qualities that he had [displayed]. And as they stood at the grave of this murdered comrade they wept. They wept for the boy, and they wept for the cause to which the boy gave his life and for which he was murdered. At the grave also stood the boy's mother. Here his voice became quiet. Pathos cannot be shouted. And she wept because her boy lay silent. She wept because the tree on which she planned to lean when she becomes weary was cut down in its youth. We stood at the grave and wept because we lost a comrade. She stood at the grave and wept because she lost a son. The effect of the pathos made the moment tense. Tense with quietness and feeling.

We know the names of the murderers. The effect was a bombshell. From every part of the Lustgarten came cries as of madmen. Name them! Name them! He stood silent. When he started again his voice was loud but slow, and the same trick that he used in the Sportpalast meeting was brought into play, the repetition of the word or the phrase until it would leave an indelible print on the mind. The murderer that committed this terrible murder is not to blame. I repeat the individual who committed this terrible murder is not to blame. The real murderers, the real murderers are the bloody Jews—the bloody Jews—the bloody Jews—who publish their *blutige*[30] newspapers on Lindenstrasse![31] Again I thought the crowd would run out of his control. For weeks they have been denouncing us, for weeks they have been lying about us, and through their denunciations of the National Socialist party they are responsible for this murder! Why are they silent now? They are silent now because the blood of this boy is on their hands. Their hands—their hands are red with the blood of young Robert Wagnitz! But let them not think that they can keep this up forever. And let them remember that for every Nazi murdered, fifty new martyrs are ready to spring forward and to carry the banner forward to victory. And let them remember this also, from now on we will protect our living. We will never forget our dead! By this time both the audience and the speaker were exhausted. The emotional peak had been reached. After a few more statements of principles the meeting was adjourned.

After the meeting I walked to the Kaiserschloss where the fifteen thousand troops were assembled. I wanted to see what they really looked like. At the time of the parade we were too far in the rear of the crowd to really see. Ninety-five percent young men, less than twenty-five, and thousands in their teens. The emotional outburst over, they stood waiting for their orders to march out of the Lustgarten like a bunch of schoolboys, and like a bunch of schoolboys bought hot dogs when the hot-dog men started to circulate among them. It may be true that men cannot live by bread alone, but if the Nazi troops are any indication, they can't live on mental excitement alone either.

◇ *Monday, January 9, 1933*

B4, F6.2

Seeing friends off on a journey in Berlin is different from seeing them off—let us say in New York or Chicago. First you buy a ticket to get on the platform of the station. That costs 20 pfennigs or about four cents. Then you had best make sure that you place the ticket in a safe place. Should you fail to do this there is no telling what it may cost you. The stationmaster may charge you with having come all the way from China without having paid your fare. You must also keep in mind that getting on the train to say good-bye to friends is absolutely unlawful. If you are caught, it's at least three marks. If you do sneak on before the stationmaster can catch you,

30. Bloodthirsty.

31. Berlin street where most newspapers had their headquarters.

make sure that you get off before he sees you. I got in because I carried one of the extra large bags and was disguised as a passenger. Above all if you value your ears, don't stay on the train even if the doors are locked before you can get out, or the next stop is say from Grand Central to 125th street. The cumulative penalties are enough to pay the national debts of half the European countries.

Except for the first I must plead guilty to all of the charges. I not only carried a bag into the third-class coach bound for Köln, but I stayed on the train after the door was locked and rode all the way from Friedrichstrasse to the Zoo.[32] And quite innocently too. How was a mere American to know he was breaking a foreign law when as often as not he doesn't know when he is breaking his own country's laws? Therefore, when I left the train at the Zoo, my troubles began, and how!

First, I handed my ticket to the ticket collector. He examined it and began raving. I caught the word Jew. Then he told me that the fine was three marks and that I would have to see the stationmaster. Inasmuch as the fare on the elevated is the same price as the amount I had paid for this ticket, I could see no crime in the offing and said so. The elevated runs parallel to the railroad, on the same elevated tracks. He turned his back on me, signifying that for all he cared I could stay there all night. I decided to see the stationmaster.

Finding the stationmaster, I started to explain when he met me with a volley of abuse that made my ears blush. I listened patiently until he was finished and then asked—Well, what now? Three marks. And must I pay them to you? Yes. I don't believe that. I believe there is a higher authority than yours; and since you won't listen to my explanation I am certain that he will. By that time I was as mad as he was and if I had had three marks in my pocket they would have remained there. Who is your superior? I have no superior in the station. So. Are you going to keep me here all night? Are you going to pay the three marks? Not to you. I'll pay it to your superior if he has the power to judge me. Moreover, if you don't release me immediately you'll have to answer for it, in addition to answering for the abusive language you and your colleague have been using. You have your choice, he answered, either to pay or to be turned over to the police. I think the police will be more sensible than you have been. Will you call them? Will you pay? No. All right you've brought it on yourself.

As I walked down to the police station in the *Bahnhof*—there is one in every railroad station in Berlin—the policeman Marquadt looked daggers.

32. The railway station called Zoologischer Garten.

Did I have my papers? Yes. Where are you staying? I named the Pension. Why didn't you pay the fine? Because he has no authority to fine me. What do you do with a German who does what I did tonight? We take his record and notify him when he is to appear in court. Then why do you follow any other procedure with me? Is it because I am a Jew? Or is it because I am an American? Speak when you are spoken to. Adolph, call up police headquarters and find out whether he is registered.

Five minutes later, apparently satisfied that my papers were in order, my passport was handed back to me and I was told to wait. Officer Marquadt left the station and disappeared. Half an hour later he reappeared. What did you say to the stationmaster when he told you that it would cost three marks? I tried to explain what had happened and he wouldn't listen. Instead he became abusive, abusive in a manner that no American will stand for. Well, he scratched his closely shaven head, he says you insulted him. Does he? Yes. Well, it simply is not true. Perhaps he misunderstood you. Well, what does he want? He wants you to come up and apologize. And if I don't? I'll have to lock you [up] to appear in court. All right. I'll pay the fine in court, if I have to. And both the ticket-collector and the stationmaster will have to appear and explain their conduct, and their calling me a Jew. You are an American aren't you? I am both an American and a Jew—but I don't see what that has to do with it. Nothing, only I have a brother in America. What part of America is he in? Saint Louis. I know the city very well. He writes me that conditions there are very bad. Are they worse than in Germany? He writes me that the *Arbeitslosen* get no aid at all. Is that true? Yes. What are you doing in Germany? Studying how you take care of the unemployed. Wait. Five minutes later he came back again. You can go home. I told the *Dummkopf*[33] that you know my brother.

◇ *Tuesday, January 10, 1933*

B4, F6.1

Nothing new. The conferences between Von Papen and Hitler seem to have been stillborn. Considerable discussion about the election to be held in the state of Lippe[34] on Sunday.

---

33. Dumbhead.

34. The Nazis made an exceptional effort for the coming regional elections in this small *Land*.

◇ *Tuesday, January 10, 1933*

B4, F6.2

There is no doubt about it. Unemployment insurance in Germany is seriously menaced. This emphatic statement came from Dr. Kuno Broecker, the social expert for the ADGB. [. . .]

Seated in his own room, I drew a copy of the January report of the Commerz und Privat Bank, and showed him the statistical table on unemployment insurance. [. . .] I feel certain that you can clear me up on some of the questions that have been bothering me. For instance, there were 21 million wage earners in Germany [in 1927], only 17.5 million were insured. Where were the others?

Dr. Broecker explained that fourteen categories of wage earners were excluded from unemployment insurance. These categories accounted for the difference between the total number of wage earners and the 17.5 million who were under the unemployment insurance act of 1927. Upon Plotkin's questions noting that as of 1932 only 14.4 million wage earners were covered by the program, Broecker reported that the difference lay in the fact that the persons missing in the first count were now classified under the emergency relief program.

Von Papen and the black reactionary crowd[35] with him, when they came into office, had their minds made up to wreck unemployment insurance and came very close to doing it. [. . .] What we resented was the damage done to the principle of the unemployment insurance, almost now superseded by something else. [. . .] Those men and women who had contributed to the insurance fund through their hard-earned contributions were entitled to what they had contracted for. Behind it stood the solemn promise of the German government. It is the breaking of this promise and pledge to the proletariat that we are protesting against. Moreover, there was no need, financially, for the von Papen regime to follow the policy that it did. To save the industrialists and landholders a few additional milliards in taxes, almost the entire principle of unemployment insurance was thrown overboard. Now we will have to start fighting all over again to rebuild the damage that von Papen did. And I am not so certain that we will succeed for a long time to come. This much is certain. If unemployment insurance is to remain, the entire makeup of the system will have to be changed, and changed in such a way as to prevent in the future any possibility of ever tampering with it again. [. . .]

35. The reference is to the landlords and Junkers of eastern Prussia.

As Plotkin was asking for more details, Broecker specified that the total number of weeks during which an unemployed person could receive benefits had been reduced from twenty-nine weeks according to the 1927 act to six. After that time, the worker could claim emergency relief, but was bereft of unemployment insurance. And after a few weeks (eight or fourteen, depending on his category) he would fall back on the Wohlfahrt, *the public assistance, financed by the cities, most of which were now on the verge of bankruptcy.*

◇ *Thursday, January 12, 1933*

B4, F6.2

Do you want to see a rent strike? I told Emil that I would like very much to see one. Then come with me and you will see the one we now have in Wedding. Twenty minutes' walk brought us to 132 Ackerstrasse. I knew there was a strike on in the house a block before we got there. The red banners flying from the windows could be seen long before the building itself could be seen.[36]

At the entrance, we were met by one of the guardsmen. Emil he knew. But I was a stranger. Who is the stranger and does he know the password? The password, I learned, was "Turmarkin." The why of the password is still unknown to me. Proving myself to their satisfaction not to be a spy was both as easily understood as easily satisfied. I showed my passport. Satisfied that I really was what I claimed to be, an American, and a trade unionist to boot, the guardsman smiled and called his wife to relieve him while he could show me the way around.

The tenement is an enormous house running around four small inner courts, five stories high. It was built in 1870, apparently before Berlin put in its modern water supply. In one of the courts, one can still see the old water pump and tank. Almost every other window in all of the inner courts had a red flag flying, relieving what otherwise would have been colorless, dreary and monotonous.

My guardsman, by this time sharing a cigarette with me and my guide, smoked almost to the lips, as I noted afterwards, now began to warm up. The strike against the landlord has been in force since November 25th, and

36. There was a wave of rent strikes in Berlin in 1932. They were mainly organized by the Communist Party but originated in the tenants' inability to pay rents in the wake of the wage cuts ordered by von Papen's decrees.

not one tenant, in spite of all the threats of the landlord and the *Polizei,* has paid his or her rent. Everyone in the house is a Communist, they stick together—*nicht wahr?*[37] And how many families live in the house? There are 355 families and altogether with the children the house has a population of exactly 1,301 persons. You have the exact figure right at your fingertips I see. Sure. We have to. Now and then the police arrest one of us and that is the way we have a daily checkup if there is anyone missing. Our people are not only facing the things that come out of a strike, but they are also active in the Communist Party. And you can never tell whether one of our house is arrested or beaten up by the Nazis, so we keep a perfect record and each day we check up. But now and then the numbers living in the house are increased by one more. Then we dedicate the new one to the revolution.

But why did the strike break out here? There are thousands of houses such as yours in Wedding, why did you undertake the fight? If you will come with me, he answered, I will show you. We entered the second court, walked up the stairs into one of the apartments and he introduced me to the tenant. The *Amerikaner* wants to know why we are on strike, he announced. Will you show him? I looked around the room, it was eight by twelve, crowded with small articles of furniture the value of which was almost zero. I had seen the same thing in Köslinerstrasse. Will you look at this? The tenant held a bottle up to the light. I looked into a small bottle of water and could see very little. Take it to the window, he urged, and turn it upside down. I did exactly as he told me, and first I noticed a dark sediment at the bottom. When I turned the bottle upside down the sediment spread throughout and turned the water into a muddy brown! What is it? It is dirt from the pipes. We drank the filth until we couldn't stand it. We live here because the rent in other houses is more than we can pay, but we made up our minds that not one cent more will the landlord get until he makes the repairs this house needs so that we won't have our stomachs eaten by the rust from the water he now compels us to drink.

Look at these walls. I looked at the walls and there was hardly an inch that wasn't either cracked or bulging. Alternate spots were rank with dampness. Accidentally I touched the woodwork of the window and it swung back to me. And as I tried to close it my host smiled. Even the woodwork is rotting with mold. When we want to keep our windows closed we have to put something heavy alongside of them. See, the wood is swollen from dampness. Now come and look at what our landlord calls rooms. We walked

37. Don't they?

into a second chamber the width of which could not have been more than three feet, and an open door showed a second chamber, used as a bedroom, no wider than the first. Our landlord was so greedy for rent space and income that he took this room which was one room formerly and turned it into two, and tried to double the rent!

What about the rent laws? The rent laws are on the books. We never hear about them. Perhaps in some other parts of the city they are enforced. Here, if any one of us had complained he would promptly have been thrown out. Then where could we go? More than half of us are on the Poor Law. We have no money to move elsewhere. That is why we decided to band together and refuse to pay rent until the landlord decides to make the changes that we ask for and comes down with the rent as well.

As it happens, only a few days ago, I saw a report on rentals, and in spite of the drop in all other prices, the average rental has actually increased by a fraction of more than one percent. More expensive apartments have dropped. But the poor have to take what they can get, and since space that can be rented for small rent is quite limited, the poor have to carry the burden for the decrease in middle-class quarters. [. . .]

You wanted to see one of the cellar dwellers, Emil tells me. I'll take you to one here. It is too late to go and see the real cellar dwellers today; but you can get an idea from the one you will see here. I agree. We cross the court and enter a basement through which we have to light our way. It is the equivalent of storage cellars in the old houses in New York or Brooklyn. But when we enter, I notice that the room, eight by twelve, is both cheerful and freshly painted, although the dampness already has created whitish splotches through the green paint. Here I meet Martha. When I ask Martha her last name, she tells me, but adds—what does it matter? [. . .] She is living alone. This, she tells us, is just what I need. But the others in the rooms alongside of me, they are crowded like pigs in a sty. Martha looks about forty, but already her face seems heavy with bloat, and her hands are thick from work, the skin inside looks hard and heavy. Her hands fascinate me. I ask her what work she does. I am not working. There is no work. She is half resentful at being questioned, so I let Emil do the talking. But Emil has seen her. He asks her whether he hasn't seen her in the same shop where he worked on radios. She feels that Emil is one of her own kind and is more at ease and becomes even a little more friendly towards me. A moment later Emil asks her what rent she pays, and the question releases all of the pent-up emotion that tortures her. Eighteen marks for this hole. Eighteen marks! She almost weeps as she speaks. Eighteen marks for this hole, and twelve marks a month for heating and light. And I get thirty-six marks a month from the *Wohlfahrt*. This leaves me six marks a month for food! I know that the dogs on the streets live better than I do, better than the workers do. I take her hand in mine and turn the palm toward me. As I hold it I feel it trembling, but the hand itself is hard and firm, as if suffering had steeled it with a purpose, stronger perhaps than the rest of her body.

Perhaps it is so with the others who live in 132 Ackerstrasse. Whether they will get communism, I do not know, neither do I know whether they will like it if they should get it. But they have a purpose, and a will, and for once let me share their hope that their will to change their holes will be realized.

◇ *Friday, January 13, 1933*

B4, F6.2

Dr. Haertel, chief of the Berlin *Arbeitsamt*, took me in hand. The literature on unemployment insurance is as muddy as the waters of the Mississippi. He had been asked to explain to me the actual workings of the unemployment insurance and emergency relief. This he was kind enough to agree to do.

Dr. Haertel presented Plotkin with official data and clarified the technicalities of the several insurance and assistance programs. His information confirmed and complemented what Plotkin had learned in his conversation with Kuno Broecker. Unemployment insurance and emergency relief, both national in scope, had been severely reduced, owing to the unexpected rise in the number of claimants since 1931. Recipients now received one-third less of the 1927 benefits, and they had to have worked longer to qualify for these programs.

I could see that Dr. Haertel was definitely worried about the status of unemployment insurance, but it was quite obvious that his official position made it impossible for him to voice any open criticism. Before leaving me he was kind enough to offer copies of all of the blanks and forms used by the Arbeitsamt in the hope, I suppose, that eventually we will have use for them in America. [. . .]

◇ *Monday, January 16, 1933*

B4, F6.1

Out of 98,451 ballots, the Nazis got 38,844 in yesterday's election in the state of Lippe. In the last election the Nazis got 33,038, a gain of almost

6,000 votes. Enough to make them feel that they won something of a victory. The Socialist vote also rose by 4,000. The two parties that lost were the Communists—who lost 3,500 votes—the rest of the votes gained by the Nazis and Socialists were lost by the Hugenberg[38] crowd. There is room enough for both the Nazis and the Socialists to celebrate.

The Socialists point out that through the entire campaign Hitler himself spoke at 16 mass meetings and concentrated all of his heavy guns in the fight for this small principality, while [they] were comparatively quiescent. The press, by and large, is not particularly excited by Hitler's victory. They regard it as quite meaningless and indecisive.

◇ *Monday, January 16, 1933*

B4, F6.2

Before going in to meet Leipart, Furtwängler explained to me that because of an important matter that has come up suddenly the interview would have to be short. He went on to explain that Leipart really wants to talk and that he wants to arrange for me to meet him again. On arriving at Leipart's office, I found William Eggert, the vice president of the ADGB, and [Peter] Grassmann, the Social Democratic Party leader.[39] All three of them greeted the *Amerikaner* quite cordially and asked all sorts of questions about Colonel House,[40] whose statement in *Liberty* was given a limited summary in the Parisian edition of both the *Chicago Tribune* and the *New York Herald*. According to these short summaries, unless conditions change in America, within two years a dictator may be expected, "closer to Lenin than to Mussolini."

---

38. Alfred Hugenberg (1865–1951), an industrialist and nationalist politician, leader of the German National People's Party (Deutschnationale Volkspartei). He would become minister of agriculture and economy in the Hitler cabinet, January 30–June 1933.

39. In fact, Peter Grassmann (1873–1939) was ADGB vice president and Wilhelm (William) Eggert (1880–1938) a member of the ADGB Executive Board. Grassmann had also been the SPD representative in the Reichstag for the Hamburg district since 1924.

40. Colonel Edward Mandell House (1858–1938) had been President Woodrow Wilson's diplomatic adviser and one of the American delegates at the peace conference in Versailles. In a January 7, 1933, article to *Liberty,* he had expressed the fear that the present conditions in the United States might lead to a revolutionary situation and to the emergence of a "dictator." "If we are to have a dictator, our people and institutions of wealth would like him to be of the Mussolini type. However, he is more likely to be of the type of Lenin, that, for obvious reasons, would not suit them at all," Colonel House concluded ("Does America Need a Dictator?" *Liberty* 10, no. 1).

Grassmann told me that he expects the Reichstag to open on the 30th—or was it the 31st?—and when I suggested that it would be nice to walk up to the *Polizei* who pushed me around when the Reichstag opened the last time and show him a pass, he laughed and asked Furtwängler to make certain that I would get the pass.

Later, before I leave Germany, I want to see Leipart, when I have a more comprehensive picture in mind of things here. Before I left, he told Furtwängler to make certain that any sources of information that I may want or need be opened to me. One can't help liking him. He reminds me of the pictures I have seen of August Bebel, ruddy-faced, silver pompadour over a high temple, short mustache and Van Dick beard, and the keenest pair of blue bespectacled eyes I have ever looked into. He strikes one as being the kind of fatherly type of German whose love of comfort is being sacrificed for a work of love.

◇ *Thursday, January 19, 1933*

B4, F6.1

Alarm, the Berlin newspaper that devotes itself to exposing Hitler, is out with an extra announcing that Hitler admits owing five million marks in debt.

◇ *Friday, January 20, 1933*

B4, F6.1

It is rumored that the application of the Nazis for permission to hold a demonstration on Sunday in front of the Liebknecht House[41] has been granted. Everyone agrees that to give permission to the Nazis to hold their demonstration there would lead to bloodshed. So far none of the political parties have been permitted to meet in front of their opponents' headquarters. Overnight there has come into the air a tenseness that is new and startling. Already it has resulted in sporadic street fights between Communists and Nazis, and the Communists have announced that they will never permit such an insult. Even the conservative *Tempo* and the democratic *Berliner Tageblatt* join the *Vorwärts* in denouncing the application and editorially demand that permission for the meeting be not granted.

---

41. The Karl-Liebknecht-Haus, on Bülowplatz, was the Communist Party's office building.

◇ *Friday, January 20, 1933*

B4, F6.2

Are you a Jew? Dr. Kurt [Zielenziger], chief of the Berlin Press Bureau, was talking. I admitted my religion. So am I. I had come to get information on the expenditures of the city on the *Wohlfahrt,* and remained to discuss the Jewish problem.

Slight, dark, dapper, Dr. Zielenziger comes from one of the oldest Jewish families in Germany. His uncle, Alfred Zielenziger, at present is the President of the Berlin Bourse, or stock exchange. Keen as a razor edge, he is alive to the problems of the day and misses no opportunity to show his distaste for the present anti-Semitism that is running amuck in Germany.

The Jews in Germany, he explained to me, were a business people. There were a number of workers, but the number was very small. I have written a book on the subject,[42] if you care to see it. He wrote the name of his book on a sheet of paper. Perhaps later I shall read it. The Jew in Germany rose high. In every division of our national life, before the war, and immediately after the war, Jews occupied leading positions. Rathenau[43] is today recognized as one of the greatest statesmen Germany ever had. Dr. Hilferding[44] is another. How many men can you point to today that occupy leading positions in the nation who are of Jewish origin? Very few. Finance Minister Bruno Asch[45] is about the only one left. The rest, since Hitlerism, have been forced out.

---

42. Probably *Juden in der deutschen Wirtschaft* [Jews in the German Economy] (Berlin: Welt-Verlag, 1930).

43. Walter Rathenau (1867–1922), a leading industrialist in the German Empire and the early Weimar Republic. President of the Allgemeine Elektrizitäts-Gesellschaft (General Electricity Company), a progressive economist, he was in charge of the management of supplies in the War Department Ministry during World War I, then became minister of reconstruction, and later foreign affairs minister. He was assassinated in 1922 by a right-wing organization.

44. Rudolf Hilferding (1877–1941), a Social Democratic leader, Marxist economist, main theoretician of the SPD, and minister of finance in 1923 and in the Müller cabinet until December 1929. A refugee in France during the Nazi regime, he was arrested by the Vichy police in 1941 and surrendered to the Gestapo. He was assassinated (or committed suicide) in prison in France in February 1941.

45. Bruno Asch (1890–1940), a specialist in finance and local politics and finance minister for the City of Berlin since 1931. He escaped to France in 1933, then settled in the Netherlands, where he committed suicide when the country was invaded by the German army.

Hans Gosler, an uncle of mine, for 10 years in charge of the Press Bureau for the Prussian government, was forced out, and the son of an officer, a von Karlowitz, put in his place. I am what you call a black sheep. I am about the only one in Berlin who occupies a similar position.

In my book I go into this material more fully than I can tell you about it now. Many of our people still retain leading positions in the national life of Germany. Men of the type of Oscar Wasserman, the Rothschilds, D. K. V. Westen, and the Warburgs[46] are still active, and they will be as long as they are permitted to be. How long that will be, we do not know.

But that is not the worst of it. These men are men with power, influence and wealth. Moreover, there are many functions of the German economy that need their services, and however the Nazis or the Hugenbergs try to get rid of them, the force of their ability will always give them a certain standing in their community. The vast majority of Jews have not that. Thousands of Jews with small shops have been driven out of business, many thousands more who were in white-collar occupations also have been driven out. Where can they turn to? If you care to dig deeper into this problem I will call up the chairman of the committee who is handling our "social" problems, I am certain that he will be glad to see you and go into details. I answered that I would be glad to have an opportunity to talk with him. He promptly called and made an appointment for sometime during the coming week.

The future of the Jew in Germany is uncertain, he went on, in response to my question. We have a mountain of readjustment work, and much of it will never be finished. The problem ahead of us is one of waiting, but I doubt whether they will ever adjust themselves so that they will be what they were before the anti-Semitism developed. The Jew in Germany is rapidly becoming proletarianized. The old occupations, I am afraid, are closed to him. But what occupations he is turning to I cannot answer. That you will have to get from the man you will talk to next week.

◇ *Saturday, January 21, 1933*

B4, F6.1

Permission for the meeting on Bülowplatz in front of the Liebknecht House has been granted to the Nazis. All day yesterday and today committees

46. Names of prominent Jewish personalities in the world of finance. Oscar Wasserman was the spokesman of the executive board of the Deutsche Bank. Dismissed in 1933, he died one year later.

pleaded with Dr. Bracht,[47] the Prussian commissioner of Police, to rescind the order permitting the demonstration but up till midnight no results were obtained. The Communists on the other hand have announced a counter-demonstration and have ordered their followers to appear at Bülowplatz presumably to oust their antagonists. The place where the meeting is to be held is in the heart of a working-class district: that blood will be spilt is a dead certainty. The police officials contend that the place was promised to the Nazis for a demonstration a long time ago. It seems curious therefore that permission was withheld until now. At the same time it appeared to me that it was inconceivable that Schleicher was unaware of what this meeting may result in. The newspapers are quite frank in calling it a bloodbath. In talking to one of the labor leaders he diagnosed it as deliberately provocative. He is of the opinion that Schleicher is going to let the Nazis and the Communists battle it out and when it gets quite serious to step in and get rid of both at the same time. The cafés tonight were jammed with men and women who could talk of nothing but what tomorrow may bring. Tomorrow the excitement will run riot. Lines of parades, already *verboten* by the police, will form themselves in Neukölln, Wedding, Pankow, Charlottenburg, Lichtenberg, Schöneberg and Friedenau, suburbs of Berlin, and try to march on Bülowplatz. I wanted excitement and I must confess that I am getting it.

◇ *Saturday, January 21, 1933*

B4, F6.2

This looks pretty bad. They should never have allowed it.[48] Plettl nodded his head in agreement. He had invited me to a lecture on "From Capitalism to Socialism" by Dr. Hans Staudinger,[49] an important member of the Reichstag, and we were in the Herren Chamber of the old Prussian Landstag building. [. . .]

The police are either *Dummköpfe* or there is something more behind the move than we know anything about. This may be the beginning of something bigger. You'd better stay away. It means a bloodbath. I shan't

47. More likely Dr. Melcher, as mentioned in the January 21 entry.

48. Plettl and Plotkin are talking about the Nazi meeting in Bülowplatz.

49. Hans Staudinger (1889–1980), an economist and Social Democratic member of the Reichstag. He took refuge in Belgium in 1933, then in the United States in 1940, where, a member of the University in Exile, he taught at the New School for Social Research in New York.

be surprised to hear that heads will crack tomorrow, many of them. I don't think it will be the same thing as being chased by the *Polizei* that day in front of the Reichstag.[50]

I found it hard to concentrate on what Dr. Staudinger was saying. If I ever meet that gentleman he will receive my profoundest apologies. [. . .] But my mind simply would not forget Plettl's phrase—it means a bloodbath.

When the Nazis applied for permission to the city chief of police to hold a demonstration, during the early part of the week, and asked that they be permitted to hold their meeting in Bülowplatz, no one took the request seriously. A few smiled at their consummate gall. It was taken for granted that this request, like all such requests in the past, would be answered in the usual manner. Bülowplatz cannot hold more than 10,000 people. . . . The point was that Bülowplatz is where the Rosa Luxemburg House, the headquarters of the Communist Party, is located! On Thursday came the announcement that permission had been granted to the Nazis to hold their demonstration! Friday and today, all the newspapers that are not sympathetic to the Nazis are protesting. The permit for the meeting was granted by the *Polizeipresident* of Berlin. Efforts have been made to get him to change the permit to let the Nazis meet some other place—a place large enough to hold their crowds and where there would not be the likelihood of bloodshed. Dr. Melcher who issued the permit was a member of Hugenberg's Deutsch-Nationale Partei, [and he] has been standing his ground. Efforts have been made to have the meeting canceled through Dr. Bracht, a member of the Catholic Centrum Party, but up to now every effort has been unsuccessful . . . The meeting is slated for three o'clock tomorrow.

Fifteen minutes after [Dr. Staudinger's lecture] we were seated in one of the salons of the Imperator, one of the largest restaurants in Berlin. Those who know the length of Berlin blocks can estimate the size of this restaurant. It runs the full length of the block, easily three hundred feet long, and runs a hundred and fifty feet in depth. In addition to the orchestra in the main salon, the second floor is divided into three salons, two devoted to dancing, and the center one to those who would rather lounge in their overstuffed chairs, drink beer or coffee, and listen to one of the four orchestras playing Johann Strauss waltzes. As we entered, the place was jammed. I suppose that when one is sitting on the edge of a volcano, one might as well take advantage of the soft spots, particularly when music goes with it.

---

50. Plotkin remembers the day, on December 6, 1932, when he tried to attend the opening session of the Reichstag.

I came back to what was on my mind. What do you suppose, I asked [Plettl], are Schleicher's motives? Schleicher's motives? Surely you don't mean that Schleicher didn't and doesn't know of every step in this move? Again he nodded. He undoubtedly does. You know, he added, we faced exactly the same thing a number of years ago. But unlike the Communists, we did not fall for the bait. When the police granted them a permit, we simply said to the police, since you granted the permit, it is up to you to protect our property. We remained passive. We placed the responsibility wholly on the police department. The Communists have acted stupidly. They should not have ordered a counterdemonstration. Their demonstrations, I answered, were ordered in the localities where they live, in Charlottenburg, Neukölln, Wedding, Pankow and Weissensee.[51] They've been prohibited, was his answer. And that reminds me we once ordered a demonstration for the SPD; when we announced the place, the police came in with their *verboten,* and on the day of the demonstration had their entire police force stationed at the supposed meeting place. In the meantime we had quietly sent the word around to our leaders where the real demonstration was to be held. When the police finally learned about it and came on the scene, the meeting was over. [. . .]

All this brings me to what I want to say [Plettl resumed]. Hitler is today in exactly the same position which Hugenberg was in when our tactics on the Young Plan broke his power and laughed his prestige into nothingness.[52] Hitler has been dancing between four masters and any one of the four may break him. There are two camps now among the heavy industrialists, and there are two camps in Hitler's party. Goebbels, whom you have heard, will not listen to Hitler stepping into the ministry. Gregor Strasser, and the thirty

---

51. Working-class districts of Berlin.

52. The new program for settlement of German reparations debts was presented by the committee headed (1929–30) by Owen D. Young. This new plan superseded the 1924 Dawes plan. The Young Plan—which set the total reparations at $26,350,000,000 to be paid over a period of fifty-eight and a half years—was adopted by the Allied powers in 1930. Designed to provide a settlement under which Germany would know the exact extent of its obligations and to reduce the payments appreciably, the Young Plan divided the annual payment, set at about $473 million, into two elements—an unconditional part (one-third of the sum) and a postponable one (the remainder). No sooner had the plan gone into effect than Germany felt the full impact of economic depression, and a moratorium was called for the fiscal year 1931–32. Although the SPD had approved the Young Plan, the ADGB in 1931 was in favor of canceling the reparation debts in order to curb the mounting unemployment.

followers that he has in the Reich, insist that Hitler must either accept a ministry for himself, or permit Strasser to take one of the posts that have been offered. Hitler will lose either way. Schleicher knows it, and it may be that Schleicher is using Hitler as a cat's paw. Hitler on the downgrade, supplying Schleicher with provocative means for eliminating the Communists, will clear the roads in the coming elections for Schleicher.

This explanation sounded plausible, but somehow it did not carry conviction. I must have looked unconvinced, for Plettl went right on. Schleicher is a military man. He has been shouting for a militia. To destroy Hitler is one thing. I am not convinced that he really wants to destroy Hitlerism. For instance, I doubt whether Schleicher wants to destroy Hitler's army. They would make an excellent base for the future militia of which Schleicher has been talking. This may be a move to encourage Hitler into taking a cabinet post, not Hitler alone, but a few of them. If Schleicher could get a few of their leading figures into the cabinet, and let them twiddle their thumbs until they were thoroughly weakened, and then take over their apparatus, it would take a long time to build up another effective opposition against him within capitalist ranks. To split Hitlerism, eliminate Communism as much as it is possible, and to entrench himself so thoroughly that nothing can budge him, I think is Schleicher's game. The only effective opposition to him will come through our party, but when we will run afoul against each other is hard to say. But of all the political parties in Germany, we are the only ones who for the present are keeping our heads. Let Schleicherism, Hitlerism and Communism fight it out. The road will be a little less foggy then.

◇ *Sunday, January 22, 1933*

B4, F6.2

I am on my way to the national congress of the *Betriebsräte*. The *Betriebsräte* is the organization of the factory councils that spreads into every establishment employing more than five persons.[53] But I am not thinking of the *Betriebsräte*. I am thinking of the advice given me last night by Plettl and this morning by the man who makes up my bed. He overheard my conversation with Jerome Bayer. We had talked about today's meeting. Both he and Cora Albertieri wanted me to take them [there]. I explained to them that I had a previous engagement. Thought it would be wiser to keep them out of harm's

53. Plotkin had reported on the factory councils in the December 29, 1932, entry.

way. On the way to the car line where Plettl was to take his trolley home we stepped into the hotel where Jerome is staying and left a note again advising him not to go. But I am not thinking of Jerome. I am really thinking of what my young man told me.

Stay away from the meeting, he said. I am going to stay in the house all day. I know the district very well. The streets are narrow. Around Bülowplatz is the old Jewish quarters. I am not a Jew but I lived there. I know what the Nazis and the police have done with the Jews on those streets. Do you know where Gormanstrasse is? I saw policemen walking in six and eights, you know how their heavy clothing makes them walk slowly. When police would turn their backs the Nazis would hit the Jews. They would knock them down and then stamp on them with their feet while the policemen would slowly walk the other way. I tell him that I have no intention of going, that I have other appointments that will keep me busy all day.

It is early, so I walk to the Gewerkschaftshaus. The meeting has just started. Leipart is talking. The man is powerful in his simplicity and sincerity. He speaks in measured tones and with measured values. But there is something wrong. I can't concentrate. I see him and I hear him, but I cannot get a sense of continuity out of his arguments. It is not his fault. There is something wrong with me. I sit through the talk by Nörpel,[54] the secretary of the congress, and Frau Hanna[55] who is in charge of the Women's Division of the ADGB, and note that they and Leipart have given the tone to the congress. Elections are coming within two months. The delegates must go to their homes well prepared with arguments to help reelect the social democratic and ADGB factory councils; but for once it does not seem real.

I look for Plettl, but Plettl for some reason has decided not to come. I go below to the restaurant and run into Furtwängler and we discuss Dostoyevsky and Joyce, and he introduces me to the president of the German Building Trades Federation. Likeable. I leave Furtwängler and run into Kummer who in turn introduces me to Fr. Husemann,[56] the president of the Miners' Federation,

---

54. Clemens Nörpel (1885–1938), a specialist in labor law, author of *Die neuere arbeitsrechtliche und soziale Gesetzgebung* [The Recent Social and Labor Legislation] (Berlin: Deutscher Verkehrsbund, 1928). At the *Betriebsräte* convention Nörpel's topic was "The Factory Councils in the Economic Crisis."

55. Gertrud Hanna (1876–1944), active in the trade union movement and in the Arbeiterwohlfahrt, SPD member in the Prussian Diet (1919–33).

56. Fritz Husemann (1873–1935), Social Democratic representative and president of the Miners' Federation. He was arrested in 1933 by the Nazis and assassinated in a concentration camp.

who invites me to visit him when I come to the Ruhr. I promise that I will. We go down for a glass of beer and over the beer Kummer tells me that the congress is a huge success, that there are more than five hundred delegates representing twenty-eight thousand factories. He tells me that I look tired, and I answer that I hadn't slept all night. Then I ask him whether he had heard anything more about the coming demonstration. All he knows is that the whole police force is out. Out where? In and around Bülowplatz. Plettl thought it would be otherwise, but Kummer might be mistaken. I let it pass.

[. . .] I decide that perhaps I need some fresh air. I try the courtyard and find that it is snowing quite hard and that I had better wear my overcoat. I return, get my coat and start. I know by this time where I am going. I tentatively promised Plettl and my chamber man that I would not go to the demonstration. I looked at my watch. It was two thirty. I was on my way.

The snow and the wind beat in my face, and the snow crunches under the weight of my body. It feels good. I keep on walking. I pass the Transport building at the corner of Engelufer and Michaelplatz. Then I notice the Lutheran church at the east end of it, while on the lake in front are hundreds of youngsters skating, and as I pass the north side of Michaelplatz, I also notice that there are hundreds of youngsters with their sleds and their parents. Things don't look so bad. I keep on walking until the cold gets into my feet, and then I decide to take the subway. But when I get to Inselbrücke, opposite the ADGB building, I am told that the subways are not running. [. . .]

◇ *Sunday, January 22, 1933*

B4, F6.1

It was impossible to get into Bülowplatz. Only men in Nazi uniforms and newspapermen admitted. The Nazis claim they had 16,000. The place itself is so small that I doubt whether they had more than twelve thousand. To make certain that these 16,000 were protected the city used 16,000 policemen. Cora Albertieri told me that the roofs around Bülowplatz were manned by officers armed with machine guns. All windows around the open space where the meeting was held were ordered closed tight and policemen with high-powered rifles stood pointing their rifles at the windows anticipating any possible snipers. The Liebknecht House was invested by the police, thoroughly searched, everyone sent home and the house filled with police who stood at the windows so that anyone hidden in the building making a rush for the window could be intercepted.

The parades that had been *verboten* were intercepted and broken up in the different parts of town. The entire city therefore was affected and to all intents and purposes under martial law. When the parades were intercepted, the crowds scattered and walked in twos and threes to the district where the Nazis were holding forth. Those who had the means tried riding in the subway only to find that the subway and the elevated shot past Bülowplatz and took them away beyond it. And every approach to the Platz was cleared and squadrons of police thrown around it. Those inside could get out, but no one, unless either in uniform or possessing a pass, could get in.

Long before three o'clock, the time of the meeting, every approach to Bülowplatz was closed. As I came up to Alexander Square, I found the streets choked with counterdemonstrators. Not long afterwards, the Communists, on the street where the elevated runs, threw up ash cans as barricades and a hand-to-hand fight with the police resulted. When I turned into Alte Alexanderstrasse I ceased to be an independent agent. I was carried along by the crowd, many of them singing the International, others cursing and jibing at the police, some of whom were on horseback, others on foot, high-powered rifles slung across their shoulders, and others in the *"Tanz"* wagons, rifles on the surface and machine guns on the bottom of their trucks ready for an emergency. The mass moved, and I moved with it. When a rifle cracked, the crowd stopped and I stopped with it. All sense of personal motion seemed to have oozed out of me, and I am by no means a coward. Later I saw a boy who had been beaten by the police until his face showed nothing but glistening eyes, eyes that spoke of the pain and horror within him. . . . It was a sheer miracle that the day didn't end in a wholesale massacre. Only two were killed, sixty-odd taken to the hospitals. And how many more beaten up, both by the police and the Communists when they could catch Nazis, will never be known. Nine o'clock this evening the *Polizeipresident* was on the radio and announced that everything on the [Bülow]Platz was quiet and peaceful. In addition to the killings, 118 were arrested.

◇ *Monday, January 23, 1933*

B4, F6.1

The Nazis are out with an extra, "Berlin Belongs to Us." The Communists have applied and obtained permission to demonstrate on Bülowplatz on Wednesday. The Iron Front[57] is applying for permission to demonstrate on Sunday coming. The Communists also announce that they will have an antifascist week commencing with their parade on Wednesday. In the meantime the unemployment problem is growing apace. The army of unemployed stands 250,000 more than on the 15th of December. Schleicher is being criticized by the industrialists for counteracting von Papen's industrial program, by the Communists for failure to solve the unemployment problem, and by the Nazis for encouraging the trade unions and the Jews on Lindenstrasse and Jerusalemerstrasse.

At a meeting of the Metalworker's section of the National Shop Council's Congress[58] today a member of the Reichstag spoke to the *Amerikaner* and intimated that something exciting would develop in the coming meeting of the Reichstag. He said something about a scandal in the use of funds that had been allocated several years ago by the Reichstag to relieve the landowners in East Prussia.[59] I wanted to ask him the particulars but other matters connected with the Congress came up and our attention was called elsewhere. I left the National Congress yesterday afternoon to go and see the demonstration, but what I saw was enough to indicate that they were in a two-sided fight. The elections in the factories take place two months hence, and after Leipart and the others set the tone of the program of the Congress I left. They are fighting the Communists on the one hand and the Fascists on the other. As Leipart, the president of the Social Democratic German Trade Union movement, declared, they want neither the soviets nor fascism; they want an orderly progression towards socialism. Today I thought I would go and see a definite industry handling its specific problems rather than a general congress dealing with general problems.

◇ *Tuesday, January 24, 1933*

B4, F6.2

There is no letup in discussing Sunday's protest meeting of the Nazis in Bülowplatz. *Angriff*, the Nazi paper, is quite jubilant. *Tempo* carries the an-

---

57. The Iron Front (Eiserne Front) was a paramilitary organization founded in December 1931 by the ADGB, the SPD, the Reichsbanner, and other less numerous groups to defend the republic and democratic institutions.

58. The National Congress of the Factory Councils *(Betriebsräte)*.

59. The subject of the East Prussian landowners' scandal is developed in the February 1 entry.

nouncement of anti-Semitic riots in the University of Breslau. This is nothing new. The riots were directed against Prof. Cohn. According to this newspaper, the university authorities have taken disciplinary measures against the students. Cora Albertieri tells me that she witnessed a students' riot in front of the University of Berlin on Friday, the day I talked to Zielenziger.

The discussion centers mostly around the effect the meeting will have on the political situation. From all opinions I gather that the effect it will have will be to strengthen the Nazis in the other cities throughout Germany. To the rest of Germany it will mean that the Nazis control Berlin. One may therefore expect more riots and more killing throughout the interior. The toll of the wounded has risen to eighty and one killed. How many of the eighty will die is still uncertain. Hartig thinks that the Communists will lose tremendously in prestige among their own people. On the other hand, I doubt whether the Nazis can get much satisfaction out of what has happened. Their handful of fifteen thousand men would have been scattered to the four winds without the protection of 16,000 *Polizei,* tank cars, machine guns on the roofs of the buildings surrounding Bülowplatz.

Now the SPD has come out with its announcement of a protest meeting for next Sunday in the Lustgarten. I have been waiting for this meeting for a long time. It should offer an interesting comparison both of temper and methods between the different groups in Germany.

◇ *Wednesday, January 25, 1933*

B4, F6.1

The *Mittag* was on the streets at noon today with the extra of the slaughter in Dresden. Nine dead and eleven wounded! All presumably Communists. Last night a meeting, of communist origin according to the *Tageblatt,* enraged the police when the speakers roundly denounced them. They ordered the meeting to disperse. According to the police someone in the balcony started shooting and they answered in kind. It is curious that not one policeman got shot. Only the people in the balcony. The authorities announce that they will thoroughly investigate the affair.

◇ *Thursday, January 26, 1933*

B4, F6.2

The end of the meeting on Sunday is not yet in sight. It is sometimes easier to open the box of Pandora than to shut it. But it is not so certain that those who have opened Pandora's box are so eager to close it. [. . .]

In the afternoon, here, the Communists answered Sunday's meeting of the Nazis with a demonstration of their own, and eighty thousand are reported to have marched through Bülowplatz; this time the police kept perfect order.

Now the Social Democratic Party is answering the demonstration of last Sunday with an order for a mass meeting in the Lustgarten to be held next Sunday afternoon. The posters announcing the meeting answer the Nazi's boast that "Berlin belongs to us" with a counterslogan, "Berlin Is Still Red!"

◇ *Thursday, January 26, 1933*

B4, F6.1

This evening the *Tempo* published a sensational story that a new government was being formed, composed of Hitler, von Papen and Hugenberg! I got the edition on the street at eight o'clock. I promptly called several friends who are supposed to be in the know. One laughed at the report and said they would never dare resurrect von Papen again. Von Papen is the most hated man in all Germany. The second one told me that the *Tempo* was a sensation monger and to pay no attention. Herbert Kline of the *Chicago Tribune* told me that anything is possible.

◇ *Friday, January 27, 1933*

B4, F6.1

There is something brewing. Hugenberg has announced himself against Schleicher and for a cabinet including Hitler. What does this mean? Hugenberg and Hitler are old enemies. If not for Hitler, Hugenberg today would be where Hitler is now. Hitler took Hugenberg's followers away from him, and much of the financial backing as well. And will Hitler get what he wants, sufficient power to put over those things that he has promised the Ruhr industrialists, and to fascisticize the country along the lines of Mussolini in Italy? So far Hindenburg has stood in the way and has refused to be budged from his course of constitutionalism. I ask questions, but the answers are as clear as mud. Everyone is doing exactly what I am doing—guessing; and no one knows exactly what will happen, although everyone agrees that the whole thing is impossible.

What adds to the tower of Babel is Hugenberg's announcement that he is in favor of building a cabinet of the three parties whose combined strength would give them a majority in the Reichstag, Nazis, Nationalists, and the Catholic Centrum. It is possible but hardly probable. The Catholic Centrum, I hardly imagine to go against its Catholic Trade Unions. And the Catholic Trade Unions hate and fear Hitler not one whit less than they hate Communism or von Papen.

◇ *Saturday, January 28, 1933*

B4, F6.1

Early this morning there seemed to be something stirring. Friends were restless, but seemed unwilling to talk. I surmised there was something in the wind but no one would or could say just what. Finally I talked with Hartig of the Transport and Municipal Employees. They will try to bring von Papen back, and Hitler will go into the cabinet, he told me. How do you know? They've been working on the old man for some time, he answered, and on Hitler too. Hugenberg must move fast to protect his landowners against the impending scandal in the Reichstag. Hitler must move fast to protect himself against his losses in the general elections, his losses in financial support, and against the revolt in his own ranks. The ADGB is worried.

The afternoon papers carried the news of Schleicher's resignation. With his resignation he also warned Hindenburg of what was before the country. Among other things he warned Hindenburg that a presidential cabinet without a majority in the Reichstag behind it, exercising dictatorial powers, would meet with opposition in all quarters.

In the evening to a mask ball given by one of the socialist magazines. Later newspapermen who attended another ball in the vicinity came over. It was intended to be a gay affair, but somehow I feel that the laughter is slightly forced.

◆ *Saturday, January 28, 1933*

B4, F6.2

[. . .] The season for masked balls is now in full swing. The costumes, many of them homemade, were better than ordinary, although Hartig tells me that when you see one you see all of them. The dancing to my surprise was exactly what it would have been in an ordinary jazz palace on Broadway. The orchestras blared their jazz and the young boys and girls of Berlin shook as mean a leg of jazz as the best. What was of more than ordinary interest to me was that there were three salons, each of them with a different orchestra, and in each of them enormous crowds making merry.

All around the dancing space in the halls were wine tables where for seventy-five cents one bought an enormous bottle of wine. Our party, six in all, with frequent casual guests, drank three bottles of wine. I did not see a single man or woman even slightly intoxicated. We left at three o'clock. The dancing went on until five.

◆ *Sunday, January 29, 1933*

B4, F6.1

A demonstration of the Iron Front in the Lustgarten. Twenty thousand men in uniform marched. Eighty thousand more filled the grounds. Another hundred thousand choked the streets leading to the approaches of the peninsula where the Lustgarten is located. This was my first sight of the Iron Front army. They marched with a zip as effective as that of the Nazis. With their red banners flying high they made a stirring sight as they marched past the stand, alongside of the canal and then up in front of the old palace of the Kaiser. These Iron Front men are the combined military forces of the Trade Unions, Socialist Party and even Catholic troops among them, sworn to protect the Republic.

Whether Hitler will be appointed is not definitely known. Neither is it known precisely what the composition of the new cabinet will be. Künstler,[60] the speaker of the afternoon, who is president of the Berlin section

---

60. Franz Künstler (1888–1942), former secretary of the Berlin union of metalworkers (1919–22), president of the Berlin section of the SPD (1924–33), and member of the Reichstag. Arrested by the Nazis in 1933, interned and tortured in a concentration camp, and liberated in 1934, he died in 1942 as a result of the torture he had been subjected to.

of the Socialist Party, with his first statement sent the crowd into a frenzy of cheerings. Paraphrasing *Angriff*'s boast of Monday that the city belongs to the Nazis, he shouted through the microphone so that it reached part of the grounds, against the walls of the building which threw it back at him. "Berlin," he shouted, "belongs to the Reds." Within a second the pent-up excitement of the last few days, the worry over the possibilities of terror arising out of last Sunday's demonstration, and the self-assurance of the speaker swept everything before him and released all that was within him. They felt their strength. And he fed it. "The Catholic Unions,"[61] he shouted, "have joined us in warning the government that any effort to destroy those things that we have won since 1918 will be [prevented], if need be with the lives of all the workers of the nation. The Iron Front on two occasions has saved the Republic. It may be necessary for the Iron Front to save it again. We will not permit the Nazis nor the monarchists to destroy the edifice that we have so painfully built." He spoke only fifteen minutes, but it was the most effective fifteen minutes of oratory I have ever listened to. I understand that the speakers in the Lustgarten are limited to twenty minutes. It takes so long to get in and out that the time left for the speakers is very short. He made the best possible use of it in the time he had at his disposal. The crowd sang the International, and happily started slowly to file its way out of the grounds.

Later, with a group of friends in a coffee shop, warming our chilled bones after the sharp weather in the grounds, I was told that the Catholic Center leader Dr. Kaas[62] and Otto Braun, the Socialist Prime Minister of the state of Prussia, the largest state in Germany, signed a joint letter to the President warning him that a nationalist government with dictatorial powers would be regarded as a move towards the reestablishment of the Monarchy and that a revolution might be in the offing. This is the first time that responsible groups have made the threat. Whether it will be effective remains to be seen.

---

61. Unions affiliated to the Christian Deutscher Gewerkschaftsbund allied to the Catholic Centrum.

62. Ludwig Kaas (1881–1952), a theologian representing the right wing of the Catholic Zentrum and president of the party since 1928. In February 1933, he was willing but failed to form a parliamentary coalition with the Nazis. Again after the March 5, 1933, elections, he offered his party's collaboration to Hitler, with no success, and on March 23 he required his party to grant full powers to Hitler. In July 1933, Kaas participated with von Papen in the negotiations in Rome for the Vatican's concordat with Nazi Germany, then withdrew from politics.

◇ *Monday, January 30, 1933*

B4, F6.1

The new cabinet was appointed today. *Tempo* was right and apparently had the inside information. How easily wish thinking will often make something impossible of belief was illustrated to me today. All of this morning, Furtwängler of the ADGB kept assuring me that the appointment of Hitler was impossible and that the old man Hindenburg would resign before he would do it. That Hindenburg regarded Hitler as an upstart who did not really belong in Germany. While we were talking, at eleven o'clock, Hindenburg called in Hitler and charged him with the task of forming a cabinet! This was a mere formality. The details were arranged before Hitler was called in. Disregarding the [momentary] popularity of the different figures in the cabinet, and for once disagreeing with my friends here, it seems to me that the cabinet is not a Hitler cabinet, but a Hugenberg-Papen cabinet, with all the strings in Hugenberg's hands and not in Hitler's.[63] Out of 10 ministers now in the cabinet, one vacancy still open, only four posts have gone to the Hitler people, six to the Hugenberg crowd. The army remains in Hugenberg's hands. Dictators are not in the habit of trusting each other with armies.

Tried to get tickets to see *Faust* at the State Theater on Charlottenstrasse. Jerome Bayer, Cora Albertieri and Margaret Chalise succeeded because the girls got their tickets earlier in the week. Coming at the last moment, it was impossible, and fortunately for me that it was so. The show opened at seven and I turned down Margrafenstrasse towards Leipzigerstrasse to get some coffee when I ran into the first torchlight parade of the Nazis. They were on their way to the Kaiserhof Hotel where Hitler is staying. Thousands of them were marching from all parts of the city to hail their chief. Occasionally one would also see troops of Steel Helmet,[64] Hugenberg's troops, fraternizing and marching along with the Nazis. After passing and saluting Hitler, they then marched to Hindenburg's palace and again hailed to their hearts' content. There is something of an automatic hysteria about it that is disquieting.

---

63. Though widespread at the time, this belief was quickly proved wrong.

64. The Steel Helmet (Stahlhelm) was a nationalist organization of World War I veterans, founded in 1918 by Franz Seldte and violently opposed to the Weimar Republic. With a membership of three hundred thousand uniformed men, it took part in the Harzburg Front. It was dissolved in 1935, and its members were integrated into the Nazi SA.

◇ *Tuesday, January 31, 1933*

B4, F6.1

The cabinet is not yet complete. The ministry of Justice is still unfilled. Neither has the Catholic Centrum indicated whether it is going to support the new government. Hugenberg and Hitler combined have only 248 members in the Reich[stag] out of 560. They need thirty-seven additional votes to rule within the constitution. Otherwise, when the Reichstag is called, a vote of no confidence will be passed and the new government will go the way of its predecessors.

Talked today to Dr. Bading, the expert for both the Social Democratic Party and the trade unions. Thinks that Hitler had to go into the cabinet or face disruption of his own ranks. Also thinks that Hitler will be able to do exactly nothing in the way of reforms that will solve the unemployment problem. On the contrary, according to Bading, should Hitler succeed in breaking the trade unions and in eliminating the social legislation of Germany, he will only succeed in intensifying the contradictions within capitalist Germany. The tangible result will be that the purchasing power of the German workers will be reduced still further and will add still more to the numbers out of employment. Moreover, he said, the unemployed are the backbone of both the Nazis and the Communist followers. When Hitler disappoints his followers he will be through. How much damage he can do in the meantime is uncertain. One thing he said sticks in my mind. Hitler, he said, had to be taken into the cabinet by the Hugenberg crowd. Just as the trade unions want Hitler out of the way, the Junkers and the Monarchists also want him out of the way. At the head of an antimonarchist movement, Hitler would be the most popular man in Germany. Now he is where he can spend himself with comparatively little damage to the royalist Hugenberg crowd.

Also talked with Naphtali and Mendelsohn,[65] the two economists who are responsible [for the] political and economic program of German Social

---

65. Fritz Naphtali (1888–1961), a journalist and economist, head of the SPD and ADGB joint Research Center on Political Economy (Forschungsstelle für Wirtschaftspolitik), and exponent of the notion of economic democracy. Exiled in Palestine in 1933, he worked for the Jewish labor organization Histadrout. Kurt Mendelsohn was a social democratic economist and author of *Kapitalistisches Wirtschaftschaos oder sozialistische Planwirtschaft?* [Capitalist Economic Chaos or Socialist Planned Economy?] (Berlin: Dietz, 1932).

Democracy. Both lean to Bading's opinion that Hitler will not be able to do anything, except perhaps to make sharper the crisis of unemployment that exists in Germany today. They pointed out that in Germany today there are at least fifteen hundred cartels existing to regulate the market prices of their commodities. Within these cartels the amount of business is apportioned to each firm and their goods sold through a joint marketing syndicate. Chemicals, steel, iron, linoleum, gasoline, margarine, textiles, coke were named among the trusts; building materials, paper goods, furniture, leather goods, etc. were named among the cartels. And while the trust indicates an absolute control and ownership through which the most efficient production units only are maintained and the less efficient closed, it is otherwise among the cartels. Here thousands of units of production are maintained that are inefficient but are maintained nevertheless. Both lead to monopoly prices. The program of the [SPD] was not to interfere with these groups. They realize that they are a natural development under capitalism, and in spite of the fact that their dissolution might break down prices and thus increase the purchasing power of the masses, the [SPD] has been planning to attack the problem from the other end. They have on several occasions already introduced bills, drawn for them by Naphtali, empowering the government to take over those groups who fall into the monopoly group. But up to the present time, they have not had sufficient power with which to go through with their program.

Now assuming that Hitler wants to do something, there are two ways open to him. One is to do what the Socialists have been demanding. Take over the monopoly price-controlled industries, reduce the prices and increase the purchasing power of the workers so that industry can start humming once more. The other is to do what you have been trying to do for a quarter of a century in America. Break down the cartels and make illegal the regulation of prices that now exists among them. Should he succeed in that policy, then he will bring into Germany the most intense competition between the employers that Germany has ever seen. Thousands of factories will be compelled to close and additional millions of workers thrown out of their employment. It is not likely that he will follow this program. It is more likely that he will try and break down the trade unions and destroy their legal wage standards as von Papen did. The result of von Papen's policy is now clear enough for children to see. During the time he was in, 160,000 additional workers lost their jobs, and since he left office, the jobless have increased by another half million. It is impossible to reduce wages and recreate work at the same time.

The first cabinet meeting was held today. Rumor has it that the question of suppressing the Communist Party was discussed and decided against. Hugenberg wants to announce a state of national emergency and cancel the meeting of the Reich[stag] slated for the 7th. Rumors also have it that armored cars are ready and waiting to bring Wilhelm II back to Germany. It is more likely that Hitler does not want at the present moment to go too far. Any other guess is just as good. I think I can understand his objection to declaring a state of national emergency. With the army in the hands of Hugenberg, a state of emergency directed today against the Communists may tomorrow be directed against present or former allies as well. Drawing of the resolutions at this meeting that endows von Papen with powers quite similar to Hitler's does not speak well of future peace between them.

While the cabinet met, it is nevertheless not certain that it can remain in office after the Reichstag meets on the 7th of February. So far the Catholic Centrum has not indicated its support. The Centrum has submitted four questions to Hitler dealing with his politics on foreign affairs, labor problems, social legislation and education. They want ample guarantees that he will rule within the constitution and that he will not tamper with labor legislation and social legislation. It is to meet again tomorrow and by that time it should be known whether the Catholic Centrum will tolerate them.

In the meantime disorders are spreading throughout Germany. After the torchlight demonstration of last evening two men were killed in Berlin, one a leader of the Nazi shock troops and a police officer. In Breslau a Communist was killed. How many were wounded in the riot that took place, no one knows.

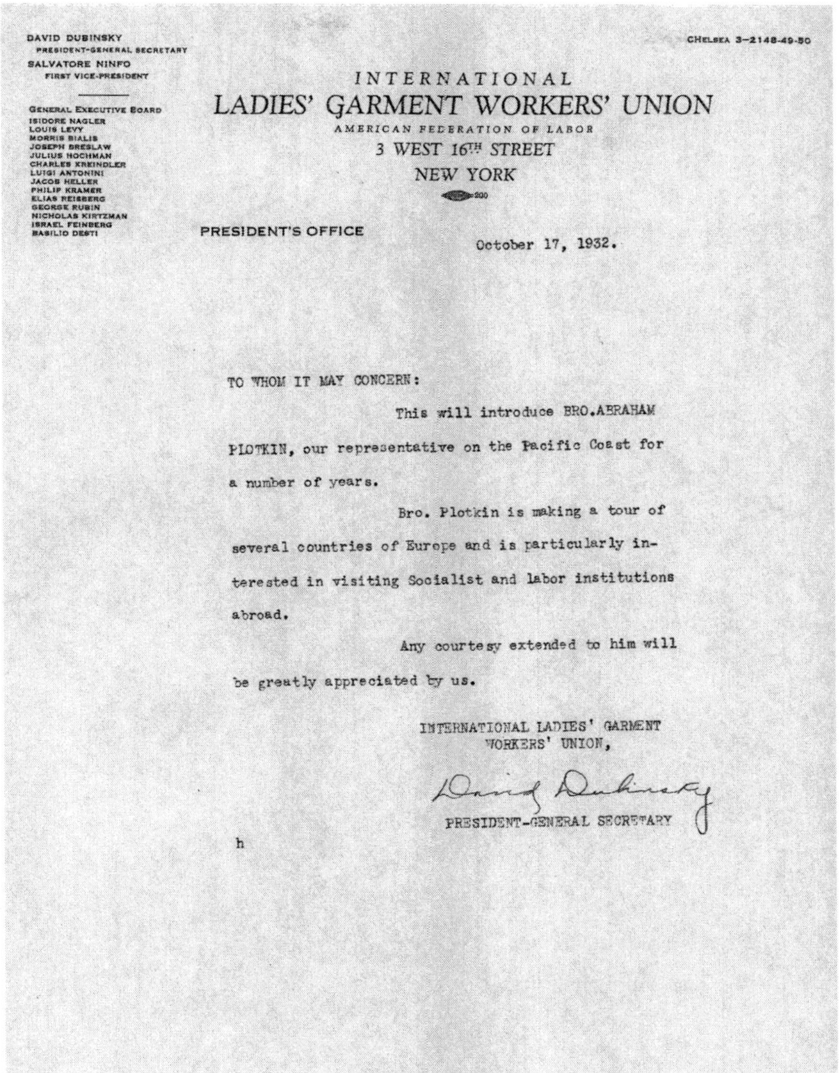

DAVID DUBINSKY
PRESIDENT-GENERAL SECRETARY
SALVATORE NINFO
FIRST VICE-PRESIDENT

GENERAL EXECUTIVE BOARD
ISIDORE NAGLER
LOUIS LEVY
MORRIS BIALIS
JOSEPH BRESLAW
JULIUS HOCHMAN
CHARLES KREINDLER
LUIGI ANTONINI
JACOB HELLER
PHILIP KRAMER
ELIAS REISBERG
GEORGE RUBIN
NICHOLAS KIRTZMAN
ISRAEL FEINBERG
BASILIO DESTI

CHELSEA 3-2148-49-50

INTERNATIONAL
LADIES' GARMENT WORKERS' UNION
AMERICAN FEDERATION OF LABOR
3 WEST 16TH STREET
NEW YORK

PRESIDENT'S OFFICE

October 17, 1932.

TO WHOM IT MAY CONCERN:

This will introduce BRO. ABRAHAM PLOTKIN, our representative on the Pacific Coast for a number of years.

Bro. Plotkin is making a tour of several countries of Europe and is particularly interested in visiting Socialist and labor institutions abroad.

Any courtesy extended to him will be greatly appreciated by us.

INTERNATIONAL LADIES' GARMENT
WORKERS' UNION,

David Dubinsky
PRESIDENT-GENERAL SECRETARY

h

ILGWU president David Dubinsky's letter of introduction for Plotkin. *Source:* AP Coll., 6036/016, B1, F10, Kheel Center, Cornell University.

Fritz Kummer and Abraham Plotkin in Berlin, January 1933. Kummer was the editor of the German Metalworkers' journal *(Metallarbeiterzeitung)*. Referring to their many friendly and more technical conversations on the German labor movement, Plotkin wrote, "Kummer and I have taken to each other like a pair of ducks" (AP Diary, January 6, 1933). *Source:* AP Coll., 6036/016, B2, F21, Kheel Center, Cornell University.

Abraham Plotkin and Martin Plettl in Berlin, 1933. As president of the German Clothing Workers' Union, Plettl introduced Plotkin to many other German union leaders. Upon his return to the United States, Plotkin was able to obtain support for Plettl and his secretary and companion, Dorothea Heinrich. *Source:* AP Coll., 6036/016, B2, F21, Kheel Center, Cornell University.

Abraham Plotkin and Tonnis Van der Heeg, secretary of the International Federation of Clothing Workers (whose seat was in Amsterdam). Van der Heeg's visit to Plettl in Berlin is reported in Plotkin's diary of February 11, 1933. In June 1933, Plotkin met Van der Heeg again in Amsterdam before reaching Paris. *Source:* AP Coll., 6036/016, B2, F21, Kheel Center, Cornell University.

Postcard photo sent by Martin Plettl to Abraham Plotkin, March 1933: "Nazis in the office of the Clothing Workers' Union in Leipzig, throwing typewriters, papers, etc. out of the window." *Source:* AP Coll., 6036/016, B2, F21, Kheel Center, Cornell University.

Alexanderplatz, Hermann Tietz Stores. *Source:* Mario von Bucovich, *Berlin 1928* (Berlin: Albertus-Verlag, 1928), 70.

Imperial Castle and Unter den Linden, view from the air. *Source:* Bucovich, *Berlin 1928*, 17.

Lustgarten and museums. *Source:* Bucovich, *Berlin 1928,* 29.

Waldsiedlung Zehlendorf. Modern worker houses in the woods on the outskirts of Berlin, built between 1926 and 1931. *Source:* Paul Ortwin Rave, *Berlin in der Geschichte seiner Bauten* (Munich: Aufnahmen von H. Urbschaft und H. J. Fischer, S.I., Deutscher Kunstverlag, 1962), 78.

Headquarters of the German Metal Workers' Union. Built between 1929 and 1931, this building was one of the "modern temples of labor" that Plotkin admired. *Source:* Rave, *Berlin in der Geschichte seiner Bauten,* 83.

Nazi squads (SA) marching in front of the Karl Liebknecht House, headquarters of the German Communist Party, on Bülowplatz, on January 22, 1933. *Source:* Helmuth Günther Dahms, *Vom Kaiserreich zum Bundeshaus: 50 Jahre deutsche Geschichte in Berlin* (Berlin: Staeck, 1964), 123.

18. Jahrg. / Nr. 20a Preis 10 Pfennig Auswärts 15 Pf.

Berlin, Dienstag, 24. Januar 1933

Die Rote Fahne

Zentralorgan der Kommunistischen Partei Deutschlands (Sektion der Kommunistischen Internationale)

Karl Liebknecht und Rosa Luxemburg

Morgen dem Faschismus unsere Macht gezeigt!

Rotes Berlin, heraus zur Sturmwoche der Antifaschistischen Aktion

Alle, Alle zum Bülowplatz!

Aufmarschplan zum Bülowplatz siehe umseitig!

Ein Extrablatt des „Vorwärts“

Einheitsfront oder Einheitsfrontmanöver

Hitlers Mordhetze fordert wieder zwei Arbeiterleben

Die Rote Fahne, official organ of the German Communist Party, calling members to a meeting on Bülowplatz on January 24, 1933. *Source: 1933, Wege zur Diktatur* (Berlin: Heenemann, 1983), 106.

Torchlight parade of SS, SA, and Steel Helmet on the evening of January 30, 1933, at the Brandenburg Gate. *Source:* Dahms, *Vom Kaiserreich zum Bundeshaus,* 123.

The Reichstag on fire, February 28, 1933. *Source:* Dahms, *Vom Kaiserreich zum Bundeshaus,* 127.

The Karl Liebknecht House occupied by the Nazis. *Source: 1933, Wege zur Diktatur,* 108.

Nazi occupation of the Trade Union House (Gewerkschaftshaus), May 2, 1933. *Source:* Deutsches Historisches Museum.

November 1st, 1933.

Dear Friend Plettl:-

Wellcome to America.

I wish I could have come to New York to greet you. Unfortunately I am in the midst of a strike and it compels me to stay here until the thing is finnished. Even then, it is extreemly doubtful whether I could get away.

However, I am certain, since I got the wire from Van Der Heeg, in reponse to the wire I sent you, that Dubinsky and tha Amalgameted will succeed in finding work for you that will be in line with what you should be doing- acquainting America with the terrible tragedy that happened in Germany.

If a lecture tour is arraigned for you, let me know what the boute will be and if it is anywhere near Kansas City, or even Chicago, I'll take the time and run down to greet you. For the moment, however, I don't dare to think of leaving.

I got a long letter from Fritz Kummer yesterday. In it he describes the terrible conditions that he ran away from, and the equally horrible conditions of our refugees in Belgium, where he is now. Fortunately his wife got his savings out of the labor bank,- so that he isn't exactly in want,- but the conditions of the others are horrible, simply horrible . He also wrote me of the killing of Engelbert Graf in the concentration camp. It is simply organized murder. I cannot think of it in any other terms.

Please give my love to Miss Heinrich, to Van der Heeg when you write to him, and let me know what your programme is. Little did I dream that on my return I would find myself in the last place you were in when you came to the states on your last visit,- I certainly hope that your lecture trip will head you westward at least to Chicago.

Abraham Plotkin greeting Martin Plettl upon his arrival in New York, November 1, 1933. *Source:* AP Coll., 6036/016, B2, F9, Kheel Center, Cornell University.

Valtin Hartig and his wife among friends, Clamart, France, June 1934. One of the leaders of the Transport and Municipal Workers' Union, Hartig found refuge in France after May 1933. On the back of the picture sent to Plotkin, Hartig had scribbled, "Have you heard something of Mrs Heinrich and Mr Plettl?" *Source:* AP Coll., 6036/016, B2, F21, Kheel Center, Cornell University.

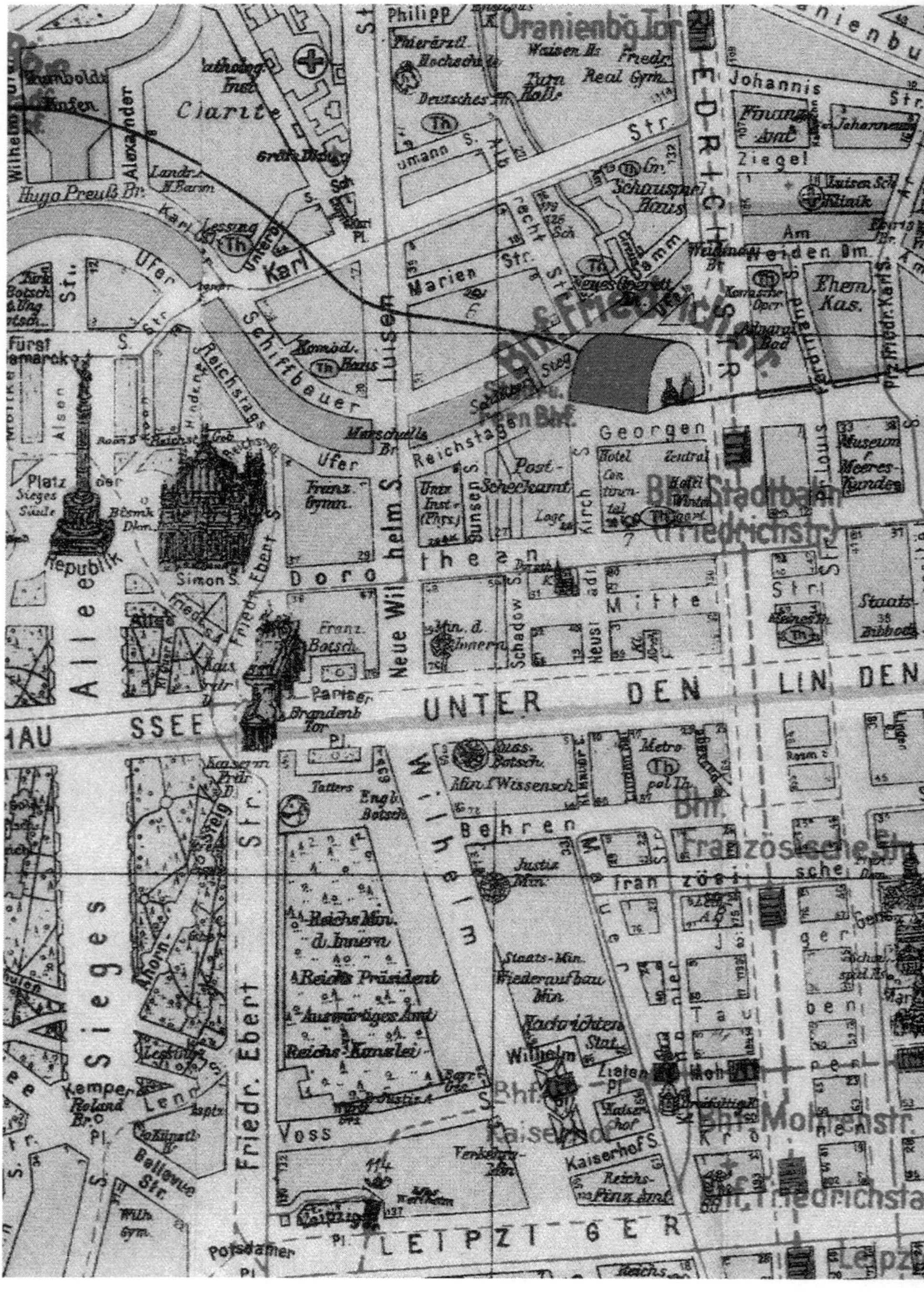

Map of Berlin (1930; reprint, Berlin: Pharus-Plan, 2006).

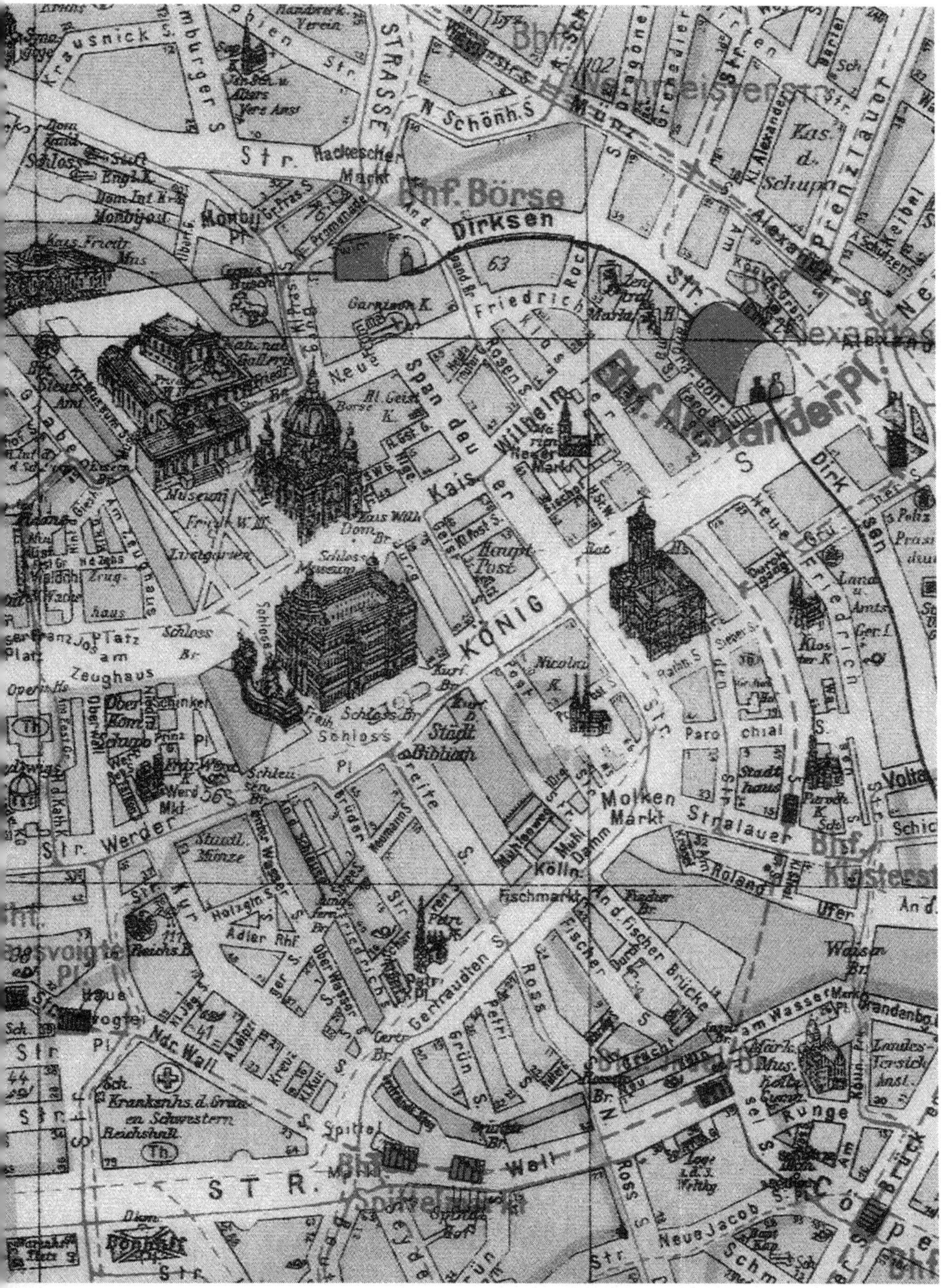

Krausnick S.
Hackescher Markt
N. Schönh. S
STRASSE
Bhf. Börse
Dirksen
Garnison K.
Friedrich
Neue
Span dau er
Kais er
Wilhelm
Neuer Markt
Münz
Kl. Alexander
Kas. d. Schupo
Prenzlauer
Alexander
Str.
Bhf. Alexander Pl.
Museum
Lustgarten
Zeughaus
Schloss
Schloss Museum
Schloss Br
Haupt Post
KÖNIG
Nicolai K.
Neue Friedrich
Klosterk.
Parochial
Stadthaus
Molken Markt
Stralauer
Bhf. Klosterstr
Werder
Str.
Städt. Münze
Breite
Brüder
Fischmarkt
An d. Fischer Brücke
Roland
Ufer
Waisen Br.
Gertrauden S.
Petri Pl.
Kur
Adler
Hausvoigtei Pl.
Krankenhs. d. Grauen Schwestern
Spittel
Wall
STR
Runge
Neue Jacob S.
Märk. Mus.
Landes-Versich. Anst.

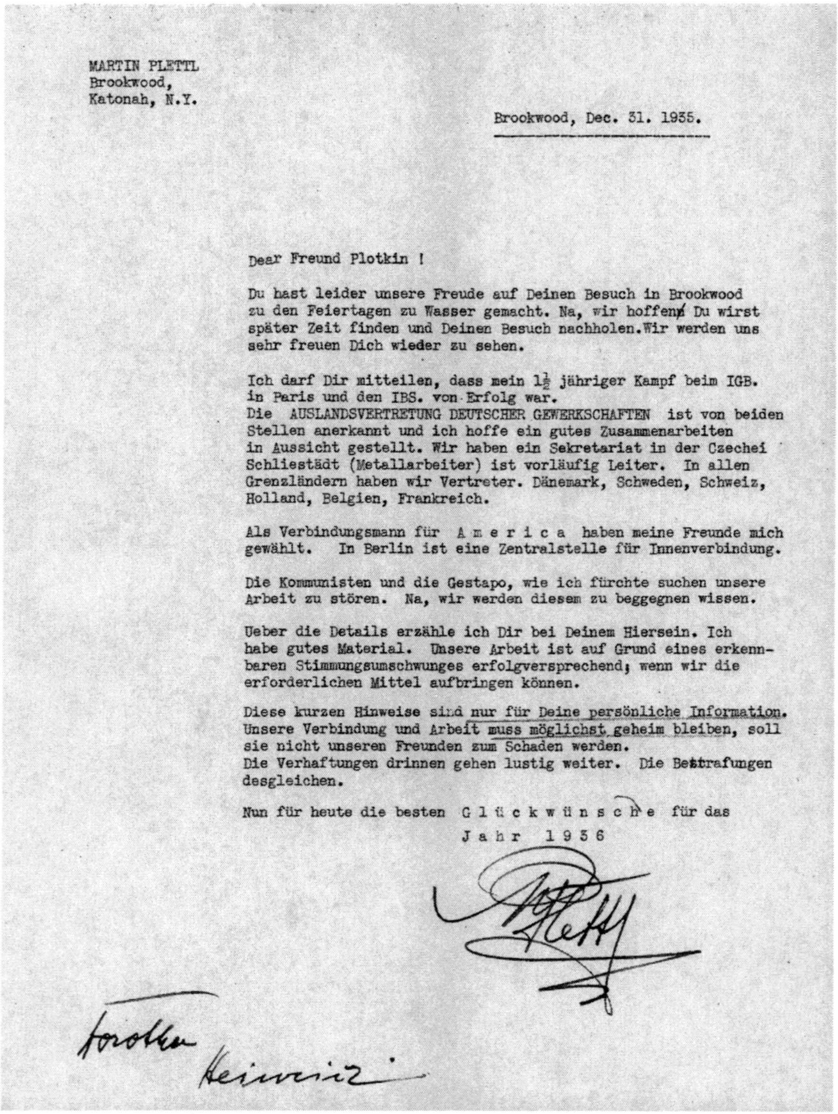

MARTIN PLETTL
Brookwood,
Katonah, N.Y.

Brookwood, Dec. 31. 1935.

Dear Freund Plotkin !

Du hast leider unsere Freude auf Deinen Besuch in Brookwood zu den Feiertagen zu Wasser gemacht. Na, wir hoffen Du wirst später Zeit finden und Deinen Besuch nachholen. Wir werden uns sehr freuen Dich wieder zu sehen.

Ich darf Dir mitteilen, dass mein 1½ jähriger Kampf beim IGB. in Paris und den IBS. von Erfolg war.
Die AUSLANDSVERTRETUNG DEUTSCHER GEWERKSCHAFTEN ist von beiden Stellen anerkannt und ich hoffe ein gutes Zusammenarbeiten in Aussicht gestellt. Wir haben ein Sekretariat in der Czechei Schliestädt (Metallarbeiter) ist vorläufig Leiter. In allen Grenzländern haben wir Vertreter. Dänemark, Schweden, Schweiz, Holland, Belgien, Frankreich.

Als Verbindungsmann für A m e r i c a haben meine Freunde mich gewählt. In Berlin ist eine Zentralstelle für Innenverbindung.

Die Kommunisten und die Gestapo, wie ich fürchte suchen unsere Arbeit zu stören. Na, wir werden diesem zu beggegnen wissen.

Ueber die Details erzähle ich Dir bei Deinem Hiersein. Ich habe gutes Material. Unsere Arbeit ist auf Grund eines erkennbaren Stimmungsumschwunges erfolgversprechend; wenn wir die erforderlichen Mittel aufbringen können.

Diese kurzen Hinweise sind nur für Deine persönliche Information. Unsere Verbindung und Arbeit muss möglichst geheim bleiben, soll sie nicht unseren Freunden zum Schaden werden.
Die Verhaftungen drinnen gehen lustig weiter. Die Bestrafungen desgleichen.

Nun für heute die besten G l ü c k w ü n s c h e für das J a h r 1 9 3 6

In this letter to Plotkin, written from Brookwood Labor College in New York on December 31, 1935, Martin Plettl announced that the Delegation of German Trade Unions in exile had been recognized by the International Federation of Trade Unions and by the International Trade Secretariats and that it had an office in the Czech Republic and representatives in all West European countries adjacent to Germany. He also informed Plotkin that he had been appointed liaison officer for the United States. *Source:* AP Coll., 6036/016, B2, F9, Kheel Center, Cornell University.

FEBRUARY 1933

◇◇◇◇◇
◇◇
◇

◇ *Wednesday, February 1, 1933*

B4, F6.2

This morning with William Verter, Berlin Secretary of the Hat and Millinery Workers' Union. Tried to discuss trade union matters with him, but the von Papen–Hitler bombshell overshadows everything else. Not even the visit of one of the oldest members of the organization, past ninety, a pensioner who gets his weekly allowance from the union, aroused much enthusiasm. The interest is centered in only one thing: what is Hitler going to do and how will the trade unions meet his onslaughts?

Verter takes a different view of Hitler and regards him as a tool of the von Papen–Hugenberg crowd. Von Papen's appointment as Vice-Chancellor—a new office created for him, in Verter's opinion—limits Hitler's power from the very start. Nevertheless, Hitler will get the cooperation of the von Papen–Hugenberg machine. It is a case of barter. Hitler will be given a free hand in dealing with the Communists and the trade unions so as to satisfy the Ruhr, and perhaps go in for a policy of inflation by way of compelling the Reichsbank to reduce the interest rate—dangerous because it will make Germany's debts rise in proportion to the inflation of currency—while von Papen and his machine can further their plans for a restoration of the monarchy. It sounds far-fetched. Rumors have it that armored cars already have been sent for the Kaiser!

This afternoon, the communist press carried the announcement that the Liebknecht House had been invested by the *Polizei*—although it was quite indefinite as to whether it was merely a raid or whether the *Polizei* had taken it over. At the same time, the communist press carried pictures of the *Polizei* scattering crowds that had gathered on Gormanstrasse, where the Labor Exchange office is located. It is in the neighborhood of Bülowplatz, where a demonstration had been broken by the *Polizei.*

In the afternoon, I swung over to Wedding to see how the crowds were taking it there. Everything was quiet and peaceful. The only sign of activity was a handbill given out by the Communists calling for a general strike against the *faschistische Terror.* The young man who gave me the leaflet told me that the workers in the Ruhr had been called out! I phoned several friends in the ADGB and they answered that it was quite likely that the Communists had called a strike, but so far they had very little information about it.

In the evening, along Friedrichstrasse, Communists were selling the *Rote Fahne,* the official newspaper of the Communists, without molestation. They again carried the announcement of the [siege] of the Liebknecht House, and that permission for a demonstration by them had been *verboten.* At the same time, the early morning newspapers that come about the same time as ours carried the announcement that the Reichstag [meeting] had been postponed and that a general election will be held on March 5th. [. . .]

◇ *Wednesday, February 1, 1933*

B4, F6.1

The Catholic Centrum has refused to sanction the Hitler-Hugenberg regime. Dr. Kaas, the leader of the Catholic Party, was received by Hitler today. Hitler asked a free hand for one year. Dr Kaas, it is understood, was willing, provided Hitler would give the guarantees asked for his party. This Hitler refused. The result was an immediate announcement calling a new election on Sunday, March 5th. The noon papers carried stories of rioting on Gormanstrasse and in the Alte Schönhauserstrasse, both in and around the Alexanderplatz section.

Spent the afternoon[1] with Kummer of the Metal Workers' Union, the largest trade union in Germany. Says, quite logically, that the trade unions cannot make a move until the government oversteps the legal lines marked out for it. Joint meetings between the trade union leaders and the Socialist Party are held every day. That they are alarmed goes without saying. In Hitler they see Mussolini and in Hugenberg they see the return of the monarchy. The Social Democratic Party in Germany, he contends, has its own historic

1. The time mentioned for this conversation overlaps that of the previous entry also dated February 1, where Plotkin reported spending the afternoon in Wedding.

origins, and is now tied hand and foot by them. The origin of the social democratic movement in Germany, he pointed out, was a struggle for the right to cast the ballot at a time when the workers were not enfranchised. It was a struggle for democracy in industry. This early faith in democracy is still the governing psychological factor in the ranks of the adherents of both the party members and the trade unionists. This faith is today endangered from three different angles: the Communists' sovietism through the dictatorship of the proletariat, the Hugenberg monarchists, and the Nazis. The Catholic Centrum, he added, is also a form of dictatorship in the offing, but somewhat more subtle. With the three leading parties in Germany denouncing democracy in the bitterest terms they can find, it is not difficult to understand why the future, to some of us, looks quite dreary. We are waiting for the other crowd to make a move that will warrant drastic action, and then you can look for a repetition of the general strike that met the Kapp putsch.[2]

While we were at it I asked Kummer to give me the details of the land relief scandal that like Pandora's box threatens to open and create much mischief for the Hugenberg crowd. His answer was quite simple. The East Prussian lands are very poor. Much of the acreage there has never been profitable. In the old days under the Kaiser, the landowners and nobility there were either subsidized, or had their taxes remitted, or were given sinecures in the government to help them go on. Many of them were army officers and formed the old Junker crowd. When the war was over and the revolution developed they found themselves [without] their former benefits and positions. It is this crowd that organized itself under Hugenberg and slowly started to fight their way back to power. Under Hugenberg they formed an alliance between the landowners and the large industrialists in the Ruhr, and up to the adoption of the Young treaty, Hugenberg had no competition. The Young treaty broke his party in two and gave Hitler the opportunity he wanted.[3]

---

2. The Kapp-Lüttwitz putsch (March 13, 1920). Organized by extreme-Right leaders General Walter von Lüttwitz and high Prussian civil servant Wolfgang Kapp, this attempt to seize power failed within four days, mainly because the general strike launched by the ADGB to protest against it on March 15 mobilized some twelve million persons.

3. Urged by Hugenberg, the nationalist Right managed that a referendum be held against the Young Plan on December 22, 1929. But the Right obtained only 13.8 percent of the votes, a failure for Hugenberg's party, the DNVP. The campaign, however, had allowed Hitler's party to assert itself among other nationalist forces and to publicize its claims. At the September 14, 1930, Reichstag elections, the DNVP polled 7 percent of the votes, whereas the NSDAP reached 18.3 percent. Approved by the Reichstag in 1930, the Young Plan did not apply for long; the 1931 Hoover moratorium suspended all international obligations of Germany.

Well, to cut a long story short, under the Brüning administration they got their man into the secretaryship of the Department of Agriculture and through his influence passed a relief act to help those landowners who were in a bad sort of way in that territory. By the way, there are not only large landowners but many small holdings that really are impoverished through the competition of both your country, Canada and Argentine. Later [Hans Schlange-Schöningen],[4] their own minister of agriculture, himself a landowner, resigned. He resigned under such peculiar circumstances, and with such strange criticism of the administration of the estates and the relief, that the Reichstag undertook to investigate the entire affair. Enough has been uncovered to show that those who really needed relief did not get it. Landowners with considerable political influence obtained money, as relief, with which to pay off their mortgages, others had many years of taxes rescinded, still others got so much that they let their former holdings go and bought new estates.[5]

The committee of the Reichstag would have reported their findings at the meeting of the Reichstag. It is virtually a godsend to the Hugenberg crowd that the meeting of the Reich is postponed until after the election. The Junkers, like the English members of the House of Lords, have always been regarded as reactionary, but with the tradition of personal and collective honesty; this would be a heavy blow to them, and doubtlessly would weaken them in any future elections. Now, of course, the facts cannot be charged against specific persons because we have not as yet an official report adopted by [the] Reichstag. One of their ministers, by the way, is now sunning himself on the Riviera. Expecting that the Reichstag would meet, he took a holiday so as to be out of the jurisdiction of the country. The man is honest. But he doesn't care to get himself involved against his own people. Do you suppose that Hugenberg would consent to share even an iota of his power with Hitler if he could have prevented this scandal from being broadcast throughout Germany in any other way? I doubt it. Hugenberg is not the man to share

4. Plotkin mistakenly wrote Shule Schanga, but he surely meant Hans Schlange-Schöningen (1886–1960), a DNVP member of the Prussian parliament from 1921 to 1928 and the Reichstag from 1924 to 1933. In 1928, he created an agrarian party, the Christlich-Nationale Bauern- und Landvolkspartei. A member of the second Brüning cabinet in 1931–32, he was in charge of the so-called *Osthilfe,* the relief for East Prussian agriculture. After 1945 his political career continued in the Christian Democratic Union.

5. Plotkin refers to the scandal of the *Osthilfe,* the credits allowed to East Prussian agriculture.

power with anyone. And if you will notice, the two departments through which he can best protect his people are not out of his direct control. He made certain that he would be appointed to both the Department of the Interior and the Department of Agriculture before the deal with Hitler was consummated. He holds both portfolios and will continue to hold them until the danger confronting his precious fellow monarchists is past.

◇ *Thursday, February 2, 1933*

B4, F6.1

Nine dead is the total for yesterday's street fighting throughout Germany. It is useless to keep track of the injured. A riot in Königsberg in the districts of the Nazis was started by the Communists. Faces were ripped open with knives, and heads were cracked with cobblestones. In the rioting, automobiles and trolleys were overturned. The police charged several times and in the melee two of them were injured. In Charlottenburg, a young Communist was stabbed to death. In West Berlin, a hangout of intellectuals had a gun match with the Nazis, and made the Nazis take backwater. In one place in the Ruhr, Wittenau, eleven Socialists were shot down by Nazis. Disturbances were also reported in Wanne Eickel,[6] Essen, Duisburg, and in other centers. The Communists called a general strike in the Ruhr, but so far there is no report. In Lübeck, in retaliation for the arrest of a socialist Reichstag member, the trade unions [ordered] a one-day general strike and succeeded sufficiently to compel the police to close the downtown streets. [. . .]

This evening the *Rote Fahne,* the official communist paper, was sold on the streets, and simultaneously came the announcement that all communist demonstrations were forbidden, and that the Karl Liebknecht House, the communist headquarters in Berlin, had been raided.

◇ *Thursday, February 2, 1933*

B4, F6.2

The atmosphere is so charged with politics and rumors that I was glad to get Dr. Victor Koehler's invitation to attend his court this morning. The political situation is exciting enough. But if there is anyone who really knows

---

6. Also a town in the Ruhr.

anything about it, that person is lost among the four million–odd inhabitants of Berlin. Everyone expects that the next hour will bring another wielding of the Hitler-Papen axe, but everyone is guessing and hoping that it will chop off the other man's head rather than his own. The rumor about the Ruhr is that the general strike called by the Communist Party was stillborn. The workers did not respond. Either they are waiting for orders from their unions, or are too discouraged to do anything. All demonstrations in the state of Prussia have been forbidden, and the rumor persists that the Karl Liebknecht House has been taken over by the *Polizei.* The application for demonstration on Sunday on the part of the SPD and the trade unions is waiting for an answer, and rumors in the air say that they will not get it. In the midst of all these rumors and counterrumors, it was therefore quite a relief to attend a court session that was far removed from the excitement of the streets.

*Dr. Koehler's labor court handled cases arising from disputes between workers and the officers of the labor exchange (*Arbeitsamt*) in matters of unemployment insurance or emergency relief. If the labor exchange officers refused to certify that a worker was unemployed through no fault of his or her own, then the worker was denied insurance or relief. It was the role of the court to review the case by listening to all parties (employer, worker, and labor exchange officer). After attending several cases that morning, Plotkin remarked that the court provided a legal safeguard against the decisions of the* Arbeitsamt *if they were arbitrary or autocratic. Altogether, this system, which included possibilities of further appeal in higher courts, he thought efficiently offered checks against discrimination and bad will.*

◇ *Friday, February 3, 1933*

B4, F6.1

Communist demonstrations were forbidden yesterday. This morning brought the news that the Socialist Party demonstration, for which permission had already been obtained, [is] also *verboten.* The *Rote Fahne* has been suspended for a week. The communist papers in the Ruhr and in Breslau have been suspended for various periods ranging from two to four weeks. Communist meetings will be permitted indoors under the strict surveillance of the police, and the police are instructed to close them if the speakers advocate either a general strike or utter treason utterances. I was in the Gewerkschaftshaus when the news spread that Sunday's meeting had been *verboten.* The Gewerkschaftshaus corresponds roughly to one of our labor temples. The news spread like wildfire, and on every hand questions arose—"What next?"

Following this announcement, a declaration from Hindenburg ends the easy party qualifications until now extant in Germany. Anyone who could get five hundred signatures tacked onto a petition had the right to form a party. Hindenburg's order will have three effects. It will, in the future, require 60,000 signatures for a new party to enter the field, cut down the number of parties participating in the present election to not more than 12 (there were thirty in the last election), and draw much clearer [lines] between the parties of the right and the parties of the left. The "splinters," as these offshoot parties have been called, will largely disappear.

◇ *Saturday, February 4, 1933*

B4, F6.1

The socialist *Vorwärts* was this morning suspended for three days. Yesterday it published its manifesto, it criticized Hitler's policies, and in commenting on Hitler's acceptance in America remarked that "no doubt it left the Eskimos speechless." The *Vorwärts* immediately was given to understand that to criticize Hitler or Hugenberg as individuals was one thing, but to criticize them now is to criticize the government! Later in the day, the ministry moved to dismiss the Prussian Landtag, the Prussian Diet. Von Papen, who has been appointed commissioner for Prussia and at the same time Vice-Chancellor for Germany, wants to hold the elections in Prussia at the same time as the national elections. The Prussian government must consent to this act, and since it is about evenly divided between the three major parties, Socialists, Nazis and Communists, it remains to be seen how they will take to the idea.

Tomorrow the Nazis will hold their demonstration in the Lustgarten for the two men who were killed in the torchlight procession last Monday.

The vote on dissolving the Prussian Diet taken today was the first setback suffered so far by the Hitler-Hugenberg crowd. The motion of the Nazis to dissolve was lost by 214 against 196. For the time being it ends the efforts of the crowd in power to grasp the powers both for the nation and the state of Prussia at the same time. The Diet may be dissolved in only one of two ways: by a vote of the members or by a vote of two out of the three men representing the largest parties in the Diet. Centrum's leader Dr. Konrad Adenauer[7]

7. Konrad Adenauer (1876–1967), a statesman, mayor of Cologne, and leader of the Catholic Zentrum in the Prussian Diet. Imprisoned by the Nazis (1933–34), he withdrew from politics during the Third Reich and after the war became president of the Christian Democrats and chancellor of the Federal Republic of Germany from 1949 to 1963.

and Otto Braun of the Socialist Party voted together against the Nazi Hans Kerril.[8] When the matter was submitted to the Diet, the Communists threw their votes in with the Centrum and the Socialists.

It may be that Hitler will appeal to Hindenburg to dissolve the Diet in order to get around the legal technicalities. It is questionable whether it comes within his constitutional powers to do so. We will know more about that later.

The two definite things that the Hitler-Hugenberg crowd has so far formulated, and not in unison, as a relief program for the country are: compulsory labor for the young of Germany, and a moratorium for the agricultural districts. The first is a definite move towards the militarization of the young in Germany. I have seen the camps of the "free volunteer service for the young in Germany" and if they are not a modified form of military service I must be blind. The second has been already somewhat hesitantly denied. While it would and should meet with the approval of the Hugenberg crowd, the Hitlerites don't seem to be particularly enthusiastic. The lukewarm denial that was made came from their ranks. The Bourse[9] and the banks naturally reacted unfavorably and are worried.

The suspension of socialist newspapers continues apace as do the killings. In Weimar the *Volk* and the *Tribune* were suspended, the first for three days, the second for 14 days. In Hannover, the *Volkswill* was suspended by the police president. In Jena the *Volk* and in Cologne the *Rheinische Zeitung* were likewise suspended for three days. Each of these newspapers [was] suspended for publishing the social democratic manifesto at the same time that the *Vorwärts* published it in Berlin. An order is being prepared, according to newspaper announcements, that will give Hitler and Hugenberg the full power to throttle the opposition press.

Simultaneously with the rapid fascizing of the state comes the news that those who have not given or will not give complete adherence to the new state of things will have to make way for Nazi or Hugenberg satellites. Hugenberg takes over the portfolios of National Economy, Agriculture, Crisis, and the portfolio of Labor for the Prussian government. This means that he is now holding four portfolios. The police in Berlin have been placed in charge of Count von Heldorf,[10] an old hand at Communist raiding, who already has

8. Hans Kerril, a Nazi politician, was a member of the Prussian Landtag.

9. Stock exchange.

10. Wolf Heinrich Count von Heldorf held important functions during the Nazi regime.

served notice on the police that they will have to make allegiance to Nazis or get out. At the same time, Prof. Rust[11] has been charged with the task of bringing the Nazi culture into the educational system of Prussia.

And the killings go merrily on. Two more late last night. Groups of Nazis and Communists, meeting each other in Charlottenburg, shot it out. Alfred Kollasitch was shot to death in the fracas. A similar incident in Neukölln ended with the death of Emil Sawinski, two seriously wounded and a number of other casualties. These were in the suburbs of Berlin. No reports are available on what happened in the other cities.

◇ *Sunday, February 5, 1933*

B4, F6.1

The air has suddenly turned from one in which one had a sense of personal freedom to an air of heavy feudalism. In spite of the rain, several hundred thousand people stood waiting for Hitler and the Crown Prince[12] to pass on their way from the Cathedral where their dead chief[13] lay to the cemetery. As I stood in the Crown Prince Museum,[14] I had a chance to look through one of the windows from which I had an excellent view of the Lustgarten where the Nazis and Steel Helmets were paying their respects to their dead leader. From the walls of the Kaiser's palace to the Dom the troops made a solid mass of brown, while the slow music of the Nazi funeral march joined in with the chimes of the Cathedral. There must have been at least fifty thousand troops, while the crowds under umbrellas packed the street Unter den Linden to the University of Berlin and from there on Charlottenstrasse all the way to the Lustgarten and through there to the cemetery.

---

11. Bernard Rust was a Nazi schoolteacher appointed by Hitler in 1933 to be minister of science, arts, and education for Prussia. In 1934 he was elevated to the post of minister of education for the Reich and remained in this position until 1945, when he committed suicide.

12. Crown Prince Wilhelm of Germany (1882–1951), son of former Kaiser Wilhelm II. In 1918, when the revolution broke out in Germany, both Kaiser Wilhelm II and the crown prince signed the document of abdication and went into exile in Holland. In 1923, the former crown prince had returned to Germany after giving assurances that he would not engage in politics.

13. SA chief Hans Maikowski and policeman Josef Zauritz had been killed on January 30, 1933, in a riot at Charlottenburg. They were given a state funeral on February 5.

14. Kronprinzenpalais, palace of the crown prince. See November 27, 1932.

One notes at the same time the much more bellicose utterances of the Hugenberg crowd. They are the real masters of the situation. If what I am told is true they have headed off Hitler from again running for the presidency and are every day tying him down closer to the royalist movement. Three of the royal family were in the parade today.

The evening newspapers brought the news that the *Bürgermeister,* social democrat, had been murdered by a seventeen-year-old boy.[15] Braun's cabinet in the Diet of Prussia has been set aside and Braun is going to take the case to the Supreme Court in Leipzig.[16] The order giving Hitler authority to suppress the newspapers has been signed. Göring, the state Commissioner of Police for Prussia, has ordered the police to [make] an oath of allegiance to the Nazis. In addition, four more were killed and twenty-four wounded over the weekend in the different cities of Germany.

◇ *Monday, February 6, 1933*

B4, F6.1

The Braun cabinet in Prussia was set aside by Hindenburg himself. Braun is appealing to the Supreme Court in Leipzig to confirm his authority over the Prussian Diet—confirmed once before by this court on an appeal from a decision of von Papen limiting Braun's powers. It will be interesting to see how the same court, handling the same problem, will decide in this atmosphere of reaction.

---

15. This was a false rumor. The last democratically elected mayor of Berlin was Dr. Heinrich Sahm of the German National People's Party. At the beginning of Nazi power, he was maintained in office under the surveillance of Nazi state commissioner Julius Lippert. In 1934, all Berlin elective positions were abolished, and the following year Lippert was appointed mayor to replace Sahm. After the March 12, 1933, municipal elections in Berlin, in which the Nazis had not obtained a majority (38.2 percent) in spite of the reign of terror they had created, the Social Democratic and Communist elected officials were prevented from exercising their functions.

16. Removed from power by von Papen on July 20, 1932, Otto Braun had sought redress from the Supreme Court. But the court in October confirmed the legitimacy of von Papen's action. Officially, Braun remained president of the Prussian government *(Ministerpräsident),* but his power was merely formal, real authority being exerted by the *Reichskommissar* (von Papen, Schleicher, and finally Göring). In February 1933, Göring obtained from Hindenburg an executive order that ended Braun's official function. Braun appealed to the Supreme Court again. The following month he took refuge in Switzerland.

All of the kiosks this morning carried the appeal of the "government" to be kept in power for four years. I don't know whether this method has been used in the past but it is new to me. The government issued the statement of appeal to the country for votes under the signature of the government of Germany and not that of a political party or a group of political parties. While the parties of the left are being harassed and repressed, the right to hold meetings interfered with, the freedom of the press so limited that there is nothing for them to say on political matters except to print the official statements of the government, the parties of the Right wage their campaign with all the authority of the government behind it, even to the printed propaganda distributed on the streets. It would be interesting to know who is paying the bill.

The order regulating the press is much stronger than the von Papen orders of last year that Schleicher withdrew. All of the papers carry the summary on the front page. The reasons that may be invoked for the suspensions of newspapers, weekly or monthly periodicals, are so broad that the Press Association already has voiced its protest. Hartig tells me that on Wednesday all the labor papers and the representatives of the other national weekly and monthly publications in Germany will meet to define their policy and to determine whether they can obey this order and still carry on their work. The order forbids the publication of anything that may disclose the military secrets of the country. To tell the truth about the "free service"[17] camps in which two hundred and fifty thousand of the German youth are being given military training is therefore in violation of the order! So would the charge that the Hitler-Hugenberg crowd is planning "to relieve" the unemployment problem by sending another half million of German youths to these camps! Calling on the people to refuse to obey the law; advocating the use of violence; to insult or to show malice to the representatives of the state or to the church; to advocate a general strike or a strike in any of the basic industries are a few of the reasons on which Hitler and Hugenberg can now go ahead and suppress the press of the nation.

Spent the afternoon with the people in the Central Jewish Citizens' Committee. Inasmuch as they represent the Jews in Germany that are naturalized they represent one point of view. The Jew that is not naturalized is today quite beyond the pale. The nonnaturalized Jew is hounded and frequently beaten by the Nazis on one hand, and finds himself shut out of most of the relief that is given to the others around him. Not infrequently, he is

17. Voluntary.

told to go back to the country that he came from, as we say at home to our foreigner. Hitler, as our own authorities do, constantly threatens to deport them, and the only thing that has held him back is the fact that such a policy might result in having a good many more Germans who are in Poland and in Russia shipped back to Germany. The difficulties of obtaining German citizenship are so hard that it is almost impossible for those of the first two generations of immigrants to obtain it. Only a child born of native-born parents is a natural citizen. The others have to wait ten years before they can apply, and then they are citizens if they succeed of the state in which they apply.[18] They remain foreigners in the rest of Germany.

The Central organization of [Jewish] citizens therefore represents the wealthier Jews of Germany. They showed me much of the statistical data they have gathered which effectively answers the Hitler charges that the Jews control the banks and the economic life of Germany, and with rather sly humor, one of them told me that Hitler himself does not believe it, but that it made excellent propaganda. Having heard some of it I could well believe it. Strange as it may seem and as it seemed to me, they were not concerned very much now that Hitler has come to the front. Their attitude is that it was bound to come, that he can't in an official capacity do anything worse to them than already has been done unofficially and that it is best perhaps that the Hitler fire run its course.

Since the order *"verboting"* the press also carried stringent orders regulating meetings and demonstrations, the city is quite excited about tomorrow's meeting of the Social Democrats. Some say that the police will forbid the meeting at the last minute and provoke rioting so as to furnish them with an excuse for more drastic action. Others say that with half of Berlin marching to the meeting, the police wouldn't dare. Since the deliberate provocation to the Communists on the 22nd of last month, I believe the police dare to do anything except that which isn't politically expedient for them to do.

Six more dead and thirty seriously wounded. Killings are reported in Schöneberg, where a woman was shot to death; from Stazfurt,[19] Breslau, Chemnitz, Mannheim, München, Düsseldorf and Bochum, riots, killings and wounded are reported.

---

18. The local state *(Land)*.

19. Possibly Stassfurt.

◇ *Tuesday, February 7, 1933*

B4, F6.1

Two more dead—one in Hamburg and the other in Harburg-Wilhelmsburg. The deaths are becoming such a common affair that it is doubtful whether they are reported.

Two more blows. One at the freedom of the foreign press. The other at the freedom of Prussia. The first gives the Hitler-Hugenberg crowd the right to exclude foreign papers from circulating in Germany, the other was the presidential order setting aside the Prussian cabinet. This von Papen tried once before and was overruled by the Supreme Court. Now Hindenburg as President did it. Whether the Supreme Court will now listen to Braun's plea is uncertain. Von Papen already has announced the dissolution of all communal governments in Prussia and announced further that they will hold elections on the 12th of March. Since he has already announced that the Prussian state elections will be held on the same day as the national election, it is presumed that he will go ahead with his program, unless a court order prohibits both him and Hindenburg from going ahead. It is precisely as if Hoover would set aside the government of the state of N.Y. and order new elections if political expediency demanded it.

Former President of the Reichstag Löbe,[20] who has been the President of the Reichstag from the revolution of 1918 until last July, has written to the Nazi President of the Reichstag denouncing the present campaign methods of the Nazi-Hugenberg parties. In his letter he denounces the efforts to take the election by storm and force. Germany, he intimates, is heading for a catastrophe that will shake it to its foundations unless the present efforts to repress and suppress opponents of the parties in power [are suspended]. The terror is outstripping all sense of freedom, and unless halted, will have the most terrible consequences for the entire German people. What reply, or whether any reply, will come from Göring is as yet unknown. It is hardly likely that he will answer. Only a day or so ago he demanded that the Prussian police, whose chief he is, in addition to being the president of the last Reichstag, swear allegiance to the Nazis or get out.

---

20. Paul Löbe (1875–1967), a Social Democratic politician, president of the Reichstag from 1920 to 1932, and chairman of the commission to investigate the relief scandal in East Prussia. He was arrested in 1933 and withdrew from public life during the Nazi years. After 1945 he was elected again on an SPD ticket in the Bundestag (1949–53).

At noon I began to circulate through the districts where the parades were to start for the meeting in the Lustgarten. Nine different parades from different parts of the city, wholly of workingmen, starting at different hours because of the difference in the distances they had to march, some of them had to march five miles to the meeting and five miles back again. The streets were crowded and the tenseness in the air made me feel that it would be difficult to control the crowds once they got started.

At 4:45 I joined the sidewalk crowd that walked along with the paraders out of Wedding. It was difficult to get through the crowds that jammed the sidewalks. Police on horseback calmly paraded along with the marchers, keeping them in line, and at the same time looking over the heads of the crowd to see whether at any point any disturbances developed. They marched from Gustav-Meyerallee to [Elsasserstrasse], then down to the Museum and turned South alongside the canal to the rear of the platform along the wall of the Kaiser's palace. Circulating around the square were thousands of police, rifles slung across their shoulders and the usual *"Tanz"* trucks with their quota of rifled *Polizei* and machine-gun equipment—and powerful searchlights trained on the crowd so that everything stood in the light.

Leaving the Wedding group I pushed my way though the Lustgarten to get an idea of the crowd whose thunderous singing was now filling the Lustgarten with the International. I noticed that the street opening to Unter den Linden was closed and standing at the bridgehead were hundreds of *Polizei* in uniform whose presence was slightly screened by the men on horseback in front of them. The proletariat must not be permitted to march down the sacred precincts of their wealthy German overlords and it came back to me that on Sunday the Nazis were permitted to parade down this very street . . . also that when in the museum I noticed that the pictures in the front rooms had been removed, not all of them but a number of the rooms were entirely closed and a number of the pictures in the other rooms taken upstairs.

And as I circled around, I noticed that the museum steps on the north side of the Lustgarten were filled with armed police. I then turned to the statue of one of the Fredericks facing the Kaiserschloss and the speakers' platform, again the inevitable police. And on the steps of the Dom—the leading cathedral of the Lutheran Church in Germany—stood the police in military formation—waiting for the first sign of disorder or the first misstatement that would justify the dispersing of the meeting. And as I circled around, I noticed that every entrance was closed.

As at the meeting of the Iron Front,[21] the Lustgarten was too small. Every inch of space was taken and it was with the greatest difficulty that I could shove through the crowd. I was told afterward that twice as many tried to get in as were in. Aside from the cheering crowds on the sidewalks there must have been close to three hundred thousand who either were inside the Lustgarten or tried to get in.

Otto Wels[22] spoke calmly but effectively. He had to be careful. Each word meant a possible excuse for [dispersal] of the meeting and a possible bloodbath unparalleled in the political history of Berlin. He repeated the slogan that "Berlin belongs to the Reds." He went on to enumerate the advantages that have been won by German Socialists and trade unionists for the workers of Germany during and after the revolution. He then pointed out how step by step since the Brüning regime these advantages have been slowly undermined. Unemployment insurance practically destroyed under von Papen, and at the same time efforts to destroy the legal manner of making wage agreements compulsory to both sides, that labor has fought for since it was first organized and won in 1918, and again confirmed in the Constitution of Weimar, and again confirmed in 1922. Step by step he led through the experiences of political intrigue and economic machination against the standards of the German workers since the Social Democratic Party lost control of the Reichstag. Having reached that point and [having] only a few minutes in which to continue (the speaker is limited to twenty minutes), he turned to his audience and announced—under no circumstances will [we permit] ourselves to return to either the monarchy of the past or to live under a fascism equally dictatorial. The Iron Front Is Alive and Ready. Let Hitler and Hugenberg measure the course they are pursuing. Let them think twice before they continue the road that leads to efforts to destroy the rights of the German nation. They have been answered once before. They will be answered again. The threats contained in these words were clearly understood. The audience understood them only too clearly. Spontaneously fists flew into the air, someone yelled *"Freiheit"*[23] and again fists were flung into the air and three times in succession fists and *"Freiheit"* split the air. At

21. Plotkin refers to the January 29 meeting of the Iron Front.

22. Otto Wels (1873–1939), president of the SPD and member of parliament (1920–30). After 1933, he headed the SPD representation in exile, first in Saarland, then in Prague, and later in Paris, where he died.

23. Freedom. *Freiheit* was one of the main slogans used by the Social Democrats.

that moment, I began to notice an uneasy movement through the crowd. How would the *Polizei* take it? The man on the platform had made the threat of revolution, and even the intimation of revolution was *verboten.* And the memory of Dresden, where only recently the police shot into the crowd and killed 9 workers, is still too fresh, and so are the dozens of killings that have developed since a week ago when Hitler stepped into office. But Wels is too shrewd a tactician in the handling of crowds. That is why he was chosen to speak at this meeting. Having made his subtle threat that could be interpreted in half a dozen different manners, he then proceeded again. This time with a pleading for the solidarity of the workers. The crowd understood this also and cheered every reference to the need of standing together under the banner of the Iron Front. Five minutes later he announced that the crowd would sing the German socialist marching song[24] and march out of the Lustgarten. He had stated the case for his people, he had hinted at what may be in store for Germany if the means used by the group in power step beyond the limits of the constitution, and had sent them on their way home without a mishap.

On the way out, I met with a group of trade unionists with whom I talked about the meeting in general and politics in particular. The most interesting opinion came from Hartig of the Transport and Municipal Workers' [Union]. "You must not get excited at what you see in Germany," he told me. "We have passed through such crises time and again. True, it looks more serious this time than in the past because the state apparatus is in the hands of the reactionaries, but a monarchy they do not dare declare, and as long as there is a shadow of constitutionalism in Germany there is hope that we will come through. You need only look at what is happening to Herr Hitler to realize that these two cannot live together in peace very long. Give them time and they will be drawing swords between the browns[25] and the steels,[26] killing each other as they are killing Socialists and Communists today. We are not getting excited. Not until either group attempts a *coup d'État.* Then will be time enough to get excited!" I wonder.

---

24. Probably the Workers' Hymn *(Arbeiterhymne),* often sung in the meetings of the Reichsbanner. Its words had been written in 1915 by Hermann Claudius and the music composed by Michael Englert in 1916.

25. The Nazis.

26. The Steel Helmet (Stahlhelm).

◇ *Wednesday, February 8, 1933*

B4, F6.2

Braun has taken the case to the Supreme Court of Germany and a hearing will be held on Tuesday of next week. Preparations for the election in Prussia are going ahead in the meanwhile. The atmosphere is such that no one believes that the Supreme Court will rule against Hindenburg. Nevertheless the case is having serious effects on sentiment on other states than Prussia. Both Bavaria and Hessen are talking of joining with Braun. They must have some ground for believing that, if this goes through with Prussia, Hindenburg will then appoint a Reichscommissioner to dissolve their state governments and call for new elections on March 5.

At the meeting of the commission appointed by the Reichstag to investigate the manipulation of the relief funds in East Prussia, Dr. Löbe, former president of the Reichstag and now chairman of the commission, had to adjourn the meeting. The Nazis, in agreement with the Hugenbergers, turned the meeting into a riot, calling the other members of the commission traitors and Jews. The exposure of the mishandling and stealing of funds by the Junkers, coming at this time, would have serious effects on the Junkers' constituencies.

The *Vorwärts* is quite jubilant over yesterday's meeting and feels quite proud over both the [number of] attendants which is estimated at several hundred thousands and [the fact] that there were no casualties. As a matter of fact there were a few clubbed. I did not see it but was told of it this morning. At one end of the Lustgarten when the crowd was cheering for *"Freiheit,"* a group of young Communists shouted for the Red Front. The police promptly got after them and scattered them with their nightsticks. Having watched a number of Social Democratic meetings in the past and having seen the tolerance of the Social Democratic brethren to their competitors of the left, I am certain that the SPD had nothing whatever to do with the violence of the police. It was a piece of gratuity on the part of the police department, for which there was as much justification as there is for a rabbi to laugh when one of his coreligionists goes over to the Nazis.

The propaganda of the Nazis against the Jews is still going strong. The *Berliner Beobachter*[27] today is quite indignant because a Polish Jew has been employed for seven whole years in some minor capacity, and protests ve-

27. More likely the *Völkischer Beobachter,* which Joseph Goebbels directed.

hemently against permitting them to work for the state in any capacity. The same newspaper denounces the Jews who have been admitted to the University of Hannover and demands their exclusion!

◇ *Thursday, February 9, 1933*

B4, F6.2

Seldte,[28] minister of labor of the Hitler-Hugenberg regime, announced again today his program to develop the *Arbeitsdienst.* The literal translation means "work service" but doesn't tell the whole story. It means that the present camps for the youth of Germany, in which there are at present 250,000 young men between the ages of 16 and 25 getting pretty close to the equivalent of military training, will be enlarged to include another half million of Germany's young men. These boys get, in addition to their food and uniforms (absolutely the replica of the uniforms worn by the prisoners in San Quentin penitentiary), six cents a day for which they work six hours on roads etc., and then spend four hours in "sport" drills.

At the same time comes the announcement of the Labor Exchange that the number of registered unemployment is 6,014,000. Except as an index of the number of unemployed, the figure does not warrant the feeling of some satisfaction that has been expressed by some of the newspapers here. While the drop as compared to last year is infinitesimally small (28,000), the average unemployment in 1932 over 1931 is between 20 and 25% higher.

Stood with hundreds of others at Charlotten and Dorotheenstrasse watching the bloodfest between the Republican and the Nazi students of the University of Berlin. Dorotheenstrasse is the street back of the University and between Charlotten and the street east of it there is a small *Platz* named after Hegel. The Republican students decided to have a bonfire through which to express their sorrow over the death of a fellow Republican student killed recently in a students' riot in Breslau. When the Nazis got wind of it this morning, they streamed out of the University at eleven o'clock and then everybody's fist tried to wreak havoc on everybody else's nose. Seven were badly beaten before the riot was over. Later another riot, this time between Communists and Nazis, resulted in four getting bullet wounds. This riot, in Bratankerplatz, sent two children and two men to hospital after the police

28. Franz Seldte (1882–1947), a Nationalist politician, founder of the Stahlhelm (Steel Helmet), and labor minister through the Third Reich. He was indicted at Nuremberg but died before the trial.

fired twenty shots. And outside of an effort on the part of 200 Nazis in Braunschweig to break up a meeting of the Social Democratic Party (they succeeded), out of which seven of the Nazis were taken to the hospital severely wounded, the day passed off quietly. [. . .]

◇ *Friday, February 10, 1933*

B4, F6.2

Tried to get into Hitler's mass meeting in the Sportpalast this evening and got there too late. I was there promptly at six o'clock. The meeting was slated to start at eight! When I got there the streets leading up to the hall were already closed to the crowds by arm-linked police who stretched clear across the streets. Just as well. Heard him on the radio, and was keenly disappointed. Said almost the identical things his friend and campaign manager Goebbels has said in the meetings I have attended. Attacked Marxism and accused [the Marxists][29] of having lost the war, etc. Said it was too early to submit a program and that to develop one would take a long time. Wound up with a fervent plea for a united Germany, and to be given four years in which to remake Germany and bring her back to the strength and prestige that she had before the war. Others who have heard him on previous occasions tell me that it is not the same Hitler. That he did not speak extemporaneously as he was wont to do in the past. They felt that the heavy hand of von Papen was quite in evidence both in the written speech and the manner of the delivery. Nevertheless I am sorry I missed it.

On the way there I almost got into a small riot of my own. The Communist headquarters is located on Bülowplatz and the station where I had to get out of the subway is named Bülowstrasse. With a car full of Nazis in uniform I made the mistake of asking one of them whether I was on the right train for Bülowplatz! Fortunately for me they recognized me as an *Ausländer,*[30] otherwise it would not have been very easy for me. Anyway let's hope I have more luck making the Hugenberg meeting tomorrow.

Dr. Frick[31] has forbidden all radio stations to permit anyone to broadcast political speeches. The Hitlerites and the Hugenbergs will broadcast as

---

29. In Nazi terminology, "Marxist" generally designated the Social Democrats.

30. Foreigner.

31. Wilhelm Frick (1877–1946), a Nazi politician and member of Hitler's cabinet in 1933 as minister of the interior. He was condemned to death by the Nuremberg tribunal and executed.

representatives of the government! It seems to me quite silly. The Communists will do their broadcasting out of Russia and the Social Democrats will broadcast either out of Austria, Czechoslovakia or France, or any one of the half-dozen countries around here.

◇ *[Saturday, February 11], 1933*

B4, F6.2

The kiosks this morning were surrounded.[32] Apparently there was some political announcement that held their interest so I edged into one of the crowds. On the kiosk was a manifesto signed by the leading writers demanding that the Communist Party and the Social Democratic Party combine in one united front. Among the most prominent of the signatures was that of Heinrich Mann,[33] the brother of Thomas Mann. [. . .][34]

Rumors are at it again. This time it concerns the status of the Communist Party. One group believes that Hitler will wait until the 15th and on that day outlaw the Communist Party. Just why he will wait until that day is not quite clear except that by waiting until the last moment when the lists can be filed, the other parties can be caught napping and fail to hand in lists to take care of the additional votes they may get in case of the removal of the Communists from the ballot. The real reason may be to forestall the appearance of a new party organized by the Communists, under a new name and a new slogan—although it would seem to me that they would do so anyway as a matter of precaution against being declared illegal, and being left without a party of their own in the field. Others have it that after the [lists] of candidates of the different parties are filed, the Hitler people will wait until the day before election and at the last moment disqualify the Communists in order to create confusion so that many of them will not vote altogether. The most persistent report of all deals with the election itself, and one for which I think there is considerable ground. And that is that on election day, perhaps the day before, the Nazis and Steel Helmets will make every effort

---

32. This entry is dated February 10, 1933, in the manuscript. However, the sequence of events more logically situates it on the eleventh.

33. Heinrich Mann (1871–1950), a writer, Thomas Mann's brother, president of the writers' section of the Prussian Academy of Fine Arts, and author of many novels of social critique. He left Germany for France in 1933 and emigrated to the United States in 1940.

34. One page is missing in the manuscript.

to so terrorize those districts in which they are weak that through sheer terror they will capture the election. That the day will be a bloody one for Germany is certain. Each political party, whether Communist, Socialist, Nazi or National, each of them have their militant forces, whether they are the *Reichsbanner* men of the trade union socialist groups, shock troops of the Nazis, steel helmets of the Hugenberg crowd or the uniformed red shock troops of the Communists. Add to this the fact that the police have been completely terrorized so that they have had to swear allegiance to the new government or get out, and a number of them have been forced out, and it is easy to be seen that they will, out of fear of losing their jobs if nothing else, pay less attention to the violence of their new masters than under ordinary circumstances. It promises to be the bloodiest election ever held in Germany.

And speaking of elections, the straw vote taken among the university students has shown a decided fall in the Hitler vote and a large increase in the Catholic Centrum vote.

Spent the afternoon with Plettl, president of the German Clothing Workers, and with Van der Heeg, president of the Holland clothing workers.[35] As usual, on Saturday afternoons, we went to one of the forests, walked for hours and then found an inn facing one of the numerous lakes and talked politics over coffee. Van der Heeg and I both jumped on Plettl for the seeming calmness of both the Socialists and the trade unionists. Nothing that we could and did say disturbed his placid calm. So far the campaign was just so much talk and neither the Socialist Party nor the trade unions would permit themselves to be stampeded into overt acts. I asked a dozen alternative questions—what would happen if Hitler did this or did that—to all of which he smiled and said that every one of the questions I raised had been fully discussed and the possibilities weighed. He did add, rather significantly, that in the event of a real emergency, the machinery of the trade union movement was so geared that every part of Germany could be reached within thirty minutes and every party of the ADGB machine in motion in an hour in every part of the nation. He also intimated that Hindenburg would not tolerate any dictatorship that was established through either sheer terror or through unconstitutional means.

I seem to be in tough luck this week. Before I got back to town from the hike in the forest and the conversation that followed in the inn, it was too

35. Tonnis Van der Heeg (1886–1958) was also the president of the International Federation of Clothing Workers.

late to go into the Hugenberg meeting. Here again the crowds were so thick that one had to be there at five in order to get in. Moreover I was confronted with the fact of [our] noted visitor from Holland [Tonnis Van der Heeg] to whom the idea of going to a meeting of Royalists was almost unmentionable. As a matter of fact it is hard for my German friends to understand the strange curiosity I have, but ordinarily they are tolerant. Plettl would no more think of going into a Hitler meeting, not speaking of a Hugenberg meeting, than of putting his hand into a whirling machine. We compromised therefore by going into the Scala, a variety theater of immense proportions where for 65 cents we had excellent orchestra seats. The acts were on a par with, if not better than, those seen at the Palace in New York. But even with the cheapness of the admission it was difficult for me to locate, except during the intermission when I went into the lobby, a few working men and their wives. The theater in Germany today is definitely a middle-class and tourist institution. The workers have no money for it. As we left the theater both of my friends commented on it that for the first time in their experience in a German variety show, the master of ceremony whose political sallies was one of the features seemed careful in treading on anyone's corns. In my own experience here, I have found that these masters of ceremony were so broad in their criticism of the administration that I wondered why such freedom was allowed them and was told that this institution is as old as Germany itself. Something was wrong. Either he was a Nazi himself or was a little timid about stepping on hot coals.

◇ *[Sunday], February 12, 1933*

B4, F6.2

Hugenberg's talk last night was along the lines of maintaining the present alliance with Hitler. There is need for this indeed. The followers of each of the participants in this alliance trust each other as far as the door, and no further. But Hugenberg needs Hitler, and Hitler for the moment would be sunk without [Hugenberg][36] and the two must share what they must and take what each of them can get away with. It must be said that up to the present Hugenberg, roly-poly, small, fiercely mustached as if the jumping bristles will make up for his size, has gotten by far the best of the bargain. An open exposure of the mishandling of the East Prussian relief funds has been

36. Plotkin here wrote "Hindenburg" but obviously meant Hugenberg.

prevented by his new allies, the price of meats will be raised through the new tariff that goes into effect on the 15th, the election prospects look quite encouraging, and in return for it he gets Hitler and the use of Hitler's army to help destroy "Marxism" in all of its conservative and radical forms—leading the road open to a restoration of the monarchy later on. He may not find Hitler so easy to deal with after the election, but on the other hand Hitler may need him far more than he needs Hindenburg now . . . all that is in the laps of the Gods. March 5th will give the answer to these questions. In the meantime, Hugenberg does well to speak against those who seek to break down the [Harzburg] front.[37] But one may venture a guess that all is not so rosy within. When a movement has solid ranks [and] is running frictionless, the leaders spend very little time on the need for solidarity, etc.

Spent the day again with Plettl and Van der Heeg. This time we took an autobus to Marquard, where we had lunch in a restaurant facing the lake and then walked eight miles, mostly along the canal to Potsdam. As we came into Potsdam we noticed that all the flags were flying at half-mast for the victims of the explosion in the Saar valley. It is perhaps characteristic of the Germans that they never speak of the territories they have lost, such as the Saar Valley and Danzig.[38] They take it for granted that these territories will eventually come back to them.

To the credit of all three of us, we did our best to avoid discussing politics in any form. For once we wanted to get away from the subject altogether. Try and hold back the Niagara. This time the subject we couldn't avoid was yesterday's manifesto of the German writers demanding that the SPD and KPD form a united front against the *Hitlerfaschismus*. Both were quite incensed at the group and thought that they were being used by the Com-

---

37. On Alfred Hugenberg's initiative, on October 11, 1931, the DNVP nationalists, the Nazis, the Steel Helmet, and the Pangermanist League (Alldeutscher Verband) organized a mass meeting in the city of Bad Harzburg—hence the name of the Harzburg Front (which Plotkin misspelled as "Hapsburg Front")—to show their determination to fight against the Weimar Republic. In response to this initiative, the Social Democrats created their Iron Front (Eiserne Front).

38. The Versailles Treaty (1919) had established special status for the Saar territory, conferring its administration to the League of Nations for fifteen years. The Saar was to be reunited with Germany by a January 1935 landslide vote. The harbor city of Danzig, a German enclave in Poland, also received international status under the authority of the League of Nations. The "Danzig question" remained a permanent cause of tension between Germany and Poland, especially after a Nazi majority was elected in the local diet. This became a pretext for Hitler to start the war against Poland.

munists who now find themselves in a tight fix, and at the same time had no hesitation in doubting the sincerity of the Communists.

According to Plettl, every time the German trade union movement moved towards a certain objective, the Communists always tried to turn it into a revolutionary objective and gave the reaction a chance to at least partially checkmate the trade unions. He pointed to what followed after the general strike in the Kapp putsch.[39] The trade unions then could have gotten much more out of the situation, but when the Communists turned part of it into a general strike to bring in sovietism they split the German people and [gave] the conservative elements a chance to checkmate. He pointed to incident after incident of a similar nature. But more important than anything else, he contended, was their utter inability to see things from the angle of the German people. Their direction and their motivation come from Moscow, and until they see that Germany is not Russia, whether inside of a united front or outside of it, the fight will be for Moscow and not for Germany. They look at Germany as a province in the Soviet system and not as a nation that industrially and even socially, in spite of all of the so-called labor legislation in Russia, is far in advance of the other nations. The moment they see Germany and German problems, not as either Germans or Russians, but as Germans, a united front will be possible. He deplored the repressive measures that have been taken against them and thinks the government is stupid in the handling of them. But as far as a united front with them [is concerned] in spite of the common danger, he gave me to understand that, unless there is a considerable change of heart among the Communists and a major reorientation of viewpoints and methods, Heinrich Mann and the other intellectuals will not be listened to.

Returning, Van der Heeg and I adjourned to the Imperator where in addition to consuming some fine München beer and listening to some excellent music, we discussed the operation of the Holland unemployment insurance. Van der Heeg tells me that the government there supplements dollar for dollar the trade unions' expenditure for unemployment insurance. He promised, if I visited Holland, that he would get me in touch with all the material on the subject and in return I promised that I would not leave Europe without visiting his country.

Sitting there the first extra was brought through the salon and apparently there has been a bloody Sunday throughout Germany. The complete reports are not in—they probably won't be in till morning.

---

39. See February 1, 1933.

◇ *[Monday], February 13, 1933*

B4, F6.2

Nine killed and more than fifty wounded and several hundred arrested is the toll for the weekend. The dead are in Bernsheim, Dortmund, Helkinger, Eisleben, Striegau, Reolinger,[40] Friedenau, Grunewald, Halle and Braunschweig. In Halle, in addition to two dead, twenty were wounded; in Braunschweig 5 wounded in addition to the fatality, in Bernsheim seven were wounded. How many of the wounded will die to swell the toll is, of course, unknown. In some cases the dead are Communists, in other cases Nazis and Social Democrats, and not a few among the dead and wounded are innocent victims who have nothing to do with any of the parties to the slaughter. It is to be expected that from now on the terror will get progressively worse. So far most of the communist papers have been suppressed, if they are permitted to publish one day's issue, the authorities find enough excuse to shut them up the next day. Twenty-eight of the social democratic papers have suffered and are suffering the same fate. One Catholic Centrum paper also has been suppressed.

In the evening to a meeting of the Tailors' branch of the Needle Trades Union. Five hundred solid Germans sitting calmly deliberating the present German crisis. Americans cannot understand the seriousness of the situation that confronts these men, and their problems are perhaps typical for all of the workers in Germany.

[. . .] These men during the past eighteen months, because of von Papen's interference, have had to take governmental decisions cutting their wages and shop conditions, and compelled to take it because a strike would be illegal! Now they are confronted with fascism, fascism that they know will make every effort to wipe out organized labor in Germany precisely as it did in Italy. Nevertheless they were quite calm and weighed their decisions in a manner that left no doubt as to where they stood.

The meeting itself, precisely because their economic demands have to be settled through political channels only, very soon turned into a political meeting. The history of the past eighteen months was recited by the secretary Faustmann. Wage [cuts] amounting to thirty percent in three successive reductions! Other firms, with the connivance of the government, had

---

40. Plotkin's spelling of some of these names is not certain: Helkinger and Reolinger do not correspond to any known locality. Possibly, he meant Hückingen and Röhlingen.

imposed a ruling that made it possible for some of the firms to evade even these lower tariffs. Their present agreement expires in April and it is not unlikely that, if the Hitler régime stays, they will be among the front-line unions to be attacked. The question therefore was twofold. First to meet the political issue. Assuming that they could meet [it] successfully, the other would automatically fall away. Otherwise they may have to face a strike that from the beginning will be declared illegal.

I was surprised at the calmness with which Faustmann presented the facts and was even more surprised at the calmness with which the men faced and discussed the issue. This union is one of the oldest in Germany and I suppose has gone through these crises before, both in the early days of organization and later through the Bismarckian period. Nevertheless I was surprised at the heavy casualness with which they spoke. It may be that they felt that it was just another crisis. Certainly they gave no indication that they were deeply stirred. The only moment when there was something resembling intense feeling was when one of their members, Shtupe by name, brought in a two-sentence resolution asking the branch to call on the general labor movement to make overtures to the Communist groups in Germany for a united front. He spoke calmly, but as he spoke, the crowd became tense. The time had come, he said, to call all groups together and to prepare for the inevitable war between *Faschismus* and the workers. Every moment lost now is demoralizing to the rank and file who everywhere are expecting the word that will guide them in their efforts to break up the *Faschismus* that is fast [en]veloping Germany in darkness. When he got through there was a sigh of relief. The chairman asked if there were others who wanted to discuss the resolution. Two others took the floor and spoke in a similar vein. [. . .] Finally Lehman, the secretary for the entire Needle Trades Union of Berlin, took the floor.

I expected that he would denounce the Communists both for their dual unionism and for their efforts to split the Social Democratic Party. Instead he analyzed the source of the resolution and stated that he believed it originated within the Communist Party whose rank and file were rebelling at the mistakes of their leaders. He got quite excited when he read some of the past leaflets issued by them in which the Communists called the Social Democrats every name in the calendar and asked whether the Social Democrats, after these diatribes, could be expected to take the initiative, but soon calmed down. The united front, he answered, was highly desirable and had always been believed in by the forces of the left in Germany. The question was whose united front? On that question the trade unionists were quite definite. It must be a united front of Germans working for Germany and not for an alien philosophy, regardless of how attractive the alien philosophy might be. On that basis a telephone call or a simple note from Communist headquarters would lead to a united front. But to expect German social democracy, that goes back to the revolution of 1848, that lived through to triumph over the Bismarckian reaction, and again through the terror of the postwar days, and that represents ninety-five percent of the organized German workingmen, to come to the Communists and ask the Communists for their terms—it was both humiliating and absurd. When the Communists really want a united front they will know where to come and what to do. The initiative will have to come from them. And as to the resolution, the matter had already been discussed in the national councils of the ADGB and the policy laid down. If the Communists want a united front let them start the ball rolling and they will find the door open to them, provided the ball they roll hasn't the Russian chain at the other end.

When Lehman got through, the chairman asked [Shtupe] whether he would care to withdraw his resolution. It was explained to me later that this was done in order to protect the maker of it in case the government should later decide to prosecute individual Communists. He declined to withdraw it and the resolution was lost by ten to one. Immediately afterward, Lehman asked that a committee of thirty be elected to take charge in case of any emergency that will require immediate action, and a committee of five to be chosen among them with full powers. This was promptly carried and without discussion. It is presumed that the committee [will] outline their program, and should a real crisis develop, know exactly what to do and how to do it, and the others will obey orders—as they have in the past.

Hessen is again alarmed. Another *Reichskommissar* has been dispatched there by Hindenburg. They expect to be dissolved as Prussia has been dissolved. In Bavaria there is considerable fear. There are rumors in the air that in Bavaria the royalists are planning to bring back their former king. Who knows? Anything is possible.

◇ *Tuesday, February 14, 1933*

B4, F6.2

The committee headed by Dr. Löbe to investigate the relief fraud in East Prussia tried again to meet today. When the meeting started the Nazis announced that the socialist and communist members of the committee had no right to be present! Dr. Frank Jr.,[41] the Nazi leader, pushed Löbe out of the chair and a general fracas developed in which a member of the committee who is neither Socialist, Communist or Nazi got banged up. The report, that may have affected the election in the agricultural districts, was therefore again prevented from being published. Complaints have been forwarded to Capt. Göring, the president of the Reichstag, but since Göring is himself a member of the Nazis it is so much paper in the wastebasket.

While Hitler's friends are broadcasting that regardless which way the election turns he will remain in office, the cabinet, presumably to strengthen its position in the agricultural districts, extended von Schleicher's order against the execution of judgments on land until October 31st. It is, in effect, a moratorium for small farmers. Simultaneously comes the announcement from other Nazi sources that as soon as the elections are over the fight against the trade unions will start in earnest.

◇ *[Wednesday], February 15, 1933*

B4, F6.2

Hints are beginning to appear in the Nazi press suggesting that the Nazi shock troops be armed and used as supplementary police auxiliaries. Twenty-two provincial police commissioners have been removed and replaced with men who are either definitely tied up with the Nazis or with the Hugenberg crowd. In the main, the new men who have been appointed are Hitlerites. Hitler controlling the police of Germany and Hugenberg controlling the army seems to have been the agreement.

Germany is on the verge of a dictatorship. Whether a dictatorship is certain, or who will really be the dictator, is still in the offing, but that Germany is pretty close to it is more than a guess. It is a hard cold reality.

One day's news includes the following items. Communist demonstrations prohibited everywhere. Nine political opponents killed in one day, among them a woman, and a policeman. Red newspapers suppressed. The Karl Liebknecht House, headquarters of the Communist Party, raided. The mass meeting of the Social Democrats in Berlin prohibited. The *Vorwärts*, official paper of the Social Democratic Party of Germany, suspended for three

41. Hans Frank (1900–1946), a lawyer, Nazi politician, and minister of justice of Bavaria (1933) and then of the Reich. He was governor-general of Poland during World War II. He was sentenced to death at the Nuremberg trial and executed.

days for publishing the Party manifesto. Two general strikes called, neither of them successful, one in the Ruhr by the Communists and the other by the Socialists in Lübeck. The first failed entirely. The second created enough disturbance to call out the entire political force and to compel them to close the downtown area.

Hardly two months earlier, Plotkin recalled, Hindenburg had refused to appoint Hitler because of the latter's all-or-nothing conditions. He also recalled that von Papen was then so discredited that the idea that he could be called back to power was considered mere folly. In addition, Hugenberg and Hitler hated each other. To understand how a Hitler-Hugenberg–von Papen government could now be possible, one needed to look back at a previous stage.

Hugenberg and Hitler have been enemies for a long time. They are different in temperament, different in their contacts within the wealthy classes in Germany, and different in both their theories and following. The first regards himself as the legitimate heir of German nationalism, has his contacts with the landowners and nobility and has a decided leaning towards the return of the monarchy. It is generally known that Hugenberg would have no hesitation in bringing one of the Hohenzollerns back and reestablish the monarchy in Germany. Hitler he has always regarded as an upstart but for whom German nationalism would never have been divided into two camps, moreover, were it not for Hitler he would have the undivided support of the large banks and the large industrialists. Hitler, on the other hand, primarily an agitator, promising everything to everyone who came into his camp, repeatedly rode roughshod over his competitors of the right, and so maneuvered that all Hugenberg got from the banks and the industrialists, since 1927, was the mere droppings from their tables. The enmity between the two, therefore, has been a long and bitter one. And it is not over yet. As soon as the present emergency that drew them together is past, the peace between the two, in all likelihood, will be dropped and Germany will witness a new war for control.

According to Plotkin, the reasons that brought Hugenberg and Hitler together were linked to Hugenberg's need to silence the mounting scandal on the use of relief funds for their own profit by the Junkers, the large-estate East Prussian landlords, while thousands of farmers were actually impoverished. Hitler's own financial difficulties, in addition, also had to be covered, while the ranks of his party were torn by inner divisions. Thus, the impending vision of a collapse of the Nazi movement left Hitler no choice but to accept the proposal made to him.

[Hitler] had either to go into the cabinet on the terms as outlined by von Papen and Hugenberg or make up his mind that as political leader in Germany he was for the time being through. It is well to keep these facts in mind. With one political group in this alliance facing a major political scandal, and the other facing decay, their sheer necessity brought them together for the time being. Anyone who imagines that they will stay together is either naive, or does not know the political antagonisms that have existed and still exist between the two. They are together now in a desperate effort to capture the state apparatus to revive their political fortunes, and it is more than likely that they will succeed in imposing their will on Germany in the next few months either towards a monarchy or towards a fascistic dictatorship, but [it is] in the very nature of their existence as separate parties that, the moment the present emergency which brought them together is past, the struggle between the two will commence. Signs are not wanting that in spite of their "[Harzburg Front]" there already is friction.

That they do not trust each other can be seen both from the composition that was made between them, and from the developments that have since taken place. The cabinet is decidedly Hugenberg. Hugenberg himself holds four portfolios. The army is also in the hands of Hugenberg, but as a sop to Hitler he was given the control of the police in the state of Prussia. To still further tie Hitler's hands von Papen was appointed Vice-Chancellor with powers that definitely delimit Hitler's. Added to that is von Papen's additional office of Commissioner appointed by Hindenburg for the state of Prussia. The Hugenberg crowd, while consenting to Hitler's control of the police in Prussia, is making certain that the largest state in the German republic doesn't swing too far out of their control. Contrariwise, Hitler is not too eager to play too far into the hands of his royalist adversaries. When Hugenberg, eager to avoid a national election altogether, demanded that a state of national emergency be declared and that the cabinet rule without the Reichstag, Hitler promptly squelched the plan. Neither does he seem too eager to completely annihilate the Communist Party. To, at this time, outlaw the Communists might swing them over to the ranks of the Social Democrats and make possible a majority for them in the coming elections, and Hitler is still dreaming that the linking of his name with Hindenburg's will swing the majority of the electors in his direction. Neither party would consent to a joint campaign under one name. And when the Hugenberg newspapers came out the other day with the announcement that the government was planning a three months' moratorium on all farm debts in East Prussia so as to strengthen the political control of Hugenberg, then Hitler's enthusiasm expressed itself in a prompt denial. It may be that Hugenberg will get his wish, but Hitler's enthusiasm in this direction is decidedly cool.

What therefore is to be expected in Germany? Were the political atmosphere in Germany different, one would not be justified in formulating conclusions. But when in Germany three of the leading political parties, Nazis, Communists and Junkers, are openly for dictatorship in one form or another; two of them looking with longing eyes on the forms existing in Soviet Russia and in Italy and the third turning back to the forms existing in Germany before the revolution in 1918, and both the Social Democratic Party and the Catholic Centrum held responsible for all the ills that have afflicted Germany during the past fourteen years, it seems to the writer that Germany is inevitably driving towards a Nazi dictatorship or a monarchy. Moreover, it seems at the moment as if the monarchists have the upper hand.

The elections will be held on March 5th. The elections will settle whether Hitler will have a majority sufficient to rule alone. If he gets it, then he will have a struggle on his hands with his present friends the Junkers. Should he fail to get a majority, then he will be precisely where he is today, dependent on Hugenberg's support to remain where he is. Should Hugenberg get a majority, which is wholly improbable, he will promptly kick out Hitler. Should the combined forces of Hitler and Hugenberg fail to get a majority, it is more than probable that they will seize the powers of government, declare a state of national emergency and through necessity for the time being continue with their alliance. In that event, the struggle between the two may be interrupted by a revolution against which they will have to use all of their combined resources. But at the present moment, a successful revolution in Germany seems to the writer quite remote. What seems more probable is that the German nation will, in the coming election, be terrorized into accepting the group that has seized power, and that on their manner of doing it will depend whether the outcome will be frankly monarchistic or fascistic. In either case, Germany is on the verge of a dictatorship, and so certain does that seem to be at present that it is logical to ask who the dictator will be, Hitler or Hugenberg. The moment the atmosphere is clearer, there is no doubt, both camps will girdle their loins and the struggle between the two will come into the open.

◇ *[Monday, February 27, 1933]*

[B4, F2]

The Last Social Democratic Meeting in Berlin, *Berlin bleibt rot.*[42]

As soon as we got halfway down the block from the Bülowstrasse underground, the chin-strapped *Polizei* became more numerous, more numerous than at any of the Social Democratic meetings I had been in attendance in Berlin—even more than at the Communist meetings. Accompanying the picked rifle-slunged *Polizei* were more than the usual number of police lorries or trucks, each carrying twenty rifle-wearing officers. I know these lorries. On the floor of these lorries are the machine guns. Something was up, and as we approached the *Sportpalast* the tension increased, although on the surface the atmosphere was quiet. Yes, there was something in the air. Perhaps it was the unusual number of *Polizei* with their rifles slung across their backs, perhaps it was their chin straps under their chin—a danger signal not to be ignored in Germany—but I am inclined to think that their number was the impressive thing. Somehow, one got the feeling, without knowing why, that tonight the *Polizei* were prepared for action.

Entering the Sportpalast we found hundreds of *Polizei* and hundreds of *Reichsbanner* men in uniform. The latter [are] the military force of the Social Democrats. I found myself wondering how effective they would be if they were matched against the rifles of the *Polizei,* or, if need be, against the machine guns that were lying on the bottoms of the lorries outside. Not much. At the same time I began to wonder what would happen if a machine gun were turned loose in the hall. The same thought must have occurred to my companion. She walked in, rather fought her way in, with me, but it was evident that going to an ice-hockey match in the same building would have been more to her liking.

---

42. "Berlin Remains Red." There are two versions of this text about the night of February 27, 1933, when the last Social Democratic meeting was held, a few hours before the burning of the Reichstag occurred. Both versions, "Berlin bleibt rot" and "The Last Social Democratic Meeting," are undated. The latter is only a section of the former, "Berlin bleibt rot," which is reproduced here. This text is classified along with other essays in AP Coll., B4, F2. However, unlike the other essays, its style of direct reporting and first-person evidence brings it closer to other diary entries than to the more abstract and general tone of the other essays. Its subject logically forms an ending—albeit an unhappy one—to Plotkin's quest for the ideal world of social democratic relations he had come to encounter in Germany.

Once in, we tried to find seats on the ground floor, but all of the entrances were blocked by the *Reichsbanner* with a polite announcement that all of the seats were filled. Not until we got to the uppermost gallery did we succeed in finding seats, the only two spaces on the benches that were left on our side of the house. The other side already was packed to the doors and no more were being admitted.

Looking down from where we were the entire hall took on a series of straight-line pattern. All the rows were filled, and at the end of each row was a *Reichsbanner* in uniform. The inside aisles also had *Reichsbanner* guards at the side of each row. In the past the meetings of every party in Germany were broken up by disturbances created by either the Nazis or the Communists. To protect their meetings the Social Democrats therefore placed a guard at each row in order to localize and to break up any disturbances that might develop. Underneath me they stood in straight lines watching every move of every man and woman in each row, scanning faces to find old troublemakers, and occasionally someone would be walked out between several *Reichsbanner* men. They were taking no chances. In the meantime I became aware of the scrutiny of the guard at the end of the row we were sitting in. I must have looked suspicious. My companion squirmed and under the close scrutiny became embarrassed and finally spoke to the guard—in English!—for which she was rewarded with a hearty German smile.

After a little while I became aware of the crowd on the stage. They were not like ordinary visitors. Their formation was somewhat out of the ordinary. Behind the *Reichsbanner* guard in front of the stage and in front of the speakers' stand the men and women who were seated seemed to be sitting as if they were holding themselves in readiness for something. They actually were. They were members of the Socialist Choir.

Since programs were not available, I do not know what this chorus of five hundred voices sang. And I was grateful to them for singing as they did. It really doesn't matter what they sang. It was a raising of voices in the songs of revolt. Not the songs of revolt that one hears every day, but the songs of revolt that stir one with the age-old desire to challenge and to dare. And I was surprised at how the audience took it. There was no effort to join in, as is usually the case in German meetings. They sat through it in the depth of the silence that can come only when a huge crowd is deeply moved. It may be that this particular chorus will never again be permitted to sing. It would be a pity.

Singing over, a woman went to the speakers' platform and for five minutes held the audience in the palm of her hand—a simple, quiet recitation, almost inaudible at first, a simple quiet recitation that grew with warmth and passion against the injustices of everyday living, and grew vivid with rage and revolt at the end as she demanded of the masses that [they] continue the age-old struggle for *Freiheit.* The audience responded by standing on their feet and three times lifting their fists in the air to the chant of *"Freiheit, Freiheit, Freiheit."*

The chairman of the meeting, Franz Künstler,[43] a member of the Reichstag for the Social Democratic Party, then walked forward and announced that the meeting had for its object the arrangement to honor the memory of Karl Marx on the fiftieth anniversary of his death! The meeting permit had been issued to the Social Democrats on this excuse. For a moment I started wondering whether the meeting [would] really be a political meeting. The chairman then continued. It was known that there were people who wanted to break up the meeting if that were possible. The Social Democratic Party had undertaken to see to it that order would be maintained and he hoped that the crowd would be helpful and at no time get too excited. He asked each man and woman in the audience to bear in mind that they were policing their own meeting and to help them keep order. For a moment he stood in silence, as if he alone shared the knowledge of what was coming. And then, without further ado, [he] introduced the veteran editor of the social democratic *Vorwärts,* [Friedrich] Stampfer.[44] Then the storm broke loose. Stampfer had been at [what] the Germans call the *"Spitz,"* in the foreground of all the press battles in the campaigns of the last few years. An old veteran in the social democratic movement whose aged body is bent with the weight of his years, gray-haired, lean, he leaned towards the crowd as if he were talking not to a crowd, but to each person in the crowd. The storm that broke loose was their tribute to this old man who in this campaign alone had been

---

43. See January 29, 1933, which describes the Iron Front meeting where Künstler also led the crowd on the theme of "Berlin remains red."

44. Friedrich Stampfer (1874–1957), a Social Democratic leader and journalist, belonged to the right wing of the SPD. He fled Nazi Germany in 1933, spent years as a refugee in Paris and then in the United States, and returned to Germany in 1947. Stampfer that evening was replacing the speaker announced for the meeting, Arthur Crispien, who was forbidden to speak by the authorities. The meeting was banned shortly after Stampfer started speaking. The Reichstag was burning. Stampfer's interrupted speech was fully printed during the night in the *Vorwärts,* but Stampfer was arrested and the headquarters of the *Vorwärts* raided a few hours later. See Friedrich Stampfer's memoirs, *Erfahrungen und Erlebnisse: Aufzeichnungen aus meinem Leben* (Cologne: Verlag für Politik und Wirtschaft, 1957), 260–61.

"questioned" several times by the police, the *Vorwärts* twice *verboten* because of his attacks against the Nazis. They recognized in him a fearless fighter and a man of action in whom their faith and their loyalty [were] well placed.

Stampfer leaned over and his head shone under the strong lights as he groped for words that would express his ideas. When I was young, he started, I joined a trade union. At that time I knew nothing about Socialism, Anarchism, or Marxism. All I knew was that I ought to be a member of a trade union. It wasn't much. Here the audience roared. It was an indirect [answer] at the anti-Marxist campaign of the Hitlerites. They took it as sarcasm. Whether it was intended as sarcasm I do not know. It probably was. But, he went on after the laughter subsided, as I grew older I learned that in order to learn something about trade unions I had to read Karl Marx, and to read Karl Marx and understand him I had to read much of sociology, history, law and a good deal of philosophy too. And this I have learned, and the old man's words took a biting sarcasm, [that] to agree with Marx you have to have a wide knowledge of almost all of the social sciences; to attack Marxism you have to know nothing.

What came after is both hard to remember and to put together. From out of the seats behind a table in front of the speakers' stand unwound himself a figure of a *Polizei* in uniform. Only one policeman. All he did that I could see was to raise his hand. Stampfer stopped talking and simply stood on the platform. The officer stood there motionless. In the front row I saw some figures raising themselves from their seats and shaking their fists in the air. The officer continued to stand motionless. Suddenly everyone in the orchestra was rising and waving fists in the air and shouting *"Freiheit."* I turned to the *Reichsbanner* man at the end of the bench and asked him what the trouble was. He shrugged his shoulders and answered *"aufgelöst,"* the meeting is dismissed. Here Stampfer left the speakers' stand, and Franz Künstler, the chairman, came back. He started pleading with the audience, but the audience had become a mass of moving fists and was demanding *"Freiheit."* Franz [Künstler], fearful that a riot would develop, tried to lead them in a cheer and at the end of it to advise them to peacefully leave the hall. He succeeded in the first cheer and then was ordered to stop by the lonely policeman in front of the fifteen thousand yelling and shrieking men and women—and for the moment I was fascinated by the shining helmet of the officer and his granite-like appearance in the storm of emotion that was sweeping the hall. I turned for a moment and looked at my companion and found her eyes in dumb wonder and her [complexion] as white as her olive-brown skin would permit. Suddenly out of the crowd came a booming voice that echoed itself in every part of the hall—*"Polizei macht Mord"*—the police are committing murder! Others took up the cry until [it] became a chant in which all of the fifteen thousand men and women joined—*"Polizei macht Mord—Polizei macht Mord—Polizei macht Mord"*—until the cry became one of hysterical redundance with a note of madness in it. One felt the utter helplessness, the kind of helplessness that makes one want to cry; and for a moment I was fearful that someone would come through the mass and do something that would provide an excuse for the machine-gun squads in the rear of the hall to turn loose. Fortunately at this moment Künstler had the presence of mind to order the chorus to start singing the International. He too was fearful of the machine guns in the rear, and depended on the singing of the crowd to bring them under his control again. In this he succeeded. When the song was over, the police who were in the rear of the hall now made their entrance and began to wield their [gum] sticks on the backs of those in the front benches, while from the side entrances came dozens of officers pushing the men and women into the aisles. Nevertheless the shouting and shaking of fists continued; until the same bellowing hall-filling voice raised the cry *"Berlin"* and the crowd answered in unison, as if the thing were premeditated and rehearsed, *"bleibt rot."* Berlin remains red. This somehow released the anger of the crowd that by this time had turned into a milling mob seeking the entrances out. But the cry was not only taken up in the hall, but was taken up on the street as well. It was not only a release, but it was a challenge as well, and at the same time formulated in a single phrase both their wish-thinking and a defiance of their enemy as well.

Coming out of the Sportpalast the first sight that greeted us was the several hundred steel-helmeted *Polizei* standing in front of the gates of the building. We were not to cross the street. We must move on our side of the street only. I felt Miss Wortis's arm link itself through mine. We were not out of it yet. On the other side of the street, at a few alternating yards, were the lorries with twenty *Polizei* and their rifles ready and waiting. Suddenly the *"Berlin"* cry rang against the building, and *"bleibt rot,"* the response, rang back again. Everyone was either shouting Berlin or shouting back the answer. Fifteen thousand people strung along for blocks each one his cheer master—the street resounded time and again to the volume of these lusty throats that were hysterical with anger and could find no other release than in shouting. Lorries began to shoot up the length of the block, trying to find who started the shouting, and officers got out of their lorries to spread themselves along the edges of the sidewalk so as to be able to trace the shouters, but it was hopeless; the few arrests they made and the few clubbings made no effect on the crowd. When we finally reached a corner, we turned and stood on the sidelines. The shouting continued for a good half hour.

An hour later I had deposited my companion at destination, and started on my way home. On the way I decided to drop in and have some coffee in Aschinger's, near Charlottenstrasse just off the Friedrichstrasse-*Bahnhof.* As I got out of the *Bahnhof,* I saw some crowds, but crowds are not unusual in Berlin. I drank some coffee and read a paper for an hour. Then on leaving I decided to walk down Charlottenstrasse, and as I walked down the crowds grew more numerous and I realized something was up. Approaching a group of people who were talking I overheard the remark that "the Reichstag had burned to the ground." The Reichstag! That is as if the Capitol in Washington were burned! Yes—the Reichstag was burning, and the glow could still be seen faintly above the buildings. I decided to go and see. I got as far as Wilhelmstrasse, here [stood] the police, arms linked across the entire street entrance. The street was closed.

An hour later I called a friend. The possibilities for reaction in the burning of the Reichstag were evident at once. The word was going around that the Communists had burned it. Also that a Communist had been arrested, caught in the act; and the first editions were just beginning to reach the streets. Somehow, news of this sort spread more rapidly than even the newspapers can get hold of it. The city was turning out to see what had happened to their Capitol. Soon after we met. Again the inevitable coffee. And over the coffee he gave me the latest news. Stampfer had been arrested. The lorries you saw in the streets will work all night and every night from now on. Thousands will be arrested as suspects. The socialist papers everywhere have been suppressed because Stampfer made the remark that it looks like *"provokatorische Arbeit"*[45] of the Nazis. The reaction is on. *"Berlin bleibt rot."*

45. A provocation.

THE DESTRUCTION OF THE LABOR MOVEMENT IN GERMANY

[Abraham] Plotkin

(General Organizer, International Ladies' Garment Workers' Union)

The factors that made it possible for the German fascists to take over the trade unions in Germany are many, but there are a few of first and immediate importance.[1] To those who were on the ground between January 30 and the middle of May it was clear that the trade unions were incapable of withstanding prolonged resistance. What follows is an outline of the rapid developments that brought about their final destruction.

1. This article appeared in the American Federation of Labor's monthly organ, the *American Federationist,* in August 1933. Historical evidence as to where and in what language it was first published is somewhat contradictory. According to a letter written by Plotkin to Georg Stolz on July 1, 1933, the article had been sent to Abraham Cahan, the editor of the *Jewish Daily Forward,* who agreed to publish it in Yiddish translation in several installments starting on July 1, 1933 (AP Coll., B2, F15). However, our attempts with the help of Yiddish-reading scholars to find this article in the July issues of the *Forward* have been to no avail. In his later oral history interviews Plotkin remembered that "Cahan felt that the article was important enough to refer it to [AFL president] William Green in Yiddish. So they had to retranslate it back into English because [they] lost my original. So this is the translation from Yiddish into English" (AP OH, B16, F3, p. 834). The fact that the article probably appeared only in the *American Federationist* may also be corroborated by Plotkin's letter to Stolz on November 14, 1933, in which Plotkin stated that "the only article I have published

The Press

The first drive of the Nazis after police power was placed in their hands was against the trade-union press. It started on March 2, when the *Jungbuchdrucker* and the *Textilarbeiter*[2] were suspended for two weeks. The *Deutscher Eisenbahner,* organ of the railroad workers, and the *Metallarbeiter* of the Metal Trades Federation, edited by Fritz Kummer, were suspended on March 10. All the other eleven publications of the Metal Trades Federation, the largest single federation in the Allgemeiner Deutscher Gewerkschaftsbund, were suppressed in rapid succession. The newspapers and magazines of [Gesamtverband],[3] an organization of 600,000 civil and municipal employees and in public-service utilities, were closed in short order.

Whole issues of the *Holzarbeiter Zeitung,* corresponding to the organ of the carpenters' union in the United States, and the *Gastwirtsgehilfen Zeitung,* issued by the Restaurant and Food Workers' Union, were seized and destroyed. At the same time, the leading organs of the central councils throughout Germany were either seized or *verboten.* As a result of this muzzling of the trade-union press by the Nazi police power, the workers were left without communication between themselves and their leaders. In a country like Germany, where the sources of information for trade-union members were almost wholly concentrated in their daily and weekly press, the shutting off of their news sources was like the cutting of an artery.

It may be asked why the workers did not fight back, as they did when their press was forbidden during the latter part of March, through the calling of a general strike until the *verboten*'s were lifted? The answer is that it was impossible to call an effective strike against the Nazi press. In Vienna the S.D.P.[4] unions controlled the printing rooms even of the Nazi and monarchist groups. In Germany that control never was in the hands of the Social Democratic Party. A protest strike, therefore, would have brought no results,

---

so far was the article I read to you when I was in France, it was in the August number of the *American Federationist* and apparently had its effect because our President used it as a basis for the boycott that the Federation passed at its convention last month" (AP Coll., B2, F15).

2. Respectively, the *Young Typographer* and the *Textile Worker.*

3. The full name of the union of public employees was Gesamtverband der Arbeitnehmer der öffentlichen Betriebe und des Personen- und Warenverkehrs.

4. Plotkin here uses the English acronym SDP (Social Democratic Party) rather than the German SPD. Note too that SDP stands here as an adjective to simply mean social democratic unions.

except perhaps to intensify the spirit of reactionism and add, no doubt, to the already growing lists of those who were in Nazi *Casernas*[5] and concentration camps.

Physical Terrorism

Three lines of terrorism were followed by the Nazis. The first was to visit the headquarters of the different trade unions and demand that the Nazi flag be hung on the flagstaff of the building. The first squads were small, but if they met with a refusal, they would come back with several hundred more in squads of fifty, surround the building, search the premises for firearms, then make a bonfire of everything that displeased them. Pictures of Marx, [Engels], Bebel, Liebknecht, Legien, Leipart, flags and banners that had been the treasures of the unions for many years and marked definite historical epochs for them, records of inestimable value—all were thrown into the flames while the Nazis held a solemn festival around the fire.

In many cases they went further. In the Berlin Central Labor Council Building they wrecked the furniture in many of the rooms, opened the cash boxes and safes, and walked out with whatever they found. In Dresden, where the top floor of the Central Labor Council Building had been used as a hotel, the Nazis fitted up several rooms in sumptuous style, scattered condoms and whips about, and then invited the populace to come and see the [orgiastic] headquarters of the workers' leaders! The hotel in this case was turned into a Nazi *Caserna* and is now one of the Nazi military barracks.

There was hardly a trade union in Germany that, during the months of March and April, did not suffer from these visitations. Nazi striplings would walk in, with the police usually in the background, cock their revolvers, demand the keys, and proceed to search the premises. Invariably they would ask if there was any wine around, and would look surprised when there was none to be found. Refusal to meet their demands met either with a prompt beating or arrest. In one case witnessed by the writer, two girls in the Berlin Transport Union Headquarters, who could not explain the blurred writing on a mimeograph stencil, were arrested and kept in jail for several days. An appeal to the police was useless. Frequently the police were a party to the outrages that were committed. Moreover, the police themselves were in-

5. With this word (from the German word *Caserne*), Plotkin refers to the yet unofficial barracks held by the stormtroops that belonged to neither the police nor the army and where opponents to the regime were detained and tortured.

timidated and would do nothing against the Nazi troops. In some cases the unions resisted the raiders with force; in other cases the Reichsbanner men (the former military force of the S.D.P. and trade unions) fought alongside of the trade unionists against the Nazis, but it was a hopeless battle.

The Nazis were armed. The trade unionists were without weapons of any kind, and the Reichsbanner troops had been ordered by the government to turn in their weapons, such as they had, to the local authorities.

A second form of terrorism was used directly against trade union leaders. Husemann of the Miners Union was among the first to feel the effects of this policy. Arrested, he was kept in a Nazi *Caserna* for ten days, and when released he was too ill to resume his activities. The chairman (also a member of the national executive committee) of the Transport Workers' Council in Berlin was arrested by the Nazis, taken to one of the Nazi *Casernas* and forced to drink a quart of castor oil, and thrown out unconscious on the street for strangers to pick up and take home. Not satisfied with their failure to properly intimidate him the first time, they re-arrested him and gave him a fearful beating.

These persecutions, perhaps, were most virulent in such districts as Mecklenburg, [Brunswick], [Würtemberg], the Palatinate, and in Bavaria. In these districts hundreds of organizers and secretaries of local unions had to leave for other parts of the country, or, as many of them did, take refuge in the forests. Even Leipart and Grassmann, two officials of the A.D.G.B., had to be taken to the hospital after their arrests. All of the trade-union leaders under arrest were first taken to the Nazi *Casernas* (the Nazis have been permitted to set up their own courts and maintain their own jails!); and once in there the men and women under arrest were treated with a brutality that has no parallel in any civilized country.

A special kind of terror was introduced in the factories. It consisted in ousting, by force, the social democratic members of the factory councils, either through dismissal or arrest. It should be remembered that every factory in Germany must, in conformity with the law, elect a factory council, whose work it is to enforce the national wage scales agreed upon between the employers and the union, the regulation of working conditions, discharges, lay-offs, etc. For many years the Nazis had entered the elections and placed their own tickets in the field in these factory council elections, but had never been successful. Now that Hitler was in power, they proceeded to oust these factory councils that had been elected. Thus in Bochum, the transport workers elected eight men as their industrial representatives, of whom five were S.D.P. men. (The elections in this case were held prior to the taking of power by Hitler.) Immediately after the March 5 elections, the five S.D.P. men were arrested and jailed. The same thing occurred in the [Siemens]' Electrical Plant in Berlin (similar to the General Electric Company in the United States), and here some of the men were jailed and others dismissed. Among those dismissed was [Erich Lübbe],[6] a member of the Reichstag, chairman of all the [Siemens] factory shop councils in Germany and labor's representative on the board of directors of the [Siemens] corporation.

After April 1 there was somewhat of a lull in these persecutions. Seldte, Minister of Labor, accommodatingly issued an order setting aside the factory elections that already had been held, and announced new elections some time in the future. On the day when the anti-Jewish boycott[7] was at its height and the newspapers had no space for anything else, this decree was hidden in an obscure corner of the average newspaper.

The third method of direct physical force against the trade unions was to occupy or *besetzen* the trade union buildings. The *[B]esetzung* is different from the raids. The first lasted only a few hours. The Nazis would come in during the night, hand up their flag, break through the doors and search the building, and then disappear. The *[B]esetzung* was the actual taking over of the buildings by the military forces of the Nazis. These preceded the final investment of the buildings on May 2, and were local actions, usually under the guidance of the local military post of the Nazis. Usually an incident would happen, as in Breslau where a number of Nazis were hurt during the riot following a parade past the [Gewerkschaftshaus], that would give the local arm of the Nazis an excuse, and a few hours later they would take over the buildings, bank accounts, books, etc., "in the interest of the Nazi state and to protect the workers' rights." The writer saw the *[B]esetzung* of the [Gewerkschaftshäuser] in Berlin, Dresden, Munich and in Bochum.

During the two months prior to May 2, there was hardly a city in Germany where the [Gewerkschaftshaus] was not occupied at one time or another. Every city in the state of Saxony suffered. It became a matter for congratulation if one visited a city where a *Besetzung* had not taken place. In

---

6. Erich Lübbe (born 1891), a Social Democrat member of parliament, president (1921–33) of the Central Factory Council (Gesamtbetriebsrat) of the Siemens factories in Berlin, president of the Factory Councils Commission of the Berlin labor unions, and member of the executive board of the Metal Workers' Union. He was arrested and jailed in 1933 and interned at the Sachsenhausen concentration camp from 1939 to 1945. After 1945 he was active again in the SPD and DGB.

7. April 1, 1933, was the first day of the anti-Semitic violence and boycott organized by the government.

one city, Frankfort on Main, the congratulations offered by the writer were premature. Three days after leaving, a short notice in the press announced that a cache of firearms had been found on the grounds of the [Gewerkschaftshaus] and that it too was occupied. But through these occupations three important factors developed.

The first, as in Saxony, the military announced that Hitler had promised them work, and that they would not give up the houses until the work promised them would be forthcoming. The second was the impounding of the funds, not only of the trade unions, but those of a number of the labor banks as well, and only enough funds were released as were needed for current expenses. The result was that many of the unions that had planned to get at least a part of their funds out of the country were thus checkmated.

But the most important results of these *Besetzungen* lay in a development not foreseen by the Nazis. They had expected that the masses would respond to this show of physical force and would welcome them with open arms. Nothing of the sort took place. If the masses were rapidly becoming demoralized, they were not, as far as the writer could see, taken in by the phrases and promises made to them by the Nazis.

Espionage

Still another factor made the lives of the trade-union leaders in Germany anything but a bed of roses. The censorship of the mails played no small part in contributing to the final breakdown. That letters were opened and read was the least problem for many organizations. The problem was how to have their mail reach them. In numerous instances, information dealing with the *Besetzungen* could not be gotten through to Berlin except by courier from the Gewerkschaftshaus involved.

When the Gesamtverband was invaded on May 2 all of the employees were marshaled into the main hall of the building, and when the officers asked if there were any Nazis among them, the mail clerk, an old and trusted employee of the Gesamtverband, and the telephone operator stepped out of the ranks.

Later it developed that Reuter, private secretary of Polenske,[8] president of the organization, was constantly in touch with the Nazis, as was Buchhalter,

8. Carl Polenske (1876–1956), president of the Municipal and Public Employees' Union (Gesamtverband). In 1933, he emigrated to Switzerland, then to Czechoslovakia, and finally in 1938 to Sweden, where he played an important role among German exiles.

a member of the national executive committee! The subjects discussed and the decisions arrived at were known to the Nazis before the members of the organization, and in many cases members of the unions never knew what the decisions of the officers were because the communications got "lost" in the mails. In this case, even the communications of the president, confidential orders from the chief to his subordinates to all parts of Germany, were known to the Nazis before the ink on the signatures was dry.

In the matter of the mails the difficulties became so great that the international secretary of one of the largest unions in Germany asked permission of the writer to have his confidential mail sent on the writer's name and address. A second official, the president of a large organization, came to the writer in desperation. He heard that I was going into southern Germany. Would I get in touch with some of his people there and arrange some method of underground correspondence? He had written repeatedly and there had been no response for weeks.

It gave the writer an opportunity to see something of the labor movement in the rest of Germany. The story everywhere was the same. In Dresden, Munich, Frankfort, Coblenz, Cologne, Essen and Bochum, the trade-union houses either had been or were *besetzt,* except in Frankfurt, where the *Besetzung* came later. Trade-union leaders either had been arrested or were in hiding, or were working under terrible difficulties. Each city was a repetition of the last one. The moment the military took over the trade-union buildings the workers stopped attending meetings, whether called by the Nazi labor "cells" or by their own leaders. Even as in Munich, where the military quickly decided to loosen its hold, the workers answered: "No dues for Hitler to steal." Until the buildings were returned to the trade unions, all activities came to a dead stop, and even after they were returned the greatest difficulties were encountered in reviving activity. In many instances, officials had to pledge themselves to their members that they would sequester the moneys paid in for dues, etc., until the status of the trade unions under the Hitlerian régime was clarified.

A General Strike Impossible

To meet this terror with a general strike, as the communists demanded, was impossible. In itself, excepting during the period pending agreements on wages, etc., and even this was subject to arbitration, the strike in Germany is not a legal weapon. Orders issued by the Government a few days after Hitler came into power made the general strike a capital offense. As far as the leaders were concerned, these orders had very little effect. It is known to the writer that a general strike was seriously discussed in the councils of the trade unions as late as the end of March. But it soon became evident [that], except as a grand gesture, to call a strike would be useless. One single factor that made the leaders realize that it would be suicidal to call a general strike was the eight millions unemployed. Among these unemployed are 1,400,000 young men between the ages of 18 and 25 who are denied any form of state aid or poor law relief, young men who have served their apprenticeship, who are eager to displace those who have what work there is. These young men have been promised work by the Nazis, and in their present state of mind to take the places of Marxists[9] and Communists would take on the color of a holy crusade. With only 12,000,000 wage-earners employed in Germany today, and of these less than half in industrial establishments, and a much smaller number in those industries that are decisive in a general strike—railroads, public utilities, such as water, gas, electricity and local transportation—it would not have taken the government long to break a strike in these fundamental industries and to keep them running. Of the other industries we need consider only one. In the building trades there are 400,000 members, and of these only 15 per cent are employed. Assuming that the 15 per cent would respond to a general strike call, something which was extremely unlikely—how long would it have taken to replace these 15 per cent? As one trade union leader put it, with the press muzzled and the lines of communications blocked, it was doubtful whether the great majority of German trade unionists would ever have known that a general strike had been called until it was too late. The general strike depends primarily on the rapidity and the swiftness with which it is called. In his opinion, it never would have gotten started.

There is still another factor that must not be overlooked. The past ten years have been filled with charges made by Nazis and Communists that the leaders of the trade unions in Germany had stabbed the German workers in the back and that social democracy was responsible both for their misery and their unemployment. The years of libel and vilification had their effect upon the masses. Not unemployment alone caused the loss of membership suffered by the trade unions; part of that loss was due to lies and slanders spread against the trade union leaders and Social Democrats. In the face of unemployment and the demoralization of the rank and file a call for a general strike would have been ineffective.

9. The Social Democrats.

Negotiations with the Nazis

At this point it were well to emphasize the factors that led to considerable and protracted negotiations between the government and the trade unions. While the raids and occupations of the trade-union houses had been going on for some time, these were the acts of local military forces and not the acts of the national government, and a sharp distinction should be made between the two. While there had been indirect negotiations since the middle of March, no definite proposal had been brought forward that could be used as a basis for negotiation. There matters rested until the local military forces throughout Germany began to take things into their own hands. It later developed that the Hugenberg members of the cabinet, distrustful of placing too much power in the hands of Hitler, were not eager to sanction a step that would make him master of additional millions of German workers. In the meantime the national leaders of the Nazis realized that these local raids and persecutions were gaining them nothing. They therefore called a truce and started conferring with the union leaders. As a result of these conferences most of the administrative buildings were ordered returned to the trade unions, and most of the trade organs resumed publication. The Nazis, on the other hand, demanded that they be recognized as part of the legal machinery in the settlement of disputes. They wanted the unification of the different trade unions, their disassociation from the Marxist internationals[10] with which they were affiliated, the lowering of dues, etc. In all of these matters, at least on the surface, progress was being made. The German trade union leaders realized that they could not function under the new régime as they had functioned in the past. They were willing to make concessions to safeguard the gains they had won under the Weimar Constitution—the system of compulsory national bargaining on wages, the labor code, the social legislation, the 48-hour [work]week. The atmosphere during the last week in April seemed, therefore, much more hopeful than at any time during the Hitlerian régime. The action of May 2 came as a complete surprise.

The Week of May 1

The week before the first of May was a week of optimism. The skies seemed clear except for one small cloud—the first of May celebration announced by

10. The International Federation of Trade Unions and the Labour and Socialist International.

Hitler. The organizations had been asked to participate, but to both workers and leaders, it seemed a travesty of the workers' holiday to celebrate it under fascist orders. Then came the government's ruling that the employers would have to pay the workers for the day. Then came the notice that those who refused to march and to take part in the celebration would be considered as being opposed to the government—no light offense in Germany at the present time. Those who refused to report and register with the Nazi shop committee would be subject to dismissal. When the leaders realized that to maintain official opposition would result in thousands of discharges, they yielded. The results were tragic.

In the morning the workers gathered in front of the factories, greeted the employers, and marched to the starting points where the parades were slated to begin. There were eleven such columns organized in the different parts of Berlin. Each line was presumed to parade one hundred thousand workers. In the three parades I witnessed, it was doubtful whether more than half of those who were expected had come. Nevertheless more than a million people were assembled in the [Tempelhof] aviation field to take part in the demonstration. As the organizers anticipated, the excitement, the crowds, the fireworks, the adulation heaped on Hitler, had their effect. Even those who were embittered by the spectacle, one that had the air of a Roman holiday, were impressed.

Week of May 2

On the morning of May 2, I had an appointment with Martin Plettl, president of the Garment Workers' Union. I phoned to make certain that he was in. The voice that answered was not the voice of the usual operator. I was asked my name, address and occupation. Only afterward was Plettl's secretary permitted to come to the phone. I overheard instructions given her that she must speak only in German. Then came Miss Heinrich's hysterical voice. She could not speak to me . . . there was trouble . . . I would understand. Thinking it was another local *Besetzung,* I called the A.D.G.B. house but got no response. I then tried the Metal Workers' Building. The phone bell rang but there was no answer. I then tried the Gesamtverband building and the same thing happened there. Fifteen minutes later I was in front of the headquarters of the A.D.G.B. It was surrounded on its three sides by the Nazi military. The staff and records of the A.D.G.B. were being loaded on police trucks. Ten minutes' rapid walking brought me to the new building of the Metal Trades Union on Jakobstrasse. The same sight there. I jumped into a taxi and drove to the Gesamtverband building on Michaelkirchplatz, at the intersection of [Engeluferstrasse], where the Gewerkschaftshaus is located. The street was roped off and the building surrounded on both sides by the military, while the complete length of [Engeluferstrasse] was lined by Nazis. It was the end. Every one of the heads of the thirty-one organizations in the A.D.G.B. had been arrested, and the important secretaries in the national office as well.

Plettl, with whom I had been intimate, Otto Schweizer of the Engineers and Technicians, Brandeis of the Metal Workers, Husemann of the Miners, Vomerhaus, organizer of the [Brandenburg] district, Otto Engel, secretary of the Agricultural Workers' Union, Franz Furtwängler, Walter Maschke,[11] Frau Hanna, Kuno Broecker, [Theodor] Leipart and [Peter] Grassmann, the two presidents of the A.D.G.B., everyone of the leaders arrested, not by the police but by the Nazi military troops. Fifty were arrested the first morning; the others were picked up in the succeeding days. This in Berlin alone—how many were arrested throughout Germany is not known and probably never will be known. For days those arrested were kept in the Nazi *Caserna.* Only later were they transferred to the city prisons.

In the afternoon the newspapers carried the first stories of the taking over of the trade unions and arrests and announcing its national character and direction. In every city and town in Germany where there was anything in the way of organized labor, promptly at 10 o'clock in the morning the Nazis marched in, arrested the leaders, ordered the office staffs to remain at their work, announced their "commissars" (the term was borrowed from the Russians by the Germans precisely as the Russians had lifted it out of the French Revolution), and that henceforth there would be only one organization, free from the taint of Marxism, and that it will be the "future cornerstone of the Nazi State."

On the third every kiosk in Germany was plastered with posters announcing the "resurrection" of the trade unions. At the same time the newspapers carried the offer of the Christian Unions to join the Nazi organization, side by side with vague charges and innuendos against the incarcerated trade-union leaders. All of the newspapers joined in proclaiming a "new day" under the bountiful blessings of the Nazi control.

---

11. Walter Maschke (1891–1980), a member of the ADGB executive board and chief of the "Young Workers" division. Active in the underground resistance in Germany, he was involved in the 1944 anti-Hitler plot, jailed, and liberated in 1945 by the Americans.

The following day brought the announcements of the appointments of Dr. Ley[12] and Dr. Engels as the chief "commissars" to take the places of Leipart and [Grassmann]; a mass meeting of the workers to be held in the Lustgarten on the fifth, where the new "commissars" would announce policy that will guide them in the handling of the workers and their problems; and that a national congress of the "new" union would be held on May 10 in Berlin.

The *Nachtausgabe*[13] listed charges against the imprisoned leaders, charging financial corruption. The heavy stress is laid on the donations that the A.D.G.B. made to the S.D.P., the Reichsbanner and to the International Federation of Trade Unions!

Standing on Unter den Linden on Friday (5th), I watched thousands of workers as they marched in from factories into the Lustgarten. Each factory's workers, as soon as the work was over, were met by contingents of Nazi troops. Squads in front and squads behind, and guards at the sides to make certain that no one slipped away; they passed in the thousands. Sickened, yet fascinated, I walked into the Lustgarten. I did not stay long. I stayed long enough to size up the crowd—there were perhaps between 60,000 and 70,000 workers present; there to hear the first principles of Nazi trade unionism as taught by their new "commissar," Dr. Ley. "I order you to stop thinking . . . I order you to keep silent and to obey orders . . . And I order you not to question the things I demand of you. . . . We will know how to treat and exterminate the poison of Marxism out of your system . . ." There was no applause and less enthusiasm. The German workers being told once more to conform and to obey. Most of them seemed bewildered and it is doubtful whether they even know what has happened to their leaders; those who do know are keeping a discreet silence.

The Aftermath

Among the first orders of the Nazis to the workers was to demand a report from their cells on the number of arrests in the different communities in Germany! They were fearful of the consequences of the acts of their own followers. Then

---

12. Robert Ley (1890–1945), a Nazi politician. He organized the destruction of the German trade unions in 1933 and their replacement by the German Labor Front (Deutsche Arbeitsfront), an organization, of which he was the leader, under the strict control of the Nazis. He committed suicide in prison in Nuremberg in 1945, awaiting trial in the international military court.

13. Night edition.

came an order forbidding workers from withdrawing from the unions—and that they must pay their dues and arrearages—or face the loss of their jobs. All of the organizations, the Catholic Unions, the A.D.G.B., etc., have been placed under one single control. They are rapidly being nationalized and their old spirit of class consciousness is rapidly being destroyed. What the Nazi aim is, no one as yet knows. They promised to formulate a program, but in the speech of Herr Hitler to the delegates attending the national congress on May 10, he said precisely nothing. Dr. Ley and Dr. Engels, aside from vague generalities, have been equally silent. The truth is that up to the present day they have no program except to destroy Marxism—and, for a while at least, will be more preoccupied with heresy-hunting than with programs. The following excerpt from one of the members of the Gesamtverband, which reached the writer through underground channels, tells its own story. It is worth quoting.

> "Our organization," he writes in behalf of this group, "continues to exist." (The letter deals with conditions among governmental and public utility employees.) "The dwindling membership has ceased. The 'Christians' have been annexed to the organization. All those employed in factories are obliged to join the organization under threat of dismissal. Yet, in spite of everything, thousands of our best functionaries" (workers in the civil service sense) "are now in the streets without receiving their ordinary or unemployment relief." (In Germany the trades unions have built their own unemployment insurance schemes.) "In spite of having belonged to the organization dozens of years, comrades have forfeited all rights. Among our employees in the Reich" (federal government) "about fifty are either dismissed or in prison, while others have committed suicide.
>
> "On Saturday we had a district leader conference at which commissars of the N.S.B.O.[14] were also present. The session lasted eight hours; it was taken up with insults against our employees and functionaries. It was the worst meeting we ever endured. All our work was made nothing of, and words like 'tramp' and 'rif-raff' were comradely expressions. Matters will fall out so that the already reduced wages will be further cut in half, and employees who have received notice will be put out upon the streets. Passports will be taken away and the demand has been made that every employee who still belongs to the party (Catholic or Centrum) shall be denounced, so as to make it possible to dismiss him without delay. No

---

14. The Nationalsozialistische Betriebszellenorganisation (National Socialist Factory Cells Organization) had been founded by the Nazi Party to establish its presence among German factory workers and employees.

more meetings take place. Only one man makes all decisions. We have only one hope—to get out of this misery as quickly as possible. We ask to be excused from writing, since we are all put under the strictest censorship . . ."

This letter is typical. It gives a hint of what may come, and requires no comment.

Did the German Trade Unions Have a Program?

When the writer arrived in Germany in November, his first impression was that the Communists had a program but no real power; that the trade unions had power but no program. He soon learned that the Communists' lack of strength was due to their failure to have a program of their own, and that the trade unions had only an outer appearance of power, and really had a program. The Communists wanted an organic unity with Russian bolshevism at a time when Russia dreaded such a possibility and would not have known what to do with it if it had come her way. The trade-unionists and Social Democrats had opened the road to socialism in Germany through democratic means, but in the process they had greatly weakened themselves. When the crisis came both went down. Since it was upon these two groups that the workers, both in Germany and outside of Germany, depended and had faith in, let us see what happened to them.

The Communist Party, in spite of its 6,000,000 votes, had no real strength. At the mass meetings of the C.P., where hundreds of thousands were present, one saw German workers in mass, but in the main they were the unemployed. If one will take the growth of the Communist vote in Germany and compare it with the growth of unemployment, he will find that the two parallel each other, yet, in spite of the rapid growth of its vote, the Communist Party in Germany was not gaining in membership. The Russian background to the movement, their many promises of revolution that did not materialize (the writer was told by Communists in Germany that the German Communists were ready but that the Russian Communists told them to wait), their splitting policy in the trade unions that won them very few adherents (but did incalculable harm to the trade unions), their occasional collaboration with the Nazis both politically and industrially, and their failure to take action when their Red Troops[15] were dissolved, foreshadowed

15. The Rotfrontkämpferbund (League of Combattants of the Red Front).

their end as a party of real opposition and revolution. One does not deny their courage or sincerity. They had both. But it must be insisted upon that they had no power and no program, and in the face of superior force, they went down, like all the other parties opposed to Hitler.

The writer saw the counter-demonstrations ordered by the Communist Party as a protest to the Nazi meeting of January 22 arrogantly held in front of the Karl Liebknecht house, the Communist headquarters. Twelve-thousand Nazi troops were addressed by Hitler; 16,000 police, with rifles and machine guns, guarded all the approaches, the roofs surrounding [Bülowplatz], and rifles were trained on all the closed windows. It seemed that most of Berlin's population milled in the surrounding streets, trying to reach the Nazis who were deliberately provoking an outbreak. But the Communists had no arms, and aside from crowding and cheering and singing, no really serious disturbance occurred. It may be said that if real opposition had manifested itself on January 22, [Hindenburg] might have considered twice before appointing Hitler. But even the Communists had to think twice before sending their unarmed followers against the rifles and machine guns of the police. From that time on, a pessimism spread through the ranks of the Communists in Germany that marked their end, regardless of the turn of future events. And later, when Hitler was already in the saddle, and they were confronted with being outlawed, they threw overboard their past policy of non-collaboration with the Social Democrats, and were willing to vote with them in the Prussian Diet in order to elect an anti-Hitlerian cabinet. Such a policy, adopted three months earlier, would have made Hitler's arrival in power an impossibility.

But if the socialist trade-union leaders had a program, by the time [Brüning] came on the scene their power and influence on the nation had already been greatly undermined. On the conclusion of the war their program of necessity had to be two-sided. They had to rescue the nation from the dangers of invasion. They had to rebuild the economic life of the nation in order that at some more propitious moment, socialism, which was their final goal, could be realized. The first presented almost [in]surmountable difficulties. The Communists wanted to introduce sovietism immediately, which would have involved civil war and intervention by the Allies had sovietism been successful; and this in a nation where hundreds of thousands were actually starving to death. And it must be kept in mind that under the Versailles Treaty all the property of the state was in jeopardy for reparations, as afterwards developed in the mortgaging of the German railways. Faced with these dangers, Carl Legien,[16] president of the German trade unions, steered away from these dangerous shoals and decided that to feed and to put the nation back to work was their first task, and at the same time to leave the doors open for the ultimate realization of their philosophic and economic doctrines. How far they were successful can be seen from both the internal and external changes that took place within Germany after the war, and the reconstruction of its external relations in the face of international hatred and opposition. The Weimar Constitution placed the German working class on a far higher plane than in any other country in Europe. Externally, the opposition to the revisal of the Versailles Treaty was slowly being destroyed.

To achieve these results, however, the socialists and trade-unionists had to pay a terrific price. In the face of the injustices, inequalities and barbarous exactions of the Versailles Treaty, these leaders had to advise patience and caution. The signing of the Versailles pact (under such terribly humiliating conditions to Germany) afterward became one of the vehicles on which Hitler rode into power. The Ruhr invasion and the inflation that followed, the signing of the Dawes Plan and later the acceptance of the Young Plan, though seemingly concessions towards Germany, actually were body blows to German Social Democracy and to the trade unions affiliated with it. With every "revision," the German people only saw another humiliation, and listened with growing eagerness and attention to criticism directed at their leaders, until large sections of them were convinced that patience and caution would lead them nowhere. With this conviction came the growth of numerous parties of opposition, the emergence of the Catholic Centrum, the first manifestation of reaction when [Hugenberg] and his Junkers National Socialists became a power in the Reichstag with 107 members whom the acceptance of the Young Plan split, the growth of the Communist opposition and the rise of the Hitlerian National Socialists. And with the growth of these new parties, particularly the Communists and the Nazis, also came a growth of trade union opposition. Thus the Communists first built their cells in the S.D.P. trade unions and tried to "capture" them. Failing in that policy, they tried to organize unions of their own. That they were not successful

16. Carl Legien (1861–1920), trade union leader, SPD representative in the Reichstag, and ADGB president in 1919–20. He underwrote the 1918 Stinnes-Legien agreement between labor and industry that allowed the German economy to start again in the aftermath of the war. The agreement provided a major breakthrough in labor relations by granting the eight-hour day, the recognition of unions as the sole representatives of the workers in collective bargaining, and the creation of factory councils for factories with a minimum of fifty wage earners.

does not measure their effect. As a trade-union opposition, they were able to circulate rumors and libels against their opponents, which too frequently were believed, and even if they led to no results for the Communists, they doubtlessly had an effect in creating a lack of faith and a demoralization in the ranks of the Social Democratic trade unions. The same tactics were used by the Nazi Party. They also established "cells" in the factories, and in some trades established their own factions as trade unions. And in some instances, in the late transport strike in Berlin, to be specific, called on the eve of the elections in November 1932, the Communists and the Nazis combined in calling the strike—obviously a collaboration between these two enemies that could have had only one object—to smash the prestige of the Social Democratic leaders of the trade unions.

The persistent undermining of the trade unions could lead to but one result. By the time [Brüning] was appointed Chancellor, with dictatorial powers, the leaders knew that their strength had been sapped and that until the dangers of Communism and Nazism, particularly the latter, were disposed of, their program and their plans were in danger. It was then that the policy pursued by the S.D.P. and the trade unions, for the time being, underwent a radical change. With Hitlerism growing at a cyclonic rate (the causes of which are too many to enter upon in this discussion), the S.D.P. and its trade unions decided that it would be wiser to adopt the policy of tolerating the "lesser" evil, than to permit power to fall into Hitler's hands. That this policy was a temporary expedient is shown by subsequent developments. The discarding of this policy during the von Papen régime undoubtedly opened the door to Hitler's entrance into power.

The policy of tolerating the "lesser" evil did not last long. With von Papen's appointment, the left wing forces in the trade unions and in the S.D.P. were turned loose, and how thoroughly they wrecked that gentleman's aspirations was indicated in the election results. At the end of the count, it was found that not a single party in the Reichstag was willing to work with him, and all that he could muster was less than 10 per cent of the membership of the Reichstag. But developments during the von Papen chancellorship pointed in new directions. For one thing, von Papen had thoroughly frightened the signatories of the Versailles Treaty and this resulted in practically eliminating reparations from the German budget. The second lay in von Papen's attacks on the social and labor legislation in Germany. He gave the industrialists even more than they expected from him. Unemployment insurance was, to all intents and purposes, emasculated. Advance taxes, over which American publicists waxed delirious with praise, were used to subsidize employers who were willing to fight the trade unions, resulting in what almost amounted to a landslide of wage cuts and strikes, and the social as well as the labor legislation of Germany was threatened with extinction. The landlords and industrialists had at last found their man! But it was not to last long. When the election returns were in, the opposition to von Papen was so strong that Hindenburg dared not reappoint him.

With von Schleicher, von Papen's successor, things took a different turn. Having learned from the experience of von Papen, Schleicher decided to be more moderate. Von Papen's antilabor decrees were promptly annulled. Other decrees followed that stopped the epidemic of wage cuts. Trade-unionists became optimistic once more. Moreover, in the November elections, Hitler lost 2,000,000 votes and 30 seats in the Reichstag, and 30 more seats were deflected from him through an internal fight between himself and Gregor [Strasser]; while the industrialists, on Hitler's failure to at least hold his own in the November election, decided that Hitler's days were numbered and therefore cut off a large portion of their financial support. The writer saw two barracks in Berlin alone that had been closed for lack of funds. During the months of December and January the Nazi troops were being sent begging on the streets of the cities in Germany to keep their organization alive and Hitler was compelled to admit being 5,000,000 marks in debt—a huge sum in Germany—the writer saw two barracks in Berlin alone that had been closed by the Hitlerians. It is therefore understandable, with these facts known, why, in spite of Schleicher's apparent liberalism, the left wing of the S.D.P. and the Trades Unions grew too optimistic. They were certain that Hitler was through, and wanted nothing to do with a man of the military caste who might have dictatorial aspirations of his own. Therefore, when Schleicher asked the socialist groups to continue the same policy of toleration that they had exercised during [Brüning's] time, they refused.

It may be added that the older heads in the trade unions and in the S.D.P. were not entirely convinced that Hitler was through, and were willing to come to an understanding with Schleicher until the Hitlerian danger would be completely dissipated, but the left wing elements tied their hands and refused to go through with the program. Unable to form a cabinet that would obtain parliamentary support, Schleicher handed in his resignation and left the door open for the von Papen–Hitler-[Hugenberg] cabal that made it possible for Hitler to become Chancellor of Germany, take over the police powers of the state, and start his campaign of suppressing all opposition. Once Hitler was in, it was certain to all observers that nothing short of war with a foreign power, or a revolution at home, would ever succeed in dislodging him. And the German trades unions, after the years spent rebuilding their national life, of fighting their way out of the injustices and exactions of the Versailles Treaty, and of withstanding criticism and vilification from their enemies at home, were too weakened and demoralized to undertake a revolution. The wonder is that the crumbling of the weakened trade union machine did not take place sooner. On the contrary, it must have taken almost superhuman efforts on the part of German trade union leaders to hold their organizations together as long as they did.

Only nit wits or those who are blind, therefore, will condemn the German trade union leaders for being without a program. Every step was carefully measured and every step carefully weighed. That their program was, because of shortsightedness and over optimism, defeated, is true. But it should be borne in mind that if they erred in their plans, the criticism hurled at their heads ought not to come from the liberals. If their program was smashed, and the trades unions along with it, it should be remembered that the error in their calculations resulted from the assumption of the left wingers' policy and not from too much conservatism!

Moreover, it is hardly fair for the socialists, liberals and trade unionists in the former allied countries, to, at this late date, criticize their German colleagues. Rather, it seems to the writer, it would be wise, and timely too, for these groups to stop and consider how much of the responsibility for the debacle in Germany should rest on their own shoulders. All of them knew the conditions in which German socialists and trade unionists found themselves after the forced armistice, and all of them knew that any party in Germany could not survive the Versailles treaty unless the injustices in this instrument were done away with; every one of them knew that Germany could not survive if the harshness and inequalities in that barbaric instrument of "peace" were applied in full force against the Germans. And in their failure to put sufficient pressure on their governments to at least mitigate the harshest features of the treaty they not only helped to bury the socialists and trade unions in Germany, but helped the reactionaries in Germany in their efforts to destroy all faith in internationalism.

One word more must be added. The writer was in Germany from November until May 8. He met, and was intimate with, many of the leaders of the German trade union movement—during the darkest hours of the tragedy. They met both their fate, and the issues that confronted them, with genuine courage. It took courage to avoid pitfalls that might have led to the slaughter of tens of thousands of workers, and the victimization, perhaps of hundreds of thousands more. It was doubly courageous to remain at their posts, as practically all of the national leaders did, until the guns of the Nazis ordered them into the lorry on their way to the military barracks. These leaders knew what was awaiting them. And they faced their arrests unflinchingly. When the real story is told to the German workers, when they realize that it was possible, through an irresponsible word or deed, to sacrifice them *[en masse]* on the altar of a gesture, and that the leaders refused and sacrificed themselves instead, then the German workers will honor their former leaders, and the world will join in the tribute.

The Future

What the future will bring to Germany no one really knows. Prognostications, especially on German affairs, are extremely dangerous. The Nazis have turned loose forces that they themselves do not understand. It may surprise many to learn that the most exciting things that have happened in Germany have come as an upsurge from below, and not from the government itself. The masses want work, and the most insistent ones are the very groups that Hitler and his adventurers have been most assiduous in organizing. It is not without reason that, at the numerous meetings the Nazi leaders are holding with the S.A. and S.S. troops they must plead for more and more discipline. The anti-Jewish boycott (not yet ended though deprived of official sanction) was started by the S.A. troops in Munich, and it gained such momentum within a few hours that not one among the Nazi leaders dared to make an effort to head it off. There is ground for believing that the same forces operating from below forced the move against the trade unions on May 2. The general belief is that Seldte and Hitler would have liked more time, but the military leaders of the Nazi party, finding their troops getting more and more restless as the days passed, took this step to appease them.

If this is true, how much more additional pressure will come from below? And in what direction will the pressure from below drive the Hitlerian government? Will Hitler, for instance, use it to drive out of the cabinet the remaining members of the Hugenberg crowd, whose tariff exactions have already sent the cost of food to higher levels, a condition which has already resulted in sporadic rioting in the cities of the Ruhr? Or, finding that the unions, "the new cornerstone of the Nazi state," are not contented with phrases about the indivisibility of capital and labor, and demand that wages, hours, social legislation, etc., be protected within the framework of the Weimar Constitution, will he restrain the large industrialists of Germany who think that now is their grand opportunity? Or, will he go still further to the right, even against his own Nazi followers in the military branch of his party who carried out the investment of the trade unions on May 2?

All these questions will be answered, and in my opinion within a shorter period of time than the world believes. Germany is moving rapidly, much more rapidly than the intellects of Herr Hitler and his crowd of adventurers. The question in my mind, and in the mind of most of the former German trade union leaders, now is: what will come after Hitler? A monarchy? A military dictatorship directed by some yet unknown head of the Reichswehr? Or a repetition of the years of terror that existed in France during her upheaval? The last is not unlikely.

Ex Tenebrae!

With faith he went to meet the sun
He heralded with song of hope,
Nor deemed himself by fate undone
That bade him in despair to grope.

Some mourn at shattered Fortune's bier,
In darkened room bewail their dead—
But others hail in vision clear,
The promise of the day ahead!

—Oscar H. Fernbach

BRIEF CHRONOLOGY OF POLITICAL EVENTS IN GERMANY, 1930–33

March 27, 1930	Fall of the left-of-center coalition (SPD, Zentrum, and German Democratic Party) led by Hermann Müller.
March 29, 1930	Zentrum leader Heinrich Brüning is appointed chancellor
July 18, 1930	The Reichstag is dissolved.
September 14, 1930	Reichstag elections: dramatic increase of the Nazi Party's (NSDAP) representation from 12 to 107 seats.
April 10, 1932	Paul Hindenburg is reelected president of the republic with the support of the SPD, Zentrum, and DDP against Hitler.
April 24, 1932	Legislative elections in the Länder; the SPD loses its majority in Prussia.
May 30, 1932	Hindenburg ends the Brüning government.
June 1, 1932	Franz von Papen is appointed chancellor.
June 4, 1932	The Reichstag is dissolved.
July 20, 1932	*"Preussenschlag":* von Papen deposes the Prussian government led by SPD Otto Braun and proclaims himself *Reichskommissar* for Prussia.

July 31, 1932	Reichstag elections. Obtaining 13,779,000 votes, 37.3 percent of the polls, and 230 seats, the NSDAP becomes the main party in the Reichstag.
September 12, 1932	Reichstag vote of no confidence for von Papen, who obtains only 42 votes against 512. Hindenburg dissolves the Reichstag.
November 3–7, 1932	Berlin transportation workers' strike jointly organized by Nazis and Communists.
November 6, 1932	Reichstag elections: the NSDAP polls 33.1 percent of the votes, SPD 20.4 percent, and the KPD 16.9 percent.
November 17, 1932	Von Papen's cabinet resigns.
November 19, 1932	Business leaders and landowners petition President Hindenburg for Hitler as chancellor.
December 2, 1932	Minister of Defense Kurt von Schleicher is appointed chancellor.
December 14, 1932	Von Schleicher cancels the low-wage policy adopted by von Papen since September.
January 4, 1933	Secret negotiations between Hitler and von Papen in Cologne on the formation of a new cabinet.
January 15, 1933	Nazi electoral victory in Lippe, one of the smallest German states.
January 21, 1933	The DNVP withdraws its confidence from the Schleicher government.
January 22, 1933	Nazi demonstration in front of the Karl Liebknecht House, the KPD headquarters in Berlin.
January 28, 1933	Von Schleicher resigns.
January 30, 1933	Hitler is appointed chancellor and von Papen vice chancellor.
February 1, 1933	On Hitler's demand, Hindenburg dissolves the Reichstag.
February 2, 1933	Interior Minister of Prussia Hermann Göring bans all KPD demonstrations.
February 4, 1933	By a decree the new government severely curtails civil liberties, the right of assembly, and freedom of the press.

February 27, 1933	Last SPD demonstration in Berlin. Reichstag fire.
February 28, 1933	Presidential decree "for the protection of the people and the state," suspending civil liberties and granting unlimited power to the Nazi regime. The SPD organ *Vorwärts* is temporarily suspended.
March 5, 1933	Reichstag elections. With the NSDAP obtaining 43.9 percent of the votes and the Deutschnationale Volkspartei and the Steel Helmet 8 percent, Hitler has a majority in the Reichstag. The SPD polled 18.3 percent of the votes, the KPD 12.3 percent, and the Zentrum 11.2 percent in these elections.
March 8, 1933	Emergency decree annuls the seats obtained by the KPD in the Reichstag.
March 23, 1933	*Ermächtigungsgesetz.* By 441 votes, the Reichstag gives Hitler full powers to legislate and even to modify the constitution. The SPD is the only party to oppose this vote.
March 31, 1933	The regional governments *(Länder)* are dissolved.
April 1, 1933	Launching of the boycott of the Jewish trades.
April 7, 1933	A law on civil service *(Gesetz zur Wiederherstellung des Berufsbeamtentums)* excludes Jews and political opponents to the Nazi regime from employment in all public services.
April 11, 1933	Göring becomes prime minister *(Statthalter)* of Prussia.
May 2, 1933	The headquarters of the ADGB and affiliated unions are raided and occupied, their leaders arrested. The Deutsche Arbeitsfront (DAF; German Labor Front) is created.
May 10, 1933	First convention of the DAF.
June 22, 1933	The SPD is banned.
June 26, 1933	Alfred Hugenberg withdraws from the government. The DNVP is dissolved.
July 14, 1933	Law forbidding the reorganization of all non-Nazi parties and institutions.

INDEX

Page numbers in **bold** indicate that biographical or historical data on the person or event mentioned are given in a footnote.

Catherine Collomp is a professor of American history at Université Paris VII–Denis Diderot. She has published many articles on U.S. immigration and labor history in French and American journals. Her previous books include *Entre classe et nation: Mouvement ouvrier et immigration aux Etats-Unis, 1880–1920* (Paris, 1998) and *Exilés et réfugiés politiques aux Etats-Unis* (Paris, 2003).

Bruno Groppo is a researcher at the Centre National de la Recherché Scientifique, Centre d'Histoire Sociale du XXe Siècle, Université Paris I. His main research fields are comparative European labor history and European exiles and political emigrations in the twentieth century, on which he has published several books and articles in various languages.

The University of Illinois Press
is a founding member of the
Association of American University Presses.

University of Illinois Press
1325 South Oak Street
Champaign, IL 61820-6903
www.press.uillinois.edu